M000103045

# THE GYMNAST

## &

# OTHER POSITIONS

# ACKNOWLEDGEMENTS

"Tall Tale" was published in *Pif*; "Flamboyant Tree" was published in *Poui* and again in *Jamaica Observer*; "Oleander" and "Terra Nova" were published in the *Jamaica Observer*; "Zemi" was published in *Poui*; "The Gymnast" was published in *Caribbean Writing Today* and again in *Caribbean Erotic*; "A Giant Blue Swallowtail Butterfly" was published in *The Caribbean Writer* and again in *The Jamaica Observer*; "Walker Family Stories" was published in *The Observer Arts Magazine*; "The Bookends Interview" was published in the *Jamaica Observer*; "Charting A Literary Journey" was published in *SX Salon*; "Sailing With Wayne Brown" was published in *SX Salon*; "Stories of a Birth" was published in *How I Came to Be*, a compilation of essays by the Opportunity Programs at New York University; "Claude McKay's Songs of Morocco" was presented May 22, 2009 at the International Center for Performance Studies Conference. Tangier, Morocco. The essay was published in *Renaissance Noire*; a different version of "The Stories We Tell Ourselves" was published in *My Mother Who Is Me: Life Stories from Jamaican Women in New York* (Africa World Press.); the poem "Recipe" was published in the collection *Snapshots from Istanbul*; "Soliloquy" was published in *Del Sol Review*; "A Clear Blue Day" was published in the *Jamaica Observer*; "A World of Superimposed Maps" was published under another title in *Pif*; "Surviving Whole" was published as the introductory essay to Roger Mais' novel Black Lightning (Leeds: Peepal Tree Press); "The Haunted Self" was published in *The Fickle Grey Beast*; "'Covering' Female Sexual Desires" was published in *The Huffington Post*; "Jacqueline Bishop, Interview with John Hoppenthaler" was published in *Connotation Press: An Online Artifact*; "Love Songs to Morocco" was published on *The Talim Blog*; "Reliving, Rewriting, Reimagining: An Interview with Jacqueline Bishop" was published in *Art, Recognition, Culture*; "Inside I Always Knew I Was a Writer" was published by *Moko Caribbean Arts and Letters*; "Jacqueline Bishop Talks About Writing Across The Diaspora" was published in *The Huffington Post*; "From Nonsuch to Bordeaux: An Inter-Island Conversation on the Work of John Dunkley" was published in *Art, Recognition, Culture*.

JACQUELINE BISHOP


THE GYMNAST

&

OTHER POSITIONS

STORIES, ESSAYS AND INTERVIEWS

PEEPAL TREE

First published in Great Britain in 2015
Peepal Tree Press Ltd
17 King's Avenue
Leeds LS6 1QS
England

© 2015 Jacqueline Bishop
and interviewers

ISBN13: 97818452323150

All rights reserved
No part of this publication may be
reproduced or transmitted in any form
without permission

Supported using public funding by
ARTS COUNCIL
ENGLAND

# CONTENTS

For Emma – my grandmother

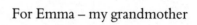

*We tell ourselves stories in order to live* — Joan Didion

# INTRODUCTION

## LOOKING FORWARD BY LOOKING BACK

She had started a reading series and she wanted me to read. Short-short stories. A format I had never tried before. The theme for the reading, for there was a theme for all the readings she was to host, was "assume the position". We both laughed at the naughtiness of it all, and, a day or two before the reading, I sat down and wrote the story. I considered myself then a writer of novels and fairly long short stories, but the minute I sat down "The Gymnast" popped right out, as if it had been waiting for me to just come along and unearth it. I wrote this short-short story in the way that I often write poetry, in a rush and in one fell swoop. Then the revising begins. After this first story, "The Gymnast", I would go back again and again to writing short-short stories and soon these short-short stories started to take on a life of their own. In this way the first third of this book came into being. As I looked back over these stories I was struck by their diversity of experiences, and I am pleased that they have an almost equal focus on the perspectives and preoccupations of men and women. I also liked the interiority of these stories, as if they were thoughts spoken to one's self. Read together they seemed to form a cohesive whole.

Still, in looking at the stories as a group, and thinking about publication, I started to feel that there was something missing, something needed to add heft, and it is in this way that this strange hybrid of a book was born. For this book with its stories, its essays, and its interviews is a strange bird indeed. Yet, in so many ways I feel that this book, of the five books I have published so far, is the most representative of who I am, because it is a coming together of so many parts of myself. My good friend Earl McKenzie, who is a creative writer, visual artist and philosopher, among many other things, has written about himself that, "many years ago a friend of mine… had prophesied that one day my… writing and painting would come together in a single praxis. With my painting on the cover of my… book of poems, this, I felt, was the nearest I had come to the fulfilment of this prophecy." Similarly, *The Gymnast* feels like the fulfilment of a personal philosophy. This book gives me a chance to reflect on the work that I have done so far and think about the work I hope to do in the future – gives a chance of looking forward by looking back. It gave me a metaphor for my creativity and my life, the collaging and quilting, the superimpositions, the piecing together of things to make somewhat of a whole. Asante Sana.

PART ONE

# THE GYMNAST

**Candlestick**: *A position where the gymnast is essentially on her shoulders with feet pointed towards the ceiling. The gymnast's arms can either be behind her head or pushing palms down on the floor to help her support and balance herself.*

Many people find it hard to believe that this was the first position he taught me. The first time, he said, he realised that I had real talent. Those long ago days of my childhood in Jamaica, the two of us behind the thick green hedge of the hibiscus, with its bright red flowers! I must have been ten that first time, and he kept insisting that he was only slightly older. 'Bet you cannot do this,' he dared, contorting himself into this weird shape. Of course I wanted to show him that I, too, could do it. Of course I had to show him that I, too, could balance on nothing but my bare shoulders. And, before long, there I was, looking at the world upside down, and him walking around, my trainer, as he would always be, his arms behind his back. 'Not bad,' he kept saying, nodding. 'Not bad at all!'

**Handstand**: *A proper handstand is extended towards the ceiling. The body is vertical, supported on the hands with arms straight and elbows locked.*

This was the position we practised next, skipping right over the arch, the aerial and the bridge – positions he said I already knew to heart. All the nights I would steal out of my parents' home to be with him! Those inky blue-black nights that he walked around me, again and again, inspecting what he saw. I must have been thirteen by then: hips rounding out, breasts becoming a handful. 'Hold it, hold it,' he kept saying. 'Straighten out those skinny legs of yours. OK, now slightly open those thin brown legs of yours. You are not afraid, are you? You could not possibly be afraid of me. How long have I been your trainer? Teaching you, training your slim young body how to assume the various positions? Breathe. Let it out. That's right. Now, you hold that position. All I am doing is looking. Nothing else. Just looking at what is flowering between your legs.'

**Lunge**: *Start by standing with feet together. Take a large step forward. Bend your front leg. Both feet should be turned out somewhat. Arms should be extended upwards so that a straight line runs up from the rear foot parallel to the hands.*

Naturally I could not wait to get close to him. I would now do anything to be with him. All of sixteen, or was it fifteen, years old. We would be going places, he promised. Far away places like New York and Toronto. Women in those places, he had heard, could do tremendous things with their bodies. A contortionist he had seen in a magazine, he said, stroking the stubble of hair that was not there, had arranged herself into so many positions all at once, a person looking at the picture, the spectacle, could never tell where a hand or a leg began. 'To have a woman like that!' he kept saying, smiling to himself. 'A woman who could assume all those positions. A woman whose body and bones are that limber. To have a woman like that!' That was the first time I ran away to be with him.

**Straddle**: *In which the gymnast's legs are spread wide.*

I am eighteen now, so this is legal. This, I tell everyone, is what I have always wanted to do; what, in fact, I was born to do: straddle this man. Straddle *my* man, my first and only trainer. Now at last I can best that contortionist! Where was it that she was located again? New York. Yes, I think it was New York. Well, I am in New York now. Attending a university here. And I won't tell you what I did to that big hairy man at the United States embassy in Kingston to make sure that my boyfriend also got a visa to come with me to the United States, as my trainer. How I closed my eyes and saw nothing but flowers, bright red hibiscus and red ginger flowers, and the pale blue sky, and, further, faster, myself swimming in the dark blue ocean. Yes, that day at the embassy I saw the look that came into that man's eyes. I could feel the flush travelling through his gigantic, well-fed body as he looked at me. 'You have such a perfect body,' he kept saying. 'A gymnast's body. A contortionist's body. The positions you must be able to assume with that body!'

**Cartwheels:** *A basic exercise in which, limbs akimbo like the spokes of a wheel, the body rotates across the ground like a wheel, hands and legs following one another. (Children love this exercise.)*

My mother was right. Cartwheels were what I was left doing, in the end. One after another, trying to get my trainer's attention; trying to get anyone's attention. Oh, I could do the hip-circle, the front split, the layout, the tuck, better than anyone else I knew. Oh, I had caused a sensation in my own right: the first Jamaican world-class gymnast.

But after a while that did not seem to matter to him, my trainer, the one I wanted it to matter to the most. So many women, so many contortionists resided in New York City! He, my trainer, got very busy. Became just like a writer. I have since dated a few of those, so I know the type well. Always something on their minds. Thinking up some new and daring position.

I don't think he told me goodbye the day he left, my contortionist, my trainer. I don't think there was even a note. I remember just coming home to an empty apartment. Then, for days, endless crying.

That was until the day when, for no particular reason, I got up and pulled my training rug out of the closet. Set it in the middle of the floor of my empty apartment. Unfolded my long, limber, dark brown arms and legs. Resting on my shoulders, with my arms behind my back, I thrust my legs up as if trying to reach the cream-coloured ceiling. My legs seemed longer, more slender and even browner than before. Such a lovely sheen! And my fingers, I thought delighted: how long and slender they, too, were! Long enough to put anywhere inside my body.

I wanted to sing, to hug myself and dance and sing. Mine, all mine, my long brown fingers! The bananas I could now see sitting on top of my empty refrigerator, the ones my grandmother had sent to me all the way from Jamaica. Their bright yellow, freckled brown, skin. My grandmother's long, slender, near-perfect bananas that she grew in the country. What was it that my grandmother had been trying to tell me, the last time I had gone to visit her, my eyes brimming with tears? She had taken my hands into hers, stroked my long brown fingers. 'So beautiful,' she kept murmuring, seemingly to herself. 'Long and slender, just like my bananas.'

'Go on, take one,' she had said, coming out of the house with some of her near-perfect fruit. 'You are, your mother tells me, someone who likes to push her body, who likes to do things with her body, who likes to test the limits of her body. The positions I have heard,' she said, smiling admiringly at me, 'you can assume!'

'Go on, take one,' she said, with a mysterious, triumphant look in her eyes. 'See for yourself what these bananas can do.'

## TALL TALE

It took her a long while to figure out what the photographs were of, and a still longer time to figure out who was in the photographs, and, when it finally dawned on that part of her brain that edits and selects who the photographs were of and just who had left them there on the breakfast table for her to find first thing in the morning, she knew she would kill him.

Yes, she acknowledged, the bile rising in her mouth, the photographs were of her daughter. Her child. In some ways their child, for hadn't Lloyd help her raise this child from knee-high to almost-a-woman? She shook her head. He had waited until her child, their child, Simone, had made it just past the age of consent to make his move. Yes, she would kill him. Of that she was sure. For here now was her child in poses that could be found only in those lurid magazines that she passed quickly wherever she saw them being sold. And there she was, her child with the almond-shaped eyes, smiling at someone – him, most likely, the man who had helped raise her; the man who had been like-a-father-to-her – smiling and sticking her fingers into various parts of her body. Effervescent flashes of pinks, purples, bruised red.

And that bedspread that their daughter was posing on, hadn't they bought it together, all three of them, on Fordham Road one beautiful spring day several years ago in the Bronx? They had gone to the New York Botanical Garden to see a show called "Andalusian Paradise" and everyone who saw them had smiled at the beauty – the rightness – of the family. Mother, father, pumpkin-coloured, talking-too-much daughter between them. Lime green and bright yellows were the blossoms on the duvet covers they had brought that day. Her daughter, Simone, had picked out the sheet because she so loved the colours, especially after such a spectacular show at the botanical garden. When she reached for her purse to pay for the comforter, Lloyd had stayed her hand. He would pay for it. He would take care of things. From now on.

It was on that very same bedspread he had positioned the laughing child in these most grotesque of photos. Perhaps it was her mind protecting her again, but it took her a while to realise that there was also a letter with the pictures, a letter written in her daughter's still childish hand. Even as she reached for the letter, she wondered why she should read anything the two of them had to say. But still she opened up the crisp white piece of paper, probably torn from her daughter's notebook, and she read a little of what it had to say, stopping once in a while to steady the bile continually on the rise in her mouth. Something about the two of them being in love. They hoped she would understand. They had taken off together.

She put the letter down. She remembered the first time she saw Simone at the Maxfield Park Children's home in Kingston. She had gone back to the island specifically to get a child, something she had always promised herself she would do. A way of giving something back, or, at the very least, helping someone from the land where she had been born and where she had grown up. Her homeland. Her motherland. The island of Jamaica. She was thirty-six years old then, had spent the better part of her life getting degrees and focusing on her career; now it was time to focus on someone other than herself. And there was the little pumpkin-coloured girl with the almond-shaped eyes, leaning against a wall, so shy and retiring. While all the other children smiled too-wide smiles to show strong white teeth, and had slender, pliant arms folded delicately on their laps, the little girl, Simone, had her back against the wall. She was told that for the many months she had been there, in the children's home, Simone had barely spoken a word.

"No," the administrator told her when she began looking closer and closer at the little girl her heart immediately told her was her own, "she is not up for adoption. Something not right with that child." The word "troubled" was used several times over.

But wasn't that what she had gone to school for? She with her psychiatric social worker eyes, wasn't that what she had been trained to do? No, this child was not troubled, but vulnerable, needy, and who could resist the pull of those sad, dark eyes? Yes, they were communicating with her, those eyes, drawing her in. Pulling her in. Like a luscious chocolate-coloured mami wata, deep into the dark blue ocean. The child was pleading with her, begging her to choose her, take her back with her to America.

Simone was nine years old by the time the adoption and immigration papers were finalised. Then, before she knew it, the child was sitting on the forest green sofa in her living room in the Bronx. Looking around, ever so shyly. All the posters of Jamaica up on the walls. The dwarf banana plant she had struggled to grow in her living room. Its flat, silver-green leaves. The crudely made wooden sculptures. All the indications, she hoped, for this child, her child with the deep dark eyes, to know that after many tumultuous journeys, she was finally home.

She had read the file on this child: her mother a lady of the purple-blue nights working the wharves in downtown Kingston; the father, judging by the child's orange-coloured, freckled face, some European sailor. And to think, the mother was supposed to have said, a smile lighting up her luminous dark face, that of all the seeds sown that would germinate and take root, it was those of some European sailor that found a fertile foothold in her body. The mother smiled again at that.

Still, that had not stopped the mother giving the child away. Someone should have told her about the responsibility. All the times she was shyly, proudly, touching her swollen body, someone should have told her about the crying at night. The endless changing of nappies. She ended up giving the child to a woman named Adina Roy, a blind old woman who had the child selling needles on the road from the moment Simone could get two words out of her mouth. Adina Roy was the one who had told the child the little she knew about her mother.

The file continued. Someone had found the child when she was four years old, her arm wrapped around herself, wandering the dangerous streets of the capital. The two-day-old dead body of Miss Adina Roy was found later. The autopsy showed her big heart had given out after a massive heart attack. The child never really spoke for years after that. And she kept having, on the evidence of what she drew, the same dream over and over again, of hundreds of thousands of needles falling down on her and digging deep into her body.

It took her, the woman who had adopted the child and brought her to America, two years, many psychotherapists and a young man with a bright yellow guitar in his hand and a multicoloured kerchief on his head to get the little girl to slowly, ever so slowly, open up like an early spring flower and begin talking. And the young guitar player with the flashing eyes did not get only the child to open up, but the child's mother, too. For years after, the mother would tell anyone who would listen that the man, the guitar player, the one at a university getting an advanced degree in film studies, was her soul mate, the person she could tell anything to. She had never felt so close to anyone in her life. Before that man came along, she would tell her increasingly sceptical friends, she had been a tightly closed flower, but that was before the guitar player transformed her into a parrot tulip, bright red and yellow, in full bloom.

Within a month they had moved in together. Years later, she still could not understand why they had never married. But now the guitar player had taken the narrative thread of her life and tangled up the order of the sentences. Everything now confused and incoherent. Everything now up for question. Had anything at all been as it had seemed? And the young woman, her daughter? There was that letter sitting there and staring at her. Something about them being in love. The two of them moving to Europe together. She had always felt, the young woman, her daughter, that her mother had died giving birth to her seventeen long years ago. That she had never had a mother. And he, the guitar-playing lover, had told her that she,

Simone, did not have an ounce of his blood flowing through her body, and since she was not his natural daughter...

How she knew the day, the exact time that she would find them, the two happy, laughing and giddy lovers at the Air France terminal at the John F. Kennedy Airport would be speculated about for weeks in the newspapers. Had the mother been going there day after day, hour after hour, after she had found the letter? Had she hired a private investigator to track them down, her lover and her daughter? But that day, there they were, feeding each other, the suitcases stacked like a pyramid beside them. Of course, nothing made much sense to her after that, and it would take her, the psychiatric social worker, days of reading through her own file to bring some coherence back to the jumbled narrative of her story. Days before, she read, she had bought a gun – there was yet another fierce battle in the New York newspapers for and against strengthening the gun laws – but, yes, she had bought a gun. One that did not have a silencer. As if she wanted the whole world to hear the shots she fired. They had both stopped laughing the minute they saw her, her daughter and her lover. He had gotten up to say something to her when she pulled something dark and powerful out of the deep pockets of the fiery red coat she was wearing.

She did not mean to kill the child, her daughter, but the child had flung herself between her man and her mother. That death she was sorry about, and would be for the rest of her life, playing it over and over again in her head as if it were her favourite sad song on some slow record player. But as for him, she told the officers who came running after they heard all the commotion, two bullets to his too beautiful face and the five more to his crotch, he was already dead by the time she killed him.

## OLEANDER

It started with one tattoo. A tattoo of a flower. Or part of a flower. She came with a photograph, but it was no flower he had ever seen before. She wanted it here, she said, pointing to her navel; she wanted it surrounding what she considered the most important part of her body. She also wanted the exact same shade of colour. Since she was chocolate brown, he, the tattooist, had to play a little bit with the mixture. When they were both satisfied with what he came up with, the tattooist wrote the combination of inks and dyes into a book, so he would always remember. He knew that she would be coming back many times thereafter.

As he readied the electric machine, the tattooist explained that the ink would be inserted into her skin through a series of fine needles, that it would be over before she knew what was happening. Still, there would be some stinging and burning and a slight swelling. He made sure that she saw the gloves that he was wearing, that he opened a brand new pack of needles and wet disposable napkins. There were no risks of any kind of infection.

To make small talk as she took her clothes off, the tattooist told the young woman that though it was hard to tell, he knew she was a foreigner. Well, not a foreigner exactly, for who could really claim to be a native New Yorker? But there was a soft lilt to her voice, an accent that was somewhat muffled. Such thick dark hair, he thought, admiring the young woman. The dark-almost-to-violet eyes. As she lay back on the raised narrow bed, he gave her what he thought was the beginning or the very centre of a flower. He noticed how, after they were finished, she stared at herself for the longest time in front of the mirror.

She came back a few weeks later with another photo. This one showed even more parts of the pale pink flower. Though he could not see all the plant, he instinctively knew that this was a flower that bloomed profusely. He saw the five petals that were beginning to flare from a yellowish centre. Could he do this, she had asked, softly, could he enlarge her flower? She lifted up her blouse so he could admire the work he had already done, that first tattoo forming a ring around the rumpled dark spot of her navel. How well everything had healed! Such vibrant colours! As he mixed a new batch of colours, she told him that she was from Jamaica, that she hadn't been home for such a long time that she could barely remember the outline and contours of the island, and she didn't really feel right in still calling the island her home. The tattooist smiled to himself. He remembered the time, years before, when he'd fallen hard for an island beauty. Every time he thought of that woman, she was conflated into a vividly coloured flower. That day he extended the pale pink colour halfway across the young woman's belly.

The next time the young woman came she wanted to round out the edges of the petals to a magenta colour. She wanted the sepals curving slightly. She wanted streaks of white mixed in with the magenta. The flower was now extending upwards to cover almost half of her body. When he was done, she kept looking at herself in the mirror, all the while mumbling, "Larger. No, larger!" He would keep working on her until the image started touching a rigid dark nipple.

The tattooist liked working on this woman's body. How effortlessly the needle sank into her skin. As if it were the very best crushed velvet. How she sighed each time she felt the piercings, almost as if it were a release to have something enter her body painfully. She wanted him to tell her all he knew about the custom of tattooing. Something of what he said about "modification" and, especially, "branding" seemed to please her immensely. Then she asked him if it was true that the ink might fade one day, in the far away future? She seemed overly relieved at his answer. That, yes, the tattoo would fade, but no one could ever totally remove it from her body. When he said this, a calm relaxed look came over her.

The next time she came she wanted lance-like, dark-green leaves to go with the flower. She had done some research, she said, had found out that many people erroneously believed the flower to be a member of the olive family. She could understand why; the leaves they grew looked so much like each other. Indeed, the night before, she had dreamt that she was applying olive oil all over her body. But, no, this wasn't some olive plant imitation flower. Anyone with any kind of sense would know that just because two things, two people, looked alike, that did not necessarily make them family. Family. In the soft lilt of her voice, she repeated the word over and over, even as he worked on the soft velvety canvas of her body, extending the flower to her back and then down her arms and legs.

But then the woman with the burnt-sienna hair had taken him aback when she told him she was working as a helper. He'd had her pinned down as someone's spoilt, rebellious daughter. But, no, she told him; the work she was doing was as a housekeeper. Still, she must be paid handsomely, this woman who kept adding more and more parts of the strange and exotic flower to her body, for she never had any problem paying him what he charged – and he knew that he charged more than any of the other tattooists in the city. They must be some very rich people she worked for.

A couple of weeks later she told him that the couple she worked for looked just like her. Had, in fact, the same warm brown colour. Did he remember what she had said before about people looking exactly like you not necessarily being your family? They were both lawyers, this couple who she worked for, with a thriving practice somewhere in midtown Manhattan. She was lying on the flat narrow bed, and this time she wanted even more branches and leaves added to the now gigantic flower that was consuming, it seemed to the tattooist, her slim young body. After a while, it did not seem right to him that this flower just kept growing and growing, up and down her arms and legs, her back, breasts, belly and even surrounding her pubic area. Was the flower sucking the life out of this once-vibrant young woman? She seemed weak and tired when she came to see him. It was then that she told him. She was but a child when she had left – had been taken – from Jamaica. And never, not once, had she set foot on or been allowed to go back to the island. Yes, she said, in a hiss of a voice that could not hide her anger, there had been a few letters over the years from a woman who claimed to be her mother, but this woman only ever wrote her when she wanted something; only ever wrote to beg her money. But she was finished with that now, the young woman busy turning herself into a flower was saying, all she cared about these days, was the style and the stigma of her flower, it's filaments and anthers.

Another day she started telling the tattooist a new story, which at first seemed to him a far-fetched, hallucinatory tale, except that she told it with so much detail and vigour. Of a little girl who had been given away by her mother. How this eight-year-old girl had just been handed over. The tourists, whom she called terrorists, had come to the island on a "visit", but had ended up taking the frightened little girl with them back to America. All the promises they made to this little girl's mother! How they would send her to school in America. How she would grow up to be a big-time doctor. The young woman told the tattooist how her mother had whispered in her ear that she was to go with these people, these strangers, and the little girl was to do what these people told her to do. They were her parents now. When the little girl started crying, her mother shushed her and told her to think of the other children. The little girl would never forget the thick wad of American dollars handed over to her mother by her new tourist/terrorist parents, and that her mother barely had time to say goodbye to her because she was so busy counting the money.

The things this couple did to the little girl-child from Jamaica! How for years she was never allowed to leave the house without one parent or the other with her. Even as she got much older. How it was that they, her "parents" – who kept handing her the begging-letters from Jamaica – also kept insisting there was no such place as Jamaica. The couple told her that her memory of a life on an island so many years before was all part of an overblown imagination, the same imagination that had landed her on the psych ward one time after another for *making-up-stories-about-such-good-*

*people*. For years she could not sort out the truth of one story from the fiction of another.

The tattooist listened without saying a word when she told how one, then the other, and sometimes both together, the couple enjoyed her; not only enjoyed her but made of her a cardboard character, filming and photographing her; sharing her with friends who eagerly came over. Calling her this horrible name – Lolita. And when the tired weakened girl left him that day, the tattooist had no choice but to trawl the Internet until he found a picture of a hardy pink plant called the oleander – a plant that the young woman said grew in abandon in the yard of a lean-to, tin-roofed house of a bedraggled woman with too many children around her. After he found the plant he sat looking at it for a long time, the tattooist, knowing, instinctively, that this would be the last time he would see her.

## TERRA NOVA

She turned to look at herself in the mirror. Legs falling away effortlessly from slender hips. This was why she always got whistles from men on the road, men who salivated when they saw her in the pants that seemed to have been sewn onto her. Yes, she admitted, she looked good, real good. That was until she turned to look at herself from the side. Then, her belly bulged slightly. Actually, more than slightly. She looked as if she were in the first trimester of a pregnancy.

*When I heard the news I couldn't believe it. I was standing in the yard washing baby clothes when someone came running up to me. I tell you my head started spinning. So many people seemed to be talking to me all at once. What was it that they were saying? Bus. Truck. Accident. Is like I couldn't understand what was happening. I needed someone to stay with the other children in the yard who I was watching so I could go to Cross Roads and go get Aunty. Before you know it I was up the road. So many people just talking-talking. Then I got to the main road. A truck. A bus. A crowd. An accident. People whispering, "That's the cousin who take care of them when the mother is at work." The police came out of nowhere. Someone was holding onto me. They would not let me see my cousin.*

Well probably her tummy was not as big as a first-trimester of pregnancy. It didn't matter anyway. Certainly not for the man she was with last night. No, she wasn't a hooker, she almost said to the reflection in the mirror. The one that was always standing there looking back at her, as if the woman in the mirror was the accuser of the woman outside of the mirror. And what was so wrong with enjoying her body, she asked the woman inside the mirror, the one who lived in a place she had come to call Terra Nova? She never took money from any of the men she was with. Not one dollar, she said, turning around to look at how tight her bottom was. She had the most perfect body. Everybody said so. Small and neat. What pleasure she could bring to others with her body! Contracting-then-letting-go. Letting-go-then-contracting. She smiled – that smug self-satisfied smile that some people accused her of.

*It was on Spanish Town Road that the accident take place. That big busy highway. The one that done claim the life of so many adults, to say nothing of little children. Especially near the passport office, which was where we were all living at the time. Sure the governmental people painted some white bridge across the road and call it a zebra crossing. As if that would help children! It certainly never help Marie. Dear sweet Marie. Buried now in Calvary cemetery. And every time… every time… I pass the spot on Spanish Town Road, all I can remember is the police holding onto me. The truck driver sitting hunched over. The bus driver with his eyes too-wide open. "The little girls," the bus driver kept saying, "the two innocent little girls!"*

◆

She looked closer at the mirror. It seemed cracked right down the middle. No wonder she thought something strange was going on. As if she had cracked right in two. How long had that crack been there, in the centre of the mirror? As if one part of her had been smiling, while the other side looked on angry, accusing. She would have thought her mother would have said something about it. But her mother had chosen to say nothing. In fact, her mother had stopped talking to her that day Marie died twenty long years ago. Of course she didn't just up and stop talking to her right away, but looking back at it, it seemed as if her mother never held another real conversation with her after that. Just a word here or there, nothing more. Never mind. She would not worry about that now. That was all behind her.

She pulled up a chair in front of the mirror. It was midday and the light pouring into the room seemed to surround her. A thought entered her mind and she pushed it away. But it entered her mind again, this time more forcefully. Soon she started to giggle. She opened her legs, slowly at first, before she flung them wide open. And there it was, the bright pink thing that gave her so much power.

◆

*The truck driver was in the wrong. That was what everyone said and that was why, that day, he had been sitting by the side of the road, his head hanging down and wringing his hands. He knew he would be going to jail. They tell me the bus driver had stopped, to let the little girls cross the road. The bus driver said later that they reminded him so much of his own two children. They tell me the bus was packed and hot, and the people were complaining. Some craned their heads through the window to see what the bus driver had stopped so long for. That was when they saw them, the two little girls in their yellow and white uniforms, crossing the road, holding hands. The people who saw them couldn't have helped but smile. The younger one, Marie, would have raised her hand to wave at them and give them a little smile. Marie was always like that. What would she have known? Did a shadow fall across her face?*

◆

She looked closer. Then even closer. There wasn't only one crack in the mirror, but many. So many cracks that now it seemed as if there wasn't one her that was rising to examine the mirror, but herself all fragmented. A breast here. A leg there. She remembered the time when her mother caught her. She must have been sixteen then and just growing into her body. Her breasts were unfolding nicely, her hips rounding out. For some time boys had been paying attention to her and sending her notes. And, to tell the truth, she had let the boys she liked touch her. Put they fingers far up into her webbed interior. She did not know how much her mother knew of what she was doing, after all, her mother was rarely at home and spent all her time going to the cemetery to visit Marie. When she was at home she was always crying. But that time when her mother came home suddenly there was no getting away for her, or for the boy hunched up naked in the far corner of her room, from the words her mother flung at her. "Slut. I wish it was you and not your sister who died!"

❧

*Everyone remember differently how Marie looked in her coffin. For me it was something I hope to never see again as long as I live. I was sorry I ever look in that coffin. No matter how hard I try to get that picture out of my mind, I can never forget it. It was the same way that I could not get them to stop what I considered a bad spectacle. Aunty was there, looking down at her dead daughter in her coffin, murmuring about what an amazing job they had done with her face, how Marie look peaceful, like she sleeping. I remember everything quite differently. Yes, Marie was in a pretty frilled white dress like Aunty always remember; but even though we give the mortician a photograph, there is only so much you could do against tons of steel on a fifty-pound little girl's body. It would have been better, I always say, if they had given the child a closed casket.*

❧

Never mind the broken parts of her that were now confronting her from the mirror, *she was pretty.* Of that she was sure. People wanted her. Men wanted her. She loved it when they told her how much they loved her. In the upscale hotel that Carl took her to last night, Terra Nova, he had told her over and over again, as she contracted-and-let-go, how much he loved her. How he could not live without her. How the fat red wife he had at home could not hold a candle to her. Yes, that was what Carl told her as he entered her. So never mind what her mother said about she was a slut and that she wished she was the one who had been crushed by that truck. None of that did not matter. No, none of that did not matter at all.

❧

*I am not no big-time specialist or pastor nor nothing and I can't talk and give advice to anyone over the radio. But I think parents should be careful how they talk to their children. Yes. Like they say in church, parents must be careful 'bout the messages they sending. Mothers in particular, for ninety* percent of the times is the mother alone raising children on this island; the fathers just gone, don't even look back on their children. So mothers in particular have to be careful. That is why I think Aunty never treat Cicely right after Marie died, never treat Cicely like she supposed to treat her. Aunty spend all her life crying over Marie, who she always said was prettier. And Cicely, she try to do everything to please her mother. But all Aunty do is call Cicely all kind of bad name. Saying that she is a slut. Saying that she wished the truck had flattened out her head instead of Marie's. Terrible things like that. Like I say, I am no radio specialist and cannot talk to people much, but I know that must hurt. Is true, Cicely have a lot of man. But if the man in the radio is right, the one they say is a specialist, the one people call in and talk to, and I listen to them talk everyday, if that man is right, I know that Cicely looking for something, something that her mother never give her. Even I, fool fool as I am and living back in the country, even I know what Cicely is looking for from all those men, even if Cicely herself don't know. She was crying when I talk to her the other day on the brand new cellular phone she send me from Kingston, crying, she said, she don't know for what reason. But I know why Cicely crying, even if she don't know, or what she looking for when she keep telling me some foolishness about how this man love her and that man love her, and she have so much power. Poor Cicely is all I can say. Poor, poor Cicely. Her mother never done right by her.

## A GIANT BLUE SWALLOWTAIL BUTTERFLY

Scott saw it the moment he opened his eyes. He immediately closed his eyes and hoped that when he opened them again, the menace with its cobalt-blue wings would be gone. It didn't even look like a real butterfly, the thing perched on the cream-coloured walls with such large blue wings.

No, it looked more like a hummingbird, one of those bright and colourful birds he had seen on his first trip to the island of St. Sebastian a couple of years before. How taken he'd been with the tiny bird, the rapid fluttering of its wings, the long arched beak and the dazzling colours.

To this day, whenever he thought about a hummingbird, he saw streaks of magenta, emerald, silver and a long thin beak pushed deep into a bright red flower. He had been fascinated, wondering what would happen if the serrated petals of the hibiscus flowers folded over, covering the tiny bird. Would it suffocate, or would it know how to use its beak to break free of the flower? He was looking out of the hotel window. Beyond were the many shades of blue of the island's waters, nearer were the trees and the many different flowers. The hummingbird, with its tall thin beak still deep inside the flower, was almost close enough to touch.

Perhaps he could catch it, he'd thought, getting up stealthily from the bed where the woman's body was still curved in sleep, perhaps he could hold this bit of magic in his hands. And he would have done it too, was almost upon the tiny bird when the woman stirred, and called his name, startling the bird, which immediately flew away. How irritated he was with the woman after that. So much so that for the rest of the vacation he kept pulling away from her, wanted her to leave him alone, telling her he had to catch up with his reading.

When he opened his eyes again the butterfly was still sitting there and looking at him. Who could he tell that he was being menaced by a giant blue butterfly? That every morning for the last two years it had been on the wall looking down at him. Was it his imagination that the stupid butterfly was laughing at him? Or was it loneliness and sadness that he saw in the butterfly's dark eyes? No, he decided, the butterfly was not sad or lonely. The insect was laughing at him. Well, no one laughed at him, he mumbled, getting out of bed. Only days before he'd gone to Home Depot and bought a large butterfly catcher, which now leant up against the refrigerator in the kitchen. He would show that butterfly. But by the time he came back, the butterfly was gone. He spent half an hour looking for it before he gave up, defeated. The butterfly had outwitted him again.

It was in St. Sebastian that he met Dora. She was one of the girls sitting in the bar in the evenings when he went down to get a drink. When they finally got together, he made it a point of honour never to ask Dora what she was doing at the bar night after night; he did not want to know the answer to that question. But there she was, the six nights that he was on the island, chatting up the bartender, a colourful drink in her hand, a big bright red flower behind her ear.

He knew she was aware that he kept looking at her, never mind that he had come on his vacation with a woman – a young woman who worked on a student program in New York, a young woman he should be paying attention to, but Rachel just did not hold his interest. What he wanted to do was get to know the woman with the big red flower in her hair leaning against the bar. He wanted to know what she told the bartender to have him smile just so.

Back at home, the butterfly was still on his mind as he made his way to work. Staring down at him as if it were both judge and executioner. No, that was not right, the butterfly acted as if it were a lawyer, looking coolly at him and waiting for some kind of answer as to what he had done with his life. Why had he never married? Why didn't he have any children? He decided that he didn't like lawyers, even though he was one. Well, he wasn't really – he had gone to law school but hadn't practised.

He was really a union man. A David throwing his stone at mighty Goliath. Just now, his little team was up against a gargantuan private university that did not want to pay its adjuncts a living-wage. What irked him even more was that the adjuncts they were treating so unfairly included those who taught on a "special program" that catered for poor students and students of colour. He could not and would not lose that case. He was transported back to the day he graduated from law school, a juris doctor no less.

"Finally," his grandmother had said, wiping her eyes, "finally we have a doctor in the family."

Well that was what he wanted for those poor and those black students; that one day someone else would get to say, "Finally, we have a doctor in the family."

But here now, in his car, was the blue butterfly. How could it have gotten in? The cussed insect must have followed him from home! So, had it taken to following him around now? The fluttering blue thing. Next thing he knew the creature would be in his office. No, he could not allow that to happen. Using one hand to keep driving, he went after the butterfly with his free hand. When that did not work, he went after the butterfly with both hands. It took the violent swerving of the car and the horns from all the other drivers to bring him back to his senses. He could have killed himself going after the creature, but still it got away.

❧

He had gone back to the island and stayed in the same hotel where he had stayed with Rachel. The woman who he had first seen leaning against the bar with the big red flower in her hair was still there, as if waiting for him. He sidled up to her. "Hi, my name is Scott."

The woman had looked him up and down, as if she was trying to make up her mind about him.

"Dora," she said, after a while.

"Can I get you something to drink?"

Again she looked him up and down.

"Sure," she answered.

Everything about her told him that she was not the kind of woman he should be buying a drink for, or having a drink with. But he was a man, after all, and didn't every man at some point in his life fall for a woman like this?

Things went fast after that. The woman under him. The woman on top of him. Riding him. So many stars exploding. The way she leaned in close and whispered something, then threw back her head and laughed as she rode him; her breasts, like two perfectly round, brown-husked coconuts, fitting perfectly in the palms of his hands; her legs like rubber that could wrap around anything. He would never forget her low soft purr. When he looked into her eyes, he thought he could see the future. So he asked no questions. Did not want to know what she was doing at the bar in the evenings. It was a clean slate for the two of them when they began their life together.

On his third trip back to the island to see her, Scott told Dora he wanted her to move to live with him in America. But instead of getting excited and clapping her hands and jumping onto him, as he expected – as he had imagined her doing on the plane ride from New York, something uncertain and suspicious came into her eyes.

"Merica?" Dora asked slowly, "you want me to pack up my life and move to Merica? You want me to give up my life on the island I born and grow on, and go live in America?"

Anybody else would have jumped at the chance he offered. There was the big beautiful apartment in Carol Gardens in downtown Brooklyn; he made a better-than-good salary.

"But who tell you," she said after a while, "who give you the impression I ever interested in living in America?"

He did not know what to say. He did not want to hurt her feelings by pointing out that it was because of him that she was living in a two-bedroom apartment in a good part of town, that she had the lovely car she was now driving. For all he knew, she'd been living in one of the zinc shacks he had seen on the island, before he came along and rescued her.

"I need you," he said slowly. "I need to see you everyday... I want to wake up and see you... see us together... in New York City."

The answer so surprised her that Dora felt herself softening. She looked away and her eyes began filling with tears. Hadn't she always longed for a man to say those words to her? Those exact words? Hadn't she always longed for a man to tell her that she completed him, and that he needed her in his life? Yes, that was exactly what she had always wanted. When she looked back at Scott, she caught a glimpse of herself in his eyes; she was already packing.

Yet, Dora could never forget her mother's words when she went to tell her she was moving to America.

"Remember I tell you" her mother had said, turning to spit out a thick wad of yellow phlegm to clear her throat, "remember I tell you that man cubbitch like star-apple leaf! Nothing change on you as fast as man! Man is green lizard. And you would be so far away from your own people! What happen if that man change on you quick-a-clock in faraway America? What if him turn out to be nothing more than green lizard or star-apple leaf? What you going do then? Who you going turn to? But I can see from the look on your face, the look in your eyes, that you done make up your mind. I can see you think you have it all figured out. You going to go away with that man that come to you like a complete stranger. You going to go away with him to that big place people call America. I won't stop you, no, for you your own big woman now and should know what you doing. No, I won't stand in your way. You is woman enough now to make your own decisions and stand on your own two feet."

"And in any case," Scott had said, when he was helping her pack, "I don't think you will miss the island as much as you think. New York has a big Caribbean community, especially in Brooklyn where I live. There is a big West Indian Labour Day parade. You will always be surrounded by thousands and thousands of your own people."

Still Dora remembered the words of her mother. "A man his age – what you say he is now? Forty-five almost fifty years old? Why he never married? Why he don't have no children? Strange. Sound like some non-soul person to me if ever there was one. Someone who can't pitch his tent and settle. Someone that deep down don't like people, all he say he working "on behalf" of people. I have met them types before, and they could kill you with false kindness, those non-soul people. But like I say, you twenty-seven years old now, old enough to know what you doing."

❧

For a short while after she moved to New York with Scott, all went well between them. The nagging doubt from her mother's warning that trailed her all the way to America had disappeared in Scott's attentiveness. Yes, she had done the right thing in leaving the little two by four island and coming to big-time America. Wasn't that what all grown-up women did? Move to go live with the man who chose them?

She still held these thoughts tightly closed as a rosebud in the centre of her chest, even when it started to bother her that Scott wanted everything done just-so in the apartment. The cleaning lady who came in once a week to do the cleaning, she knew him so well, he insisted, even though he didn't think they had physically ever met each other. He just left the key in a place where the cleaning lady knew where to find it and her payment would be in a small white envelope on the small, yellow, formica folding table in the kitchen.

This woman left everything in the apartment just as he wanted it, Scott kept insisting, when Dora annoyed him by moving things around. The cleaning lady never did any such thing, so he always knew where to find things. She even knew to arrange the milk cartons in the refrigerator in such a way that he could see the expiration dates before he reached for them.

Then there was that time they were coming back from a Yankees game in the Bronx and she wanted to talk to him about something. It was about the polyp that the gynaecologist had found during her annual examination. He'd thought that the polyp might be the source of her intense cramps. But Scott refused to listen. The commentary on the game they had just seen was on, and she should talk to him some other time about the polyp.

After a while, it seemed to Dora that whenever she tried to explain to herself just what was happening between herself and Scott, the image that came to mind was of a fruit falling in slow motion. A precious sweet-sop that she was helpless to stop from hitting the ground and smashing open; or a sweet brown naseberry that slipped from the grasp of her hand.

That was until the day Scott came home with what he thought was the answer to their problem, and Dora had to admit that, yes, he was genuinely trying hard to find the answer to the nameless thing that was ailing her. One of the local unions he worked for, he told her, was sponsoring a float in the annual labour day parade that wound it's way for miles along Eastern Parkway in Brooklyn – all the islands of the Caribbean represented in their colourful costumed finery. But one of the women – the one who was the giant blue butterfly at the head of the float – had been taken violently ill, hospitalised. The union was frantic to find a replacement, a dark-skinned island beauty who could jump and sing and carry on so. When he heard this, Scott had thought immediately of the woman he had met on the island, the one with the big red flower in her hair, and he knew that this woman, the one with the easy manner and the light-bulb smile – the one who could make you feel as if you were the most important person, if not the only person that mattered – was hiding out somewhere in the silent grey woman who now spent all her time sitting on a chair and looking out of the window. Scott had volunteered her.

When Dora went down to try on the costume, it fitted her perfectly. It clung to her body, as if all along it had been sitting there just waiting for her to step right into it. How easily she transformed into a gigantic blue butterfly with such dazzling sequins! It was her long-forgotten life. That bright blue colour reminded her of all she missed, all she had given up, and all that she now longed for. That bright blue colour pulsed through her as if it were her blood. The minute she put on the costume she remembered all the songs from all the islands; knew all the dance steps. So much so that the members of her troupe looked on in astonishment when the songs burst through her mouth, as if propelled by a force greater than herself.

As for Scott, he was on the parkway that day, pointing his Dora out to everyone, there at the head of the procession. He would remember seeing her making her way down the middle of the road, laughing and talking with everybody in that intimate way she had even in a large group of people.

That was the last day he saw her. That was the last image he had of her. A giant blue swallowtail butterfly, going down the road.

## SOLILOQUY

Dear Sister Lorna,

You don't know me, but I know you. At least I feel as if I know you. To me, you are good, honest and loving. You would have to be that way to spend thirty-five years of your life with one person. I heard he called you his queen and that in honour of that title you grew the locks that he loved seeing you in, the locks that are now mostly silver. Then you started wearing bright-coloured tams in red, green and gold. Rasta colours. I want you to know that I am a rastaman too. A rastaman who is on the lookout for a nice queen like you. I know it has not been that long since your man passed. I know they called him Pencil. I followed his case closely in the newspaper. How Pencil died of an asthma attack after he was left untreated in the Kingston Public Hospital. How for days, then weeks, no one in your family knew what happened to Pencil because no one at that hospital we have here had the sense or decency to know that perhaps it would be a good idea to contact his family. I read about how day after day, then night after night, you went out looking for him, your man of thirty-five years together; how you searched all over Kingston, all over Papine and Mona, thinking that perhaps Pencil had not gone to KPH to get treated but to the University Hospital in Mona, which everyone knows is better.

Sister Lorna, I followed your story as you appealed to the public for anyone who might know the whereabouts of your common-law husband. That you didn't have much, but you could give a little money. I tell you, Sister Lorna, I had a bad feeling in the pit of my stomach, a really bad feeling the first time I read your story, because you really do not want to go missing in Jamaica these days, especially in Kingston or Spanish Town or Montego Bay, because that is usually the last anyone hears from you. So many mothers never even get the chance to bury their sons and daughters. Bodies never show up. People just go missing. We, as a people, have sunken mighty low, Sister Lorna, mighty low. But maybe you were one of the lucky ones, because day after day the papers report on you looking for Pencil and you never stop until Pencil was found in one of the many morgues of the city. Those idiots at the hospital did not have the common decency to tell you that Pencil died. But when Pencil's brother, the big-time university professor from the United States went down to the KPH and start speaking in that American accent, and talking about investigation and American lawyers, is then one of the doctors came out and looked at the flyer you made and nodded and said, "Yes, that is the chap." Pencil had died of an asthma attack close to three weeks earlier. That was when some idiot at the hospital tell you that because of the constant killing in Kingston, the morgues were forced by the government to divide up the work amongst them. If you die of gunshot wound, you go to Morgue X. Everybody hates Morgue X because they're doing so much business. If you die of a stab wound or were a child or very elderly you go to disgruntled Morgue Y, who feel they not getting enough business and that gunshot deaths should be divided into two categories – those killed by the police, and all the others. They would be quite happy to take only the ones killed by the police, because, despite the public outcry, the police still kill about 500 people a year, mostly young men from around West Kingston, and everybody know that those same young men are busy killing each other to the tune of about 1700 murders per year. So if Morgue X just gave Morgue Y the police killings, then everybody happy and Morgue X still making more than everybody else because they'd get that much more bodies. As for poor Morgue Z, they get all the "natural" deaths and have declared over and over again that if it wasn't for accidents they would be long out of business. For how many people you know die of an asthma or heart attack or any kind of illness anymore? At one point they weren't doing so badly with AIDS-related deaths, but the government with the help of foreign people step in and manage to stabilise the AIDS crisis to 1 to 1.5% of the population, and while still high, the number of AIDS deaths is now under control – so there is not that much money to be made there anymore. In any case, everybody know that only certain people – loose and dirty people – catch AIDS. So Morgue Z was for a further division of the death by gunfire into two camps: those by head wounds and all the others. They were prepared to take all the others, because most of the shootings were head wounds and Morgue X and Morgue Y could share those between them. Well, as it turn out, Pencil was among the natural deaths and so he was in Morgue Z.

Sister Lorna, I read how you fall to the ground when the doctor confirm that Pencil was indeed dead. That when you got to Morgue Z, you did not go up to look at Pencil, but you let your brother and Pencil's brother go up to identify the body. I guess a part of you was hoping against hope that it would not be Pencil after all, because I hear that you been telling some of his close friends that Pencil had just taken off to go spend some time alone in the country, like he been saying he wanted to do for a long time now; he was tired of all of the killing and violence in Kingston – even though you know that Pencil was not the type of person who would just go away for days and weeks at a time without telling anyone where he was going. But perhaps, you kept telling his friends, Pencil lost his mind and was walking around deranged. Just days before, you say how Pencil keep saying he could not make any sense of Jamaica anymore. People just killing each other like it was nothing. Young people especially.

You and Pencil live all your life in what we now call a "garrison community" and over the years you two see how things decline in that community, how people start fighting over politics, the PNP with the JLP, even going into each other's community, firing shots and killing people. Even as stupid as that seemed to you and Pencil, this made more sense than the gang warfare that was now taking over the island. At least with political warfare people expect to get something if their MP get elected – a bag of flour here or a pound of sugar there – but with this gang warfare mothers were just left with the dead bodies of their sons to bury. You and Pencil could not believe that you would be longing for the 1980s to come back, because that 1980 election was real bloody. But now boys that grew up with each other thought it alright to shot and kill each other over the smallest things – which never happen in the 70s and 80s. At least with politics, people could tell themselves they were fighting to put some food on their table.

Ah, Sister Lorna, this little note that I plan to write to you is turning out into one long letter. So, after the body was found, Sister Lorna, the body of your beloved Pencil, I know there was the whole business of the funeral. First you had to pay for the plot of land at Dovecot – that cemetery everybody say is getting bigger and bigger every year. Sister Lorna, I hear that if you go out to Dovecot, all ten twelve funerals going on at once, and some of the funerals come like party, with loud music and people dancing and carrying on and somebody selling food. Is like in Jamaica now funeral turn into celebration. I don't go to Dovecot because, like I say, I am a rastaman at heart, and rasta don't mix up in dead business. Still this singing and dancing that going on at funeral, like funeral is some kind of party, is really too much for me. I am with the pastor who I read about in the newspaper the other day who stopped the funeral of the "Area Leader" and tell them all to cart out of his church with their indecent old naygah behaviour. Ragga Ragga dancing in church? They were to get out of his church with their singing and dancing and the clothes that more fit for nightclub and weddeh-weddeh than in his church that is a holy place. That man was right on. But I know that you are a good woman and you would never let that happen to Pencil.

The first thing you told a news reporter that come to interview you is that you had to decide on the funeral home to handle Pencil's body. Depending on the funeral home you chose, that would decide what kind of funeral Pencil would have. Naturally you weren't going to go with funeral home A, because that was the home for politicians, celebrities and big time shottas. This is the home you go to if you want a glass casket drawn by a horse and buggy and you have a lot of money. You also didn't consider funeral home B, who get some shottas, but usually these were the ones that didn't have much money. Still, with Funeral Home B, you got a glass front casket and your body goes to the cemetery in a nice gold Lexus. Funeral Home B deny this, but they can also provide you with a whole bunch of dancehall queens to cry and carry on at your funeral. After that, there are all sorts of other funeral homes to choose from, because, let's face it, Sister Lorna, the funeral business is one of the most thriving industries in Jamaica these days. In Kingston, Montego Bay and Spanish Town especially. The last time I pass my place and end up at the KPH, I was surprised at the number of funeral homes around the hospital and all the people outside the hospital gate enquiring if I was looking for services for the dead. Oh my dear Sister Lorna, I just don't know what is happening in this country that we call Jamaica. *The Sunday Gleaner* did carry a little part about Pencil's funeral in a nice small Seventh Day Adventist Church, not far from where you live, and I hear that even people from foreign come down to pay tributes to Pencil, for he did sound as though he was a good man and he could draw well and that is why people called him Pencil. I hear that Pencil was driven through the community where he lived one last time, and, Sister Lorna, I know it must have moved you to see all the people who come out to wave and sing and say goodbye to Pencil.

Sister Lorna, I hear that they had to hold you up at Dovecot when they call for the last look on the body, before it went into the ground, that you didn't want to go, but then you found the strength… yes, you found the strength, Sister Lorna… to say, unnu all let me go… I can stand up on my own two feet… I have to fix something on Pencil's lapel, because this is the last thing I will do for my Pencil. And you went over and you did fix the lapel and you stood there for a long time just looking down at Pencil. Since you were fifteen years old that man was your life. That man would always bother bother you and throw pebbles after you to get your attention and tell you that when you flat-iron your hair you look like Chinee. I hear that Pencil never talk to you for one whole year when you get pregnant for somebody else, but when police kill your baby father over foolishness, him take in you and your baby, and raise up the little girl like she was his own.

Sister Lorna, I hear you and Pencil use to play sometimes as if the two of you were children, people looking at you both and shaking their heads and saying, but look these two grown people behaving as if they was children. Well, Sister Lorna, when I done follow your story in the newspaper and on the radio, I say to myself that Sister Lorna must be a good woman, and for years now I looking for one good woman. I know that it hasn't been that long since Pencil died, Sister Lorna, but I couldn't wait and I decide to write you this letter. I don't know if you have any plans to see anybody, and like I say is all a little bit early, but I putting in my word early, Sister Lorna, because, believe me when I say, I am looking for a woman just like you.

## SOLDIER

The man had been living by himself for many years, in a house on the hill, far from everyone else. Maybe, they said, the people who knew him and now felt foolish for knowing him, maybe he had gotten away with as much as he did, for as long as he did, because he did not mix much with the local people. You could see them on the news programmes, uncomfortable men and women who would shift about when the questions were put to them about who exactly was the man who had been living among them for so long.

A woman identified only as Shirley was the most succinct. She said that the man rarely spoke, but just nodded when he was spoken to. She did not know how true it was, but she remembered being told, from the time she was a little girl, that the man was from Germany. That he had been a soldier and had fought someone called the Nancys.

An elderly man named Ceebert said the man had turned up shortly after the second world war, had stepped off a boat with a few boxes and a large wooden trunk and settled into the house on the hills that had belonged to a Jewish merchant, one Hubert Janovich, who bought the place on one of his many trips to the island. Janovich, it was said, had wanted a cool place where he could stare out at the calming waters around the island. The few people who could remember him said Janovich used to have grand parties and tell tales about his time in the movie business in Hollywood, how he knew some of the most important stars of his day. One day, Janovich had gone on a trip abroad and the young blond-haired man who walked with a limp returned in his place. All this young man seemed to want to do was get to Janovich's house and be left alone to calm something that troubled him.

"That's until he gets well," the people had said at the time. "As soon as he is well, you will see him with one dark-skin girl after another, and before you know it, little half-breeds will be filling up the place. It's the same with all of the white men who come to these islands."

But things turned out differently.

A young girl, Myrtle, had made her way up to the house to be hired as a helper. This gave the people pause. As well as being deaf, Myrtle was dumb. Why would the young man take on as a helper a woman who could say nothing to him? A young woman to whom he could say nothing? What ungodly intentions did the young man have towards Myrtle? It was then they really started to think that there was something strange about the stranger in their midst, though they couldn't help but notice that Myrtle was free to come and go as she pleased, and she did not look in any way unhappy. In fact, the girl seemed to have taken to the job and was flourishing. For the first time she had respectable shoes and clothing and, before long, was able to pay down on a small house at the foot of the hill. She now helped her mother to send her younger brothers and sisters to school. You could tell that Myrtle liked working for the handsome young stranger.

From time to time, when something needed fixing, Soldier, as the people came to call him, would reluctantly let someone inside the house. The few people who went to the house said that things were pretty much the same as Hubert Janovich had left them. There were the same lemon-coloured benches on the verandah, the same huge mahogany dining room table, the same mosquito netting around the bed. It was true that things were getting older, but since only one person lived in the house, there was not that much wear and tear, and the furniture remained in a good condition. Joey, the electrician, who went up from time to time to fix some wiring, said that apart from a large wooden trunk that made the man very nervous if you got too near it, it was as if Hubert Janovich had never left the place at all.

For a while the big wooden trunk was the source of much speculation. Some even wondered if poor Hubert Janovich was in it. But since Soldier had been able to provide stamped documents that showed he had bought the house and all its contents from Janovich in a far away place called Vienna, no one could say or do anything.

In one of those rare moments when he talked, Soldier said Janovich had seemed anxious to get the house off his hands, saying that he was thinking of setting up some kind of business in the recently created home for Jews in Palestine. As far as Soldier knew, Janovich had gone home to his people.

The fire changed all that. By then Soldier had been living on the island for a long time. No one really knew how he lived, where he got his money from, they only knew that he never seemed to be in need of anything. Some people claimed that every month a cheque came from Germany. Others said that the trunk was filled with money. Still others believed he came from a rich family.

"You have to remember," a man named Rufus told the news camera, "I grown up with Soldier always here among us. For someone like myself, he was a fixture. I know that the people who had money didn't like Soldier, because he did not mix with their kind of people. The people like me, who have no money, just left Soldier alone. It is not like his house is close to anybody else's; it's behind God's back, up there in the bushes. Is not like he bothered anybody. All Soldier seemed to want was to be left alone on his verandah. This is how, from a young boy, I grown up to know Soldier."

The fire happened on the weekend when Myrtle was away, or she might have been able to help him. By then Soldier was an old man and there were so many things in that house that burned easily. No one knew for sure how the fire got started, but everybody had a story of how it moved around the house. Some people said the fire jumped up the curtains at the windows and started eating its way around the large wooden house. Like a stalking animal, it climbed the stairs in giant steps up to the second floor, and started devouring all the things it saw.

When the people in the district heard the loud crackling and saw plumes of smoke billowing up, they came running with buckets of water. But their buckets were nothing to the beast that was now roaming about the house.

When Soldier, who had been standing outside, saw that the house was going to be burned to the ground, he charged back in. He came back out, pulling and dragging the heavy wooden trunk. He had just enough time to throw the trunk over the railings and leap off the verandah before everything gave way under him.

Whatever the people thought would come out of the trunk, they never expected what actually came out: paintings in heavy golden frames and marble sculptures, things that the people would learn were worth a lot of money.

Soldier had been a soldier alright, everyone would soon find out, a member of the Führer's army. He had been studying art history at the time of the war, Soldier shouted to anyone who would listen when the police finally came to take him away from a cottage. He, like the Führer, had been a talented artist. A brilliant painter. But *those Jews*, who controlled everything, had denied him acceptance at The Academy of Fine Arts in Vienna, and when he reapplied a year later he was again rejected – *by those Jews*.

When the Führer came up with the idea of the Führermuseum as a monument to mankind, he wanted to help. Those Jews did not know how to appreciate the things they had. So he took the paintings from rich Jewish families for the Führermuseum, and yes, some of the smaller ones, he kept as his own. When the Führer killed himself and Germany was defeated, he had taken the smaller works with him from place to place for a few years, before he met Janovich and decided to come to Jamaica.

No one ever knew what really happened to poor Hubert Janovich though there would be all kinds of stories. And for the longest time all the people who lived close to Soldier could do was look at each other, shake their heads solemnly and mumble, "That is why it is better to stick to the evil that you know, because in the end you just can't trust foreign people."

## ZEMI

The three boys were there the night a fire brightened the sky. When no one was looking, they signalled to each other and took what looked like a smooth wooden sculpture and disappeared with it into the night. Since the old man whose house was on fire was going on and on about the things being burnt up in the fire, they guessed that what they had was valuable. At the very least they knew that it was valuable to the old man.

When they got to the mouth of the cave they used as their hideout and took out a flashlight to see just what it was they had taken, they could not hide the disappointment on their faces. What they had was some dark, polished wooden object that looked as though it was a dodo bird with a long thin piece down its back that ended in a flat base on which the bird could stand. Altogether, the dark wooden bird was the length of a hand.

"But what kind of old foolishness this that we waste we time to tek way?" Derek wanted to know. "This thing look exactly like what people carve up quick and sell to fool-fool tourist people down at Bay."

"The tourist things down at Bay look better than this," Carlton said. "At least with the things down at Bay, you know what the hell they carving. This thing look like it part-bird, part-man, part-something else." He shuddered. "I just hope we don't take up crosses on we-selves when we take up this thing tonight!"

For the longest time the other boy in the group, Hugh, the one who attended Titchfield High School, said nothing. He just kept running his hands over the smooth dark wood, which he was sure was mahogany. Someone had taken the time to work on the piece of wood and he vaguely remembered a teacher in first form telling them something about the first inhabitants of Jamaica, who were the Tainos, though most Jamaicans called them Arawaks, carving things that looked like this. They were not Arawaks, he remembered his teacher insisting, but Tainos. It was the first time he had heard the word Taino and he'd rolled the word over and over again in his mouth as if it was a big blue marble that when you held it up to the sky looked as if it contained the world. The boy had forgotten what the difference was between Tainos and Arawaks, but he remembered the teacher being quite adamant on the point. The teacher had told them that, whether they knew it or not, the Tainos, the original inhabitants of the island, were right there with them, in the foods that they ate and in some of the words they spoke, though most people could not see this. If they had not been so far from Kingston, the teacher said, if it had not been a four-hour drive there and a four-hour drive back, he would have taken them to see the Taino pieces at the National Gallery. The boy kept looking down at the statue. The best he could do, the teacher said, was show them a couple of drawings of pieces in the National Gallery. This carving looked like one of them.

The boy kept his mouth shut. His friends thought he was strange enough already, what with his love for girly subjects like art and literature. When he passed the examination to attend Titchfield High School, his friends, who had not passed, had almost stopped speaking to him. Only idiot boys passed their common entrance exams. They had looked at him with such scorn, said he was a sissy and that they did not want him near them because people might think they were "sissified" too. He would not say anything to upset them now. He had come on the raid with the other two because it was such an easy target, an old man's house on fire. Lately, they had been going on more and more raids and taking the goods back to the hideout. Though his grandmother did not know it, he had started skipping classes to go pick-pocketing with his friends, both of them now secondary school dropouts.

"Just plain foolishness!" the one called Derek yawned. "I cannot believe I come out of my bed for this foolishness! I cannot believe I was in and out of that house with buckets of water, pretending I helping to put out the fire, just for this!"

Derek was what most of the girls in the district considered "nice" – tall with the eyes of a cat and the pretty yellow skin of a ripe banana. His father, people said, had been a sailor, though like many of the boys in the district he did not know who his father was. He was being raised by his grand-mother while his mother worked as a housekeeper in Kingston.

Again Carlton spoke up. "When I hear the old man's house on fire, I figure they must have something in that house worth taking, for the old man always going on and on in Miss Pearl's rum shop about the valuables he have in that house." He reached over and took the carving from Hugh. "Is a good thing we luckier this afternoon with the chains and earrings we get. We won't get nothing for something looking like this."

The other two boys nodded.

"Well, all in a day's work" Carlton said, words he'd heard his uncle say after cutting and selling his bananas in the Bay. "Yes, all in a day's work."

"So what we going do with it?" Hugh asked.

"This piece of old foolishness?" Carlton was now turning the carving over and over in his hands. "Might as well we leave it in some place far in the back of the cave, which is where it belong." He tossed the carving in a corner where it landed with a loud crack.

There it remained for the next couple of years, kicked or tossed out of the way as the boys brought more things to the cave. By then they had graduated from pick-pocketing to more elaborate and daring robberies. Once, they entered a jewellery store in Buff Bay, masked, with high-powered weapons and made off with every last piece of jewellery in the store. But they had such a hard time getting the jewellery off their hands, having to travel far to sell it in other parts of the country, that they decided from now on they were going to deal only with cash. So they robbed the Courts Furniture Store in Annatto Bay, right before Christmas when people were finishing off paying for their purchases. Next it was the McDonald's on Fletcher's Lane and the haberdashery in St. Margaret's Bay.

Hugh had long dropped out of school, telling his grandmother that he had a job out at Boundbrook, though he did not tell her what exactly he was doing or who he was working for. Boundbrook was miles away from Nonsuch.

The other two boys gave their grandmothers similar stories.

The people of sleepy-eyed Portland wondered who could be preying on their parish. Nothing like this had happened before. Many felt sure that it was people outside of their community who were going on with all of these robberies, people from Kingston no doubt, though a few people kept saying that no, it must be someone local, because the robbers knew exactly when and how to strike before they melted back into the bush like duppies.

Still others pointed to the fact that these things had only started happening since the new highway was built linking Portland to Kingston and Montego Bay. One pastor preached that since the highway and all the 'new developments', things had gone downhill. People could drive in and out as they had a mind to. At least when the roads had been bad, it wasn't so easy to move about.

The boys loved hearing the talk about them. Sometimes they joined in the conversation. No, it was not someone from the parish, one of them would say. Yes, it was someone from the parish, another of them disagreed. Then they would start arguing with each other. Alone, they would have a roaring laugh about how stupid Portland people were. "Imagine, they thinking is some big-time criminals from Kingston doing these things! When is only we! Is only we! Three boys right here in the district of Nonsuch! Portland people! Fool-fool Portland people!"

Hugh, the high school dropout, was now the acknowledged brains of the operation. He talked strategy. The other two were the hands behind the triggers. They now believed in their invincibility, even talked of setting up shop in Kingston where, with their skills, they could get rich in a hurry. Hugh was careful to warn against ostentation. They should not call attention to themselves. When they made a really big haul, he encouraged them to go and reap something on their land or try to get some kind of work to account for the extra things they would be buying.

❧

One day, when they were all relaxing in the hideout from a particularly successful run at a nightclub the night before, Hugh's eyes fell on the carving. Over the years, as it was tossed here and there, more and more pieces had broken off. Carlton and Derek were for throwing it out; it gave them the creeps, but something about the statue still appealed to Hugh and he was for it staying in a dark corner of the cave. The old man from whom they had stolen the carving had since died and every time Hugh looked at the carving he winced, thinking how for years the man would talk about it, how in his carelessness he had let it burn up in the fire, and how he had found that carving in a cave painted in a dull red colour that had all sorts of strange markings and symbols. From the minute he found it, the old man said, he knew that the carving had a strange power; he was so sorry it had been destroyed. He should have taken it to the authorities, he knew he should have done that, but he had loved the thing so much he could not bear to part with it. Now everything was dust, nothing but dust, and this was all his fault.

Hugh kept looking at the carving. No, he thought, the carving could not be a zemi, for by then he'd remembered the word the teacher had used when he showed them the pictures at school. Zemis were rare and precious things and this did not look in any way rare or precious. It just looked old and tired, with more and more pieces missing. He could not understand why he kept holding onto the stupid thing.

❧

They had decided to rob the hotel at Treasure Man's Cove. Hugh would say later that he had a sense of foreboding about it, but the hotel was right there in Fairy Hill and on the days they cased the place, there was no security. This robbery would be as easy as all the others. But this time the Port Antonio Bay Police, who they had been laughing at for years, were waiting for them. When the boys arrived, wearing their trademark black and white ski masks, the police opened fire. Dexter died on the spot, Carlton on the way to the hideout. Hugh had been shot in the arm, and the police with dogs followed him all the way up to the cave where a large crowd gathered, among them his grandmother.

"Do, mister policeman do, don't finish him off right here, before his old grandmother," she said. "Don't do it. Don't do it before his grandmother. Do, mister policeman do, I know a grandmother grown you up too."

The senior officer had looked at her and said nothing.

"Do mister policeman," the grandmother had continued, "take him alive, please take him alive. If him do all the things you all say him do, one thing him never do is kill nobody. So I beg you, let me talk to him, him will surrender, don't kill him please... Don't kill him here before his old grandmother. Him is all I have. I know," she said, tears streaming down her eyes, "I know is a grandmother raise you up too."

Something about what the old woman said moved the officer, who called out to Hugh to come out with his hands in the air. His grandmother was there, and he did not want to shoot him before his grandmother. Hugh wasn't to make no funny moves, was not to come out with no weapon, not have no ski mask on his face, for that would be the end of him, the policeman said.

"Listen to the police," Hugh's grandmother said over the hushed crowd. "Come out and give yourself up, Hugh. Come out and surrender. Listen to me, Hugh, this is your grandmother talking to you."

The crowd waited until a slim, dark figure appeared at the mouth of the cave, his hands raised above his head, searching the crowd for his grandmother's face. When he found her, Hugh lowered his eyes and did not say anything. He could see her hurt and disappointment.

When an inventory of the cave was done, the old wooden carving was found, in pieces, along with a few pieces of jewellery. The carving would have been thrown away, except that it exerted a pull on a young police officer, who asked for the strange-looking object. He took the carving, wrapped up in old newspaper, to the National Gallery, where the director's eyes popped open when she saw what the policeman had walked in with. The carving was a zemi alright and when the pieces were recovered from the floor of the cave and put together, it turned out to be one of the most important zemis found on the island.

From his jail cell, Hugh laughed a sardonic little laugh as he read in the newspaper about the carving said to be worth untold amounts of American dollars. He had always known that there was something special about it, but the other two refused to listen to him when he suggested they take it to his old school teacher, who would know for sure what it was and what they should do with it.

"Put it over there," one or the other of the two would say. "Keep it in the dark. Careful you take it out and someone recognise it belong to the old man and we bring eyes on we-selves."

Hugh continued laughing louder and louder, even though a warder was coming towards him with a hard wooden baton and telling him to shut up; he was causing a disturbance with his loud laughing. It was a precious piece of Jamaica's heritage, worth more than all the things he and his two dead friends had stolen, the newspaper article was saying. A real authentic zemi. The policeman who had brought it in would be paid handsomely for his "discovery". Hugh's laughter rang out long and loud, despite the baton coming down on his head, trying to silence him. He could not stop laughing.

## EFFIGY

That Sunday, instead of going to the big Catholic Church he always attended on Old Hope Road, Howard turned the car around and headed back up the hills. The woman was still there when he returned, wearing the same bright red dress that came all the way down to her ankles, her hair wrapped tight in a high, white roll. When had the woman moved into the hills? Could it be that the woman and her little shack had been right there in Jackson Heights since the devil was a boy? No, Howard shook his head at the thought, the shack could not possibly have always been there, set back from the road almost surrounded by calabash trees. No, this was the first time he remembered seeing the woman with her croton and marigold flowers.

From the safety of his car, Howard kept looking at the woman. There was such a sureness in the way she went about what she was doing, planting marigolds and crotons, going into the little shack of a house she obviously lived in and coming back out with a small plate of food that she left beside the door. The woman then filled her mouth with what he would later know was white rum before she sent it flying in a clean clear arc about the yard. She seemed to know something he did not know and he envied her.

It had been six months since Madge died. Not died, Howard thought angrily, it had been six months since Madge was murdered. It seemed like every minute of the day he kept asking himself the same two questions: how could someone have killed Madge? What in the world would anyone want to kill Madge for? But like so much on the island these days, nothing made sense to him anymore.

He knew Madge would not have resisted. She would have given whoever killed her whatever they wanted, anything she had, yet they had felt the need to kill her. He shook his head at the insanity of it all.

He had always been in love with Madge. From the moment he first saw her, a barefoot girl at the back of his parents' house, when she came to bring something to her mother, his family's helper, he knew that he was in love with the girl with the four thick plaits in her hair. He could still remember in great detail the first day he saw her. She was about ten years old and he was going on fifteen. She had on a cotton dress that was mostly white with some tiny purple flowers. She was standing by the giant flamboyant tree in his backyard and beyond that was the thick green forest. Looking at her, he had the sudden strange urge to paint her. He wanted to capture something in her that he knew, even then, he would never be able to possess.

Privilege has its price, Howard would tell himself years later, especially in a place like Jamaica, because he knew he could never have Madge in the way that he wanted to have her. His parents would never allow it and all his friends in the hills would shun him for marrying so beneath himself.

There was the day his mother found some of the drawings he had started doing of Madge on the desk in his room. His mother had flipped through the pile before she gathered them up and sat down on the bed beside him.

"These are a lot of drawings you have done of Mae Sarah's daughter," his mother had said, looking down at the drawings in her hand.

When he did not answer, she continued, "I am just wondering, why so many drawings of just one person? Why only pictures of Mae Sarah's daughter?"

Howard looked at his mother and realised with a shock that she did not know the name of their helper's daughter, this helper who had been with his family for donkey's years.

"Her name is Madge, mother. She has three sisters and two brothers."

"I see," his mother had said. "And how do you know so much about this girl?"

He knew better than to tell his mother the truth. That he had been spying on the helper's daughter. That sometimes he would go to the ramshackle house where Madge lived with her brothers and sisters and stand under the jacaranda tree with its big beautiful lilac blossoms and watch her from a distance.

"I just know is all," he told his mother. "I just know."

His mother said nothing more to him.

❧

Everyday for the next three weeks Howard went out of his way to drive over to see the woman in the shack and to look at her shrine that everyday grew more and more elaborate. Now she had added drums and tambourines, bottles of honey, more croton plants and small calabash trees. She had drawn on the outside walls of the house in thick white chalk, and had surrounded the place with smooth, bluish-grey stones that looked as if they had been taken from the bottom of a river. In the centre of the yard was a small table covered with a clean white tablecloth, and on that table was a circular constellation of clear drinking glasses filled with pretty multicoloured marbles.

One day, after watching her for a while, Howard decided to get out of the car and talk.

"Quite a shrine you have here," Howard said, standing at the barbed wire fence that marked the boundary to the woman's house. "Everyday it just keeps growing bigger and bigger."

The woman studied him for a while, before answering. "Yes, I building up this little place."

"So how long have you lived here?" Howard asked, smiling.

Again the woman took her time answering. "Not long, a month or two… nothing more than that."

"Do you live alone?" Howard could not understand why he felt compelled to ask the woman all these questions.

A pained look came into her eyes. "Yes," she said after a while, "for the most part I live alone… but that is because I no longer have my son living with me… that is because…" She was clearly struggling with what she was saying, "I live alone now because… because somebody done shot and kill him. My son. Yeah," the woman said quietly when she saw the look that came over Howard's face. "Yeah, somebody done kill my son Eric in cold blood. And that is why I now live alone."

Howard thought of Madge and for the longest while there was silence.

"Yeah, they killed him, Eric, they killed my son… And Eric was no kind of bad boy, you know," the woman said, as if explaining something to herself. "No, he never give no kind of trouble… even from the time he was a little baby… the quietest little baby there was… never cry for nothing. The police, who is the ones that shot and kill him, they kill him for no reason. Well, that is not true," the woman said, "they kill him just because of where he was living, which is in West Kingston, and not in these hills. If he was living in these hills, in one of the big fancy houses in these hills, chances are they would think twice before coming into his house, much less killing him. But in West Kingston you can kill anybody and get away with it, especially if you are the police. Yes, in West Kingston all those things done happen. But not in these hills. No, not up in these hills. Up in these hills things like that don't happen."

"I'm really sorry to hear that," Howard heard himself saying. "Really sorry to hear what happened to you. Really sorry to hear what happened to your son."

"Yes, I am sorry too."

Howard could hear the tears in the woman's voice.

"Very sorry too…" she continued. "Let me tell you, nothing so terrible as looking down on your dead son body. Nothing so terrible like that in all the world. Your son shot and killed in his own house, minding his own business. West Kingston, those things happen all the time. Not up here in these hills." For a moment the woman looked out at the hills surrounding her, before she looked back at Howard. "These flowers that I planting… these bottles and candles and honey and all the things I setting up here, they are all in rememory of my son Eric, because I know if he had lived in these hills, in one of the big houses in these hills, chances are that he would still be alive today. Even if we only lived in a little shack-shack place like this one, he would still be alive today. I know that with all my heart. The people here in the hills, they have rights, rights we don't have in West Kingston. No one can just burst into your house and kill your son in these hills… there would be so much to answer for… so many people to answer to… but no one can give me any answer about my son. They just kill my son and that is the end of that. All because we live in West Kingston.

"So I come up to these hills… put these things together… as a rememory of my son … as a rememory of my Eric. But since you the first person to stop here and talk to me, ask me what I doing and how I keeping… I tell you something else… These things that I gathered here are not only for my son, no, they not only for Eric. They are also for someone else… they also for Effigy."

"Effigy?" Howard asked, confused at the turn the woman's story had taken.

"Yes, Effigy," the woman replied.

"What Effigy?"

The woman looked him up and down again, summing him up, before making up her mind about him.

"Effigy is the woman who tell me to make up this shrine… Effigy, when I go to her crying, after the police done killed my son for no good reason, no good reason at all, killed him because he look like bad man they say, then plant gun on him and talk about is some kind of shoot out, when the whole wide world know that nothing don't go so.

"People hear my son begging for his life, telling them him not no kind of bad man; people shouting from other houses that my son innocent-innocent, quiet boy, school boy, spend all him time locked up on the verandah, not in no bad company. Still they put the gun to his head… right at his temple… People telling me my son calling out for me, calling out for his mother… Mama, Mama, I don't do anything and they going to kill me … my son begging them to spare his life… The people around begging them not to do it … still they kill him anyway… They put the gun at him temple and kill him anyway… Pop, pop, pop… three bullet holes to the head… Fourteen years old was my son… I one grow him… My son don't have no father… I was away at work and when I come back home this is what greet me… the bullet in the walls of the verandah… my son blood and brains all over the floor… I is the one that have to clean it up… I is the one that have to get someone to come take up my son's body… and for days all I can hear is my son calling me… Mama, Mama, I don't do anything and they going to kill me… Mama, Mama, come save me… So many people done tell me the same story…

"And is so I go crying to Effigy after the police done kill my son for no good reason... I trying to get my son's voice out of my head... My own mother, God rest her soul, used to tell me... Sinclair, if you ever have a problem, go talk to Effigy... this Effigy that I put so far away from me that even when I go looking I can't find her for the longest time... I looking for her everywhere... this Effigy that my mother tell me should be the one thing hanging on my wall... the only thing hanging on my wall... but I search and search until I find her... I never stop searching until I find Effigy... and when I find her and dust her off and put her back up where she belong... put her back up on the wall... Effigy is the one who tell me... raise yourself up... build a shrine to your dead son... keep up his rememory. A rememory is important. No rememory and you go crazy.

"She will find me the place to build the shrine, Effigy said, and she will give me the energy. She will guide me. Effigy, she lead me to this spot right on this hill and then she drop right out of my hand so that I know this is where I need to build the shrine, where I need to build my son's rememory, right in this little shack-shack house where nobody else was living. Right up here in these hills. This little shack-shack house have all the calabash trees that Effigy love and it close to the river that Effigy love too.

Howard remained rooted to the spot listening intently to everything the woman was saying. Why did he now have this strange feeling that he was doing something he always knew that he should be doing, that he should have done before – listening intently to this woman?

"Effigy is the one that tell me to plant the croton and marigold flowers, put out the rum and the cream soda and the bottles of water. Effigy the one that give me the strength, even now, so I can stand up here and talk to you... Yes, now I can talk to you and stop talking-talking to myself, because for months that's what I was doing, talking-talking to myself... going crazy... but Effigy give me the strength... she give me the strength to go on and continue... she give me the strength to go on with my son's rememory... You want to come inside and meet Effigy? She been telling me that you going to come soon and we going talk a little talk and then you going want to meet her. You want to come inside and meet Effigy, yes?"

Howard found himself being propelled towards the house by a force much greater than himself.

❦

Years later, people would still be talking about it, and after his death Howard would become something of a legend on the island, this man, who, when he stepped over the ledge into the woman's yard, stepped over into a whole other life. He had stopped going to the Catholic Church on Old Hope Road that he had been going to for years and started attending a whole other church with a whole different group of people, people who wrapped their heads in turbans and danced around a centre pole. He started talking about a whole different cosmology –

heavenly spirits, earthbound spirits, ground spirits. It began when he came home one day with a wooden sculpture with two long breasts and a distended belly that looked as if it had been forged in some ancient fire.

He took everything else down from the walls in his house, all the expensive paintings and photographs that he had spent a lifetime collecting, and in their place he hung the wooden sculpture with the two long breasts and the distended belly. Before long, people started whispering about him. Then his friends stopped coming to visit. They could not bear to look at it, the wooden carving with the long sad face and the closed eyes that was the only thing on Howard's wall. They felt there was something accusatory about the wooden carving that looked as if it had come out of the deepest, darkest parts of Africa. It implicated them somehow, and they could not understand why Howard could have such a thing hanging on the wall in his house.

But what his friends said, thought or did, no longer mattered to Howard. For the first time in his life he felt a free man, unburdened of something he had been carrying for too long. Then Howard started making a shrine… an ever-growing shrine at the front of his house to the one woman he had ever loved, the woman who had been taken away from him. He would always remember Madge's dark brown eyes and the laughter that bubbled up like water. He remembered the days he would leave school early and linger outside her school, just to get a glimpse of Madge, before he started following her home, eventually getting her to talk to him. They both caught fire for their deepening friendship, Madge from her mother – we-cannot-afford-to-loose-this-one-job-that-bring-food-into-the-house-all-because-you-friendly-friendly-with-Mister-Howard; and Howard from his mother, his father and all the brown-skinned uptown girls they paraded before him. For a while they had to break off their friendship, but they could not stop thinking about each other. Howard remembered the cool spring day Madge told him that since she could not have the man she wanted, she was going to join a convent, and he remembered his frustration at not being able to talk her out of it. She was a nun, working with poor people, when she had been shot to death so cold-bloodedly. He had not been able to talk about Madge's death, to anyone. He had not been able to voice what had been turning up and down inside him. That was until the day he met Effigy, who let him know that it was okay to talk about Madge, to let the world know that he had been in love with the helper's daughter. Build a shrine for her, Effigy had told him. A rememory. A rememory for Madge.

## FLAMBOYANT TREE

*A winged bird-like creature*

They would gather beneath it everyday after class, the big flamboyant with its bright orange-red flowers, and they would talk. Oh, how they would talk. About any and everything. About what had happened that day in class. That Grenadian, how he got on their last nerve! How he dismissed some of the writers they doted on; how his voice caressed the words of the few he adored. About their characters. There was always something to say. This one underdeveloped, the actions of another did not make sense to him at-all, at-all. He was a man not known for mincing his words. Did not suffer fools. They could never understand why – and he was not one of the really famous professors that you had to fight to get into their classes – they had to meet this one at his house? So far up in the hills!

Sometimes he would go on and on about his native Grenada. What had happened to some of his closest friends there. He never gave specifics. Would only mumble about "invasion" and "disaster". It-all-happened-before-you-were-born. The "things" Uncle Sam had-done-to-Grenada. Had-done-in-his-Grenada. But, he would say, looking out into a place that he alone could see, the invasion was one thing; it was totally another what Grenadians-done-to-each-other. He always felt that he-should-have-spoken-up-sooner… had he spoken up… had he said something… all those years ago… perhaps… perhaps… He could never finish the sentence.

*That was large and extremely ancient*

The days his students were not there he would sit out on the verandah of his large airy house, dragging on a cigarette, his feet up, looking out at the tree, the large flamboyant across the road. He had read somewhere that the tree was a native of Madagascar, but he did not believe this; like the calabash, this tree with its large scarlet-coloured flowers *had* to be from these islands. Why was it, he found himself grumbling one day, that people were always so quick to point out that this-and-that thing was not *native* to these islands. As if the place was one big, dark hole populated by nothing but other people's imaginations.

He remembered not too long ago reading about reggae – a type of music
he did not particularly like, even after so many years of living on the
island. Still, he was shocked to see that the idiot anthropologist-cum-
apologist who had written the book had said the beat of the island had
originated not on the island, not in the heart-blue mountains of Jamaica,
but somewhere over in Europe. In fact, in Ireland. Had been transported
along with indentured Irish labour to the islands. He put the book in
the garbage and forgot to take it out again.

He had come to Jamaica after many journeys and two failed marriages
to write his story. Tell the world the truth of what had really happened in
Grenada. Invasion. Disaster. Him reaching for the creamy Tia Maria
always on the small coffee table, the flamboyant tree right there in front of
him, the flamboyant tree with its flat, wide crown of orange-red flowers.
This tree was supposed to blossom for only several months a year, but it
seemed as if this tree, his tree, *old girl*, bloomed all year long. Such large
flowers! They had the power to make him both sad and happy. Every time
he looked out at the tree it provoked a memory. A tree blossoming in his
childhood. Somewhere near his long-dead mother's house. He was such a
young child when she died. Could barely remember her. He never did
know his father who, before he was born, left the island for England, or was
it America? No one ever heard from him again. Not so much as a photo in
a heavy silver frame sitting on a dresser. Nothing he could have taken up
and stared long and hard at to try and get a sense of the man that everyone
said he so resembled. His mother had died of waiting, people said. Died of
a broken heart, for she had really loved that-man-your-father. Not even the
old woman, Ma Chest, who had raised him after his mother died, could tell
him much about his father. Or his mother for that matter. She had been too
new to the district, but *someone* had to raise the little boy. So all he had was
a tree. Perhaps it, too, was a flamboyant tree. Such striking burnt-orange
flowers.

*With golden red plumage*

Yet so many people walked past the tree as if they did not see it. These
Upper St. Andrew people, neighbours always waving and smiling,
but never talking to each other. The place was quiet, much too quiet,
he often felt, as if this was an inversion of all that was going on elsewhere
on the island. Lately, he had taken to avoiding the newspapers. Before
long he added popular television and radio programmes. There was
only so much death and violence that one could bear to know about.
He preferred looking out at the flamboyant, sometimes walking across
the street and leaning over the white stuccoed fence and reaching up
to touch her. Its dark green shade seemed to cool the entire island.

The flamboyant was there when his house was broken into by four youths young enough to be the children of his children. They had forced him to the ground, guns at his head, and it seemed they were about to kill him. He would always be convinced that it was only the movement of the tree, as if it were the shadow of somebody coming, that caused the four young boys with black bandanas covering most of their faces to flee, taking absolutely nothing. He became a Jamaican that day, he often said, for he realised that he could die in this damn country. After the police came and went, and after his students came and went, he went over to the tree, reached up and touched her, as if he were patting her head ever so gently, "Hey *old girl*," he heard himself saying, "Thank you *old girl*. Thank you for standing here all these years just looking pretty!"

But then came the neighbour to talk, to complain to him. He did not like the students congregating outside, this neighbour, who only smiled and waved and said nothing. Talking-talking under *his* flamboyant tree. Yes, they were on the government sidewalk; still they were under *his* tree. Could he talk to them, his students? Could he do something? If he, the writing instructor, did not do something, then he, the owner of the yard, would have to do something. No, the students were not talking too loudly. But it just did not seem right to him, them congregating under the tree like that. Where did they think they were? Downtown Kingston? Before long, the neighbour complained, there would be higglers selling right outside of his house!

*Why did this creature build herself a nest?*

The writing instructor was unprepared for what actually happened. How, one morning he would wake up and take his steaming cup of Blue Mountain coffee out on the verandah. How he stood up. How he sat down again. How he started looking around him. Where was *old girl* with her many orange-red flowers? He could not believe what he was seeing! The nothing there before him! The scoundrel could not really have done it! Not without him knowing! When he hurried across the street and looked over the wall he saw a blackened stump, heavily bleeding. He leaned back against the stuccoed white wall. How fast his heart was beating! When had the man, who only smiled and waved but said nothing, set the tree on fire? In the middle of the night? Was that the hacking, then the crackling he now remembered hearing? Before he could stop himself, he was crying. It was all his fault. He had been too stubborn. He had refused to say a word to the students. The-side-walk-government-property. He shook his head slowly as he made his way back to the verandah. How could anyone have done such a wicked and terrible thing?

He was tempted to pack up and go back to Grenada immediately, even though he knew that back home his life would be in danger. Nevertheless, for hours, he seriously contemplated taking the next plane off this godforsaken island! Be finished and done once and for all with this place. Still, he had to admit it, the place had always pulled him back, and had done so since his days as a boy on campus. Always had some kind of hold over him, as if it was a luscious, chocolate-coloured river mumma. But this time he had come near to untangling himself from the arms of the heavy-breasted woman. If only he had not fallen asleep. If only he had not been visited by a large-boned, many-bangled woman wearing a beautiful, tangerine-yellow dress, crimson-coloured bennu bird flying about her. He was not to feel sad or to worry, this woman told him. He was not the one who put the machete in that man's hand and hacked and hacked away in anger for hours. It was not he who had then collected her, trunk and branches, and doused everything in gallons of kerosene oil to light one great big bonfire. No, he was not the one who had done all that. But he was to watch and see what would happen.

*Of cinnamon twigs that she ignited*

But even then he could not have predicted how the tree would rise up out of her own ashes. How she would become even more flamboyant, prettier, larger. How she would encourage more and more people to gather beneath her. How her insistent brown pods and thousands of feathery, fernlike leaves would come raining down on the yard, so much so that it would cause quite a litter. How the owner of the house would throw up his hands in utter frustration.

This was much more than he had bargained for. As if the tree itself had conspired against her owner. Had put some kind of obeah on him. Because he noticed that from the moment the man killed the tree, nothing went right in his life. First his wife of donkey's years left him. Next the children stopped calling. Then his business went bust. One problem, one botheration after another. He had to sell the miserable house. He did not care if the new owner turned out to be an inscrutable, irascible Grenadian-turned-Jamaican writing instructor.

Sometimes people would see the new owner in the evenings, walking around the property, his hands behind his back, a certain sardonic half-smile on his face. He would invariably stop before the flamboyant. Stand there for the longest time as if in prayer. They would hear the soft distinctive lilt of his voice, as if it were two old friends talking.

*The bird that many people called the phoenix*

PART TWO

## THE STORIES WE TELL OURSELVES

My mother tells me that the day I was graduating from high school in Jamaica she sat in a friend's car in New York and wept because she could not be with me. As if to make up for this forced separation (she did not then have a green card, and I did not have a visa) she sent me three most spectacular dresses for the graduation that year. In fact, so spectacular were these dresses that two of them I never wore again, they looked so much like bridal gowns. All that day, even though so many of my relatives were with me, I kept reaching for the person who was not with me: for my mother. She had been gone years, had made the journey from Jamaica first to Miami (where she worked as a live-in "helper"), then on to a cousin in New York, seeking to provide a better life for both herself and her children back home in Jamaica. Jamaica then – the 1980s – was a place of high unemployment, sharp devaluations of the Jamaican dollar, and increasing violence. There were blackouts, gun battles, not enough food on the shelves, and not enough money to buy the food that was on the shelves. Those fortunate enough to have visas were making off in droves to Canada, England, America – elsewhere. Everyone, it seemed to me, wanted to get off the island as quickly as possible. How odd, I remember thinking, that my mother should now be working as a "helper" in America, she who often employed help in Jamaica. What manner of place was this America where such a salary could sustain a certain kind of life in Jamaica? America then was a far-off magical place, a place that almost everyone I knew in Jamaica wanted to go to; a place where many people I knew would do almost anything to get to. It was the Promised Land, New York an especially magical place: the abode of relatives, of networks, of "things", a place just three and a half hours away by plane, a place where the wealthy girls at the Catholic girls school I was attending went for vacation. In my mind New York was a place of endless possibilities, a place of more-than-enough money to buy the more-than-enough things I believed lined the streets of places with such names as Brooklyn, Bronx, Manhattan, and Queens. Yes, New York was a place that loomed large in the collective consciousness of those of us living on the island, especially those, like myself, who had never set foot off the island. But most importantly to me, New York was the place where my mother now was, a place, therefore, where I desperately wanted to be. My mother was the voice over the telephone, the sender of beautiful things, the woman we no longer saw or, after a while, truly knew. She seemed to be growing away from us, becoming more and more of a shadow. There were days I would gaze longingly at photographs of her, trying to remember everything about her, desperately trying to "fix" her in my mind. Her absence became a hole that threatened to swallow me. I missed her terribly and, when alone, often cried, because I was secretly afraid that I would never see her again.

I did not know on that day in 1986, when I gleefully accompanied my mother to the airport, how long my mother would be gone. I, along with my three siblings, had stood on the waving gallery and waved enthusiastically, believing that we would soon join our mother in that far-off magical place called America, the place where she was going to make a better life for us, the move that almost everyone agreed was the best thing for her to do. My mother herself did not know how long she would be gone. No one had any real idea of how long the separation would last. In all our minds she would send for us soon-soon, and we would be whisked away in that magical apparatus of an airplane to join her in America. We were so convinced of this that when tears finally slipped out of my younger brother's eyes at seeing our mother engulfed by the airplane, my older brother chided him, in the language of the day, that he was to stop his crying because it was all for the best. My younger brother must have been no more than seven or eight years old then – my mother's last child at the time, her "wash-belly," her baby. How frightened he must have been. How frightened we all must have been. Our family was never to recover from the shock.

My mother was to miss important milestones in all our lives, as we were to miss those in hers. The separation was almost unbearable. That first year I clearly remember newspaper articles sprouting up about the terrible consequences to children whose parents had journeyed to America and left them in Jamaica: One girl – I think she went to the same Catholic girl's school my sister and I were then attending – in a heated argument had plunged a knife into her sister and was horrified when her sister died. No parents were at home. Her father was unaccounted for in the article, while her mother, like mine, was in America. Another boy had somehow come into possession of a gun, and, in an argument with his sister, shot her dead. I remember this story clearly – his father pleading with him to come home, to give himself up, for he was on the run. A nun from the school the second girl attended wept openly because the girl had been, she said, "perhaps my best student. After her death, I began counting all the A's she received in school, but after a while I stopped. It was easier to count the B's." The way the facts arrange themselves in my head today, her mother was also in

America. Such were the consequences of our parents, of our mothers leaving.

In my home things did not go as expected after my mother left. My older brother stopped going to school and took to the streets. All the pleading and cajoling from my mother over the telephone and in letters could not get him to go back. Shortly after my mother left, my siblings and I started a process that was to foreshadow what would come later – drifting from place to place, searching for somewhere to put down roots and set up shop, a place of our own, somewhere to call "home". For a while we continued living with an aunt and an uncle in the house my mother had rented prior to leaving the island. Then my family was split up and parcelled out here and there, first with one family and then another. My sister and I ended up with our father, while both of our brothers went to live with relatives for various periods of time. This crack-up wouldn't have happened with my mother around, I kept thinking to myself. Without her everything started falling apart. Yet almost everyone agreed that my mother had done the right thing in leaving the island, and even today, when I ask her if she made the right decision to come to America, she is adamant. It was the only thing to do.

The next time I was to see my mother – and I was the one lucky enough to get to see her first, coming, as I did, to the United States to attend school – several years had elapsed. As I sat in the airplane, excitedly looking down at the watch on my wrist and timing myself, I did not realise that I was meeting a new mother, someone who was somewhat familiar, but some-one I hardly knew. I gave little thought to my father, who, I now realise, had declined to come to the airport with me for all sorts of emotional reasons, and who had instead ironed and (re)ironed the clothes I was to wear for the reunion.

From the start there was an awkwardness between my mother and me, an awkwardness that time would only slowly and painfully erase. In our years of separation, something had happened. It was as if, yes, this was my mother, and I was oh so happy to be reunited with her, but there was also a part of myself that I now kept hidden from her. It was as if I unconsciously blamed my mother for leaving us, even though I knew that it was what she felt she had to do. I saw each of my siblings go through a similar process and saw my mother question herself incessantly about the decision to leave. It was painful for all involved, perhaps most especially so for my mother. She wanted to erase the years of separation between us, to continue as if those years had not happened, as if, when she finally went to pick up my youngest brother at the airport, he were still eight years old and not eighteen; as if he did not now tower over her. She wanted to continue on as if in her absence he had not become a man.

It is a good few years now that I have been in the US, and my mother is getting ready to go to Canada to spend her Christmas holiday with my older brother and his Canadian children. Her mother, my grandmother, will also be there. There is the usual last minute bustle as she tries to get everything in order for her trip. (My mother can never get what she wants; her entire family in one place for the holidays. She has never really had this since leaving Jamaica.) I am spending Christmas in New York. As I go about my life in New York – buying gifts for friends and family, turning in my grades for the classes I teach, complaining about the weather, which has suddenly gone very cold; taking the subway back and forth – I am reading the diaries of Edna Manley, who has been called the mother of modern Jamaican art. At times I have to put the book down because her entries are so descriptive, so evocative that I get terribly nostalgic for the island. Memory has a way of intervening in the most inopportune times, and I seem to be seeing Jamaica everywhere. Daily I face issues of "home" and "place" and "belonging" and "otherness" in the United States. I do not see myself as an American, but more as a Jamaican living in America. The crux of the matter comes when I go back to the island. For even though I recognise myself in and on the island and am joy-filled that I am still there after such an extended absence, after a few weeks there a restlessness climbs upon me, comes to sit and stare at me from my lap like a long-neglected child. This restlessness is a yearning for America. What manner of creature is this that I have become, I often ask myself, looking down at the imaginary child that is my life; the person who is always in one place while longing for another? I remain nostalgic for a place that I have yet to return to live. Yet, Jamaica is home, will always be home, its significance being more the idea of a home. I live constantly between worlds, every moment a negotiation.

❧

This story, my story, is one of a series of stories that I would eventually collect and tell in a compilation called *My Mother Who Is Me: Life Stories from Jamaican Women in New York*. I collected these stories, I have now come to realise, because I wanted to counter common stereotypes I was encountering in the United States about who was and was not a Jamaican woman – even as I strove to better understand the lives of immigrant Jamaican women. I was also tired of reading reports and analyses "about" the lives of Jamaican and other Caribbean women: I longed to hear these women speak in their own voices. What is perhaps difficult to convey here is the sheer joy I felt in talking to and with each of the women whose stories I collected, of finding community, of, in a sense, coming home. As I listened to each woman tell her story – and the story was what was most important to me – each woman became, for me, symbolically, the women in Paule Marshall's kitchen when she was growing up, the women she wrote about in her beautiful essay, "From the Poets in the Kitchen", who "… [t]aught me my first lessons in the narrative art. They trained my ear. They set a standard of excellence." What these women talked about, the very Jamaican way in which they often said what they had to say stands as, to again quote Marshall, "testimony to the rich legacy of language and culture they so freely passed on…" For me, the meaning and significance of my life story and the other life stories I collected is to make immigrant Jamaican women more visible, to tell the story of our lives as we experienced it, using our voices to document the day-to-day reality of our lives in the United States. The value of such narratives, I eventually came to think, lies in the individual stories that we tell ourselves, the interpretations that we make of our own lives, recognising, as the great writer Zora Neale Hurston has said, that "[W]omen forget all those things they don't want to remember, and remember everything they don't want to forget. The dream is the truth." My immigrant story, as are the stories of the other women I collected, is a record, a testament, even a testimony of who we believed ourselves to be in Jamaica and the lives we have made for ourselves in the United States. These are the stories we tell ourselves, as Joan Didion wrote years ago, in order to live. These are the stories we tell ourselves in order to build a narrative. These are the stories we tell ourselves to make sense of our lives.

## WALKER FAMILY STORIES

Certain "facts" begin to emerge: he was born in Hopewell, Hanover, and had one – not the two of my mind – child there, before coming to Portland. He had been to Cuba at least once, cutting cane, people say, and he came to Portland to look for his sisters Aida (Aunt Caide) who lived in the hills of Nonsuch, and Ursula (Aunt Ursi) who lived in Buff Bay. It was Aunt Caide who came first. She had a job in the hotels, Aunt Caide. Brown-skinned people. Fair-skinned people. Near-white people. Those were the only ones who would get hired to work in the hotels back then.

He met his wife Celeste in the cool, blue-grey-green, ever-present hills of Nonsuch and decided to stay. Lugita was a fat, brown-skinned baby when she died; she is buried where the startlingly purple crotons are still growing below the old house on the hill of my childhood, of my imagination, the old house on the hill that I keep coming back to, unfolding again and again, like the many mountains of Nonsuch. Perhaps there was or was not a time when he, my great-grandfather, Wilfred Ferdinand Walker, won the lottery and spread the money all over the baby. He later used that same money, it was said, to buy the house I came to know them in – the small house on the hill of my childhood, my imagination, the small house on the hill that I am always coming back to, that I take with me wherever I go. Almost everything, to quote Derek Walcott, is "returning to fable and rumour and the way it was once, it was like this once…"

How they met and what they first said to each other, no one knows – children stayed out of big people's business; you had to be careful what you asked the adults – though I want to think that this small, dark firebrand of a woman, this born-ya, gave this just-come-bout-ya trouble, so much trouble! It was he, in my mind, who had to work hard-hard to get "C". Twelve children followed; eight lived to adulthood – my grandmother, Emma Louisa, was the girl who "broke the spell". Two other girls, Ufi and the nameless nine-days' baby, were born before my grandmother, but neither survived long. Yes, everyone agrees, it was my grandmother, Emma Louisa, named for both her grandparents, who broke the spell so that other girls, other girl children, grandchildren, great-grandchildren, even great-great-grandchildren, could also be born.

❧

She met him, my great-grandmother Celeste did, when some say she was fifteen-years-old. My grandmother insists that she was eighteen, and almost everyone agrees that he was twenty-one; people seem to know more about him than her. I distinctly remember that he used to talk more, almost with regret, of never going back to where he came from: Hopewell, Hanover. Not once. Not ever.

❧

"Your great-grandfather was a man of pride. He was full of so much pride! Once, his sister Ursi came to visit. That was before we put up the house that is on the hill now, and we still lived in the old house, the old wooden house. He ran away, Pupa did, rather than see his sister. He did not want his sister to see the house that he was living in."

❧

I, too, remember the whispers about there being other children in Hopewell, Hanover, and it is interesting to try and figure out – since the story diverges – whether it was that other woman's parents who did not want him for her, because he was too poor, or whether it was his parents who felt the girl was not good enough for him and hastily arranged the trip to Portland to visit his sisters. He came for three weeks only; he was not supposed to stay that long; but he had cut canes in Cuba, and there was some kind of sugar mill in Nonsuch in those days; I believe he worked there. At one time I know that he worked for the United Fruit Company.

❧

"He tried showing me how to do this once, how best to cut the canes, but I wasn't interested in all of that. I was only interested in singing. Singing was always my thing.

And then there was your great-grandmother. By then he had met your great-grandmother."

❧

Some journeys you seek. Other journeys seek you. Perhaps this too is what my great-grandfather finally came to believe. No one knows too much about his father, a shadowy dark figure who was, most agreed, a fisherman who brought home to his wife – she with hair so long she could sit on it – the best fish. The rest he sold. She was, my great-grandfather's mother, more fair-skinned; she must have been mixed-race or mixed-breed or something like that. A white man's daughter. A sailor man's daughter. The name Lyons comes to mind.

❧

Ireland-Scotland-Wales? Ireland, my Uncle Moses says, and I feel a little bit more relieved about the essay I was invited to present at Gates of Gold: An Irish American Literary & Cultural Festival in San Francisco entitled, "Stories My Great-Grandfather Told Me: The Irish Presence in Jamaica." Relieved, yes, because after a while you get to wondering whether it was you who had started telling yourself these stories, fanciful tales about Maroon, Cuban and Irish ancestors, or if you hadn't in fact heard them before, heard them in the stories that your family tells, the stories that your family insists on telling – and how seriously they take you, how much, you are quietly astonished, they are cooperating with you. The more you talk to your relatives, the more you realise that their stories, these family stories, the fable and rumour of it all, keep turning up, like some insistent heavily-scented night-blooming flower, in just about everything you think, write and dream about. Even the old house on the hill of my imagination. Especially the old house on the hill that I keep coming back to, again and again.

❧

Up close, the hills of Portland are a strong dark green. The African tulip tree with its flaming orange-red flowers dominates the landscape. I cannot separate her, my great grandmother, from the African tulip tree, or from the mountains. Those blue/gray, purple/blue mountains; the mountains of Nonsuch. One thinks of the line by the Haitian-American writer Edwidge Danticat, "Beyond the mountains are more mountains." Mornings and evenings, the mountains are a diffused bluish-gray. During the day they are dark blue and forest green and ever-present. Sometimes they are purple. Purple-blue. I could spend a lifetime, I think, looking at and writing about these mountains, encircling and cradling the district of Nonsuch like a fiercely protective womb.

❧

"During the hurricane things was bad but not too bad for us. We have the mountains, you know.

Nonsuch. You want to know how we got the name of this place? It was a man, a white man who found his way here and kept telling others or others kept telling him that there could be none such place in the world, and that is how we got our name. Nonsuch."

❧

"Your great-grandmother?"

"Well!" A distant relative of mine says and pauses. Everyone speaks first and foremost of her tongue, of her legendary temper, she did not suffer fools, though people are equally quick to tell you that she did not trouble people. That people had to bother-bother her first. And please, oh, please, do not trouble one of Celeste's children, grandchildren or great-grandchildren, because you would get-her-out. And the last person in the world you wanted to get-out was Celeste.

❧

"God alone know how a woman as skinny as a rail could wear so many dresses over such a slender frame!

When you got-her-out, she would throw one dress over another until she was stripped down to her knee-length drawers with the pockets she had sown unto them for safe keeping; she could hide things all over her person, that woman could. Don't make me take these off too!

Let me tell you something about that great-grandmother of yours. Everybody at Nonsuch All Age School was afraid of her. Jesus, my God, she was a terror. Not for you! She would tell people who called her Muma, that name is only for my grandchildren and great-grandchildren. Here, take all the salt, Ms Denny, and please, next time you see one of my grandchildren coming from shop with salt, don't beg them any more salt ever again! You could be as big as a breadfruit tree, she would not back away. Yes, that great-grandmother of yours was something else!"

*

"I remember that time the river was washing me away," my aunt Ann says. "Muma had told me not to go to the river and still I forced and go, me and Blanchie them, and the river was washing me away. And I kept telling them, shouting to them that the river washing me away and they think I was joking, everyone was laughing. When I look up, who should I see coming down the banking-side but Muma! And even though, just moments before, I was washing away, I found my way out of that river! You think she easy? Once, she throw kerosene oil on me and thank God she did not find the matches, because I still feel to myself that she would set me on fire!"

"– All because Ann kept laughing when she told her it was late at night and to stop her laughing. Imagine that: she was going to set Ann afire because she refused to stop her laughing!"

*

Her people, everyone agrees, were from Portland, from Nonsuch (Africa, my Uncle Johnny, the Rastafarian says). "Her people was from Swift River, same place here in Portland, your mother and all of us; we are Portland women through and through."

She might have been, some say, a Maroon, and for whatever foolish reasons I want to believe that she was a Maroon, this small dark woman.

"She was in Poco business you know! Once she took me to this Poco house far, far away in the bushes and we stayed there for a few days. I had to turn my wheel! They sprinkled fowl blood outside of the door!"

I have never heard of such a thing, my grandmother says, about my mother being a Maroon, but even to my father's eyes she looks like Portland Maroon people, though he is a not-born-ya, he, whose mother was Cuban-born, so what does he really know anyway? How can he really judge?

*

"Celeste's mother died when she was very young – not even a year old – and is buried same-place-here in Nonsuch, but that was before there was a cemetery. I remember this as clear as day," my grandmother says, "that some people were buried at cocoa root and others at breadfruit tree root. My mother's mother, no, she is not buried in the cemetery, but she is buried in Nonsuch, somewhere over there in Silver Hill. In fact her mother died when she, Celeste, was a year and nine months old. Did you ever hear the story? That she and her sister had gone to the market and were on their way home when she just dropped down and died. Duppy business. Celeste never knew her mother at-all, at-all. She is not the only one in our family who did not know her mother. Your cousin Vernis, she did not know her mother either. Her mother died right after she was born and her grandmother, Aunt Caide, raised her. "

❧

When her mother died, Celeste was sent to live with her mother's family in Swift River, though no one knows exactly why her father, Dr Scott, never kept her. Here is another place where the story I am now collecting diverges from the story in my head, for, in my head, in my imagination, she, Celeste, had been sent to live with her father in Swift River and when he died she was nine years old ("You have it all wrong," my grandmother says to me, "her father died when she was twelve.") Anyway, the story in my head, the story I am always writing, the story I am sure I have heard somewhere else before, was that when her father died she was sent to live with her older sisters back in Nonsuch, who treated her terribly, and it was this awful fate that my great-grandfather had been "rescuing" her from, though the woman I came to know – hot, some described her; like Scotch bonnet pepper, others said; fiery, still others said – did not seem in need of rescuing, seemed almost invulnerable and invincible, like a great Edna Manley sculpture, though I do remember her once wondering as a very old woman (she was always a very old, vibrant and powerful woman for me – even in death, especially in death) what her mother must have looked like. What must she have been like? Photographs were not readily available in those days.

"Dr Scott. Dr Scott. He was the headman on a plantation (Is that why they called him Dr Scott? Or was he some kind of herbalist? That would explain my great grandmother's immense knowledge of the bushes around her; this woman who could walk into the bush and walk out with a poultice to cure just about anything). He came from same-place-here in Portland too. He took up with another woman who did not like his children."

"They didn't have it too easy, you know," Ms Mina told me – a woman who called my great-grandmother aunt. "My mother, Aunt Irene, who was

Celeste's sister, used to talk sometimes about the bad treatment they suffered. No, I don't think they had a happy childhood. Back and forth between Swift River and Nonsuch. Portland people. Portland women."

❧

Now it occurs to me that I am not telling my great-grandparents' stories, so much as I am telling the stories of the people, friends and family members, as they intersected with Celeste's and Wilfred's stories. And stories all is what they are, and everyone has his or her story about them, and how they, my great-grandparents, functioned in their life. I am surprised at how much the people I am interviewing want the story, their story, our story, my great-grandparent's story, recorded.

Stories are an integral part of all our lives, we live our lives by the stories that we tell; the narrative helps us organise and make sense of our lives, our worlds. Helps. There has been another senseless killing on the island. This killing touches particularly close to home. The uncle of one of my dearest friends. A-waste-thing. No one knows why. A baffled and baffling story. No satisfactory narrative of that story. No satisfactory conclusion to that story. Still, we live our lives by stories.

My grandmother, for example, tells me about Nonsuch – the way it was once, it was like this once. She tells me that, long-long-ago, Nonsuch was a slave-owning place; one family owned the entire place. If you go over to Silver Hill, the evidence is still there, the remnants, the shackles. Your mother's family on her father's side, the Bishops, they are – you wouldn't believe it when looking at those black-black people – but they are the direct descendants of that slave-owning family, the Becks, Aunt Beck, Becka Chi Chi who sold my father, your great-grandfather, the land that the small house on the hill is built on. She decided to sell him the land, Becka Chi Chi did, because they were living over by old yard, and there was a river that they had to cross, and she thought, Becka Chi Chi, that that river was not safe for the children.

❧

"You remember old yard, yes? It had plenty-plenty tangerine trees. One time, I was playing over at old yard and a man who had just died came and longed-out his tongue at me. Lord, Jesus, it was the longest tongue in the world. It just kept coming and coming and coming, that bright pink tongue. I ran home, could barely talk, but when I could finally talk I tell Pupa what happened and he went over to old yard with his machete and kept telling the man to come on out. To show himself. Come out if you bad. Come and roll out your big-long tongue at me. Come so I can chop it off at the root, that tongue. Listen to me, dead man, I don't want you frightening my children again! On their own land at that! Anyway, that was after they won the money that they used to cover the baby with from head to toe. And Aunt Beck felt that that old yard was not safe for the children, because there was a river that the children had to cross, and though the small house on the hill had a dry river that came down when rain fell, the children could at least walk through her yard to get to the house. They used that money to buy that land. They used that money to build that house."

❧

– And even as a child I remember crossing a river, crossing so many rivers, to go and take him, Pupa, his lunch. It must have been in Silver Hill as he worked and worked and worked. That man was always working, picking fleas off his flesh-white belly…

❧

There are, of course, surprises. Aunty Gladys tells me, for example, that they, my great-grandparents, did not marry until after they had had several children. That in fact they only got married after he won the money that he used to cover the baby from head to toe, the money he used to buy the land where the small house on the hill still stands, the front of the house that had in my childhood, and still has today, the most astonishing red ginger lilies. The biggest, brightest, reddest ginger lilies in front of that small, unfinished white-paint-peeling old house that is being overtaken now, and perhaps was then, by the trees and bushes, the many shades of green in, around and about it.

After my great-grandfather died, my great-grandmother continued living in that house for a while. But nothing was the same, would ever be the same again, in the small house on the hill. She eventually abandoned it for one of her daughter's houses a mile and a half away in Cambridge, my great-grandmother did. After all, by then, she was old and frail. It was in this house that I saw her last, a few years before she died, her moaning and groaning late at night – she missed her husband, "Old Walk", so much. It was time for her to go on home to her husband. She longed to see him, to touch his old beleaguered face. How did she feel when she had to leave that house, I wonder? Did she look back once with longing, like Lot's wife? Did her eyes move over the house they had never finished, the house they had lived a lifetime in, and, as her small, dark, tired eyes moved over the house, did they also move over the years she and her husband, my great-grandfather, all-their-generations, had spent in that one small house? That one small unfinished white-paint-peeling old house on the hill of my childhood? Did her eyes come to rest on the red ginger lilies? The redder-than-red, astonishingly-big ginger lilies? "And you know Muma never did want me to plant those ginger lilies? Say I blocking up her eyesight and she cannot see what going on out the road."

❧

It was only then, my Aunt Gladys tells me, after they had won the money that they covered the baby with from head to toe, and moved over or were getting ready to move over to the new house, that they got married. No, they had not been married all along. Did she insist that they get married? Did she stand her ground? "Yes, is true," my grandmother says, "I know that too, but I don't see why I should tell you that, why I should tell you everything so you can put it into that book that you are always writing. How many years they were living together before they got married? How many years they were together? Why didn't you let Gladys tell you that too?"

*

There was another brother, perhaps two, for my great-grandfather. William, who died young, and an older brother – I don't know their names – though, if you ask my Uncle Johnny, he is quick to tell you that "we" have shares in hotels in Montego Bay and "we" are related to well-known-people-with-the-last-name-Jackson. He talked incessantly about going back, my great-grandfather did, but, says my Aunt Gladys, transportation then wasn't like what it is today. Then his parents died, and his older brother died – so who would he be going back to anyway? "He always felt," says my Aunt Ann, "that someone had 'done' something to him, preventing his return. I think once or twice a son came to visit him in Portland. Plus, after you leave a place for a long time, you want to go back with a little something. You want to go back with a little money in your pocket. You have to account for yourself."

*

He and Celeste had 12 children; eight lived to adulthood. My grandmother, Emma Louisa, who was named for both her grandmothers, was the fourth. She was the girl who broke the spell. "You want to know who the children were? First, there was Ufina, a girl, who died when she was a year old; Brother B, who you know; Oswald, who died in the asylum in Kingston; the 9-days baby girl who never got a name; Emma Louisa; Rueben; Calvin; Gladys; Aunty Elizabeth, who died in 1997; Theresa; the fat-brown-skinned Lugita buried at the bottom of the hill where the purple crotons are; and the one who is always singing, Johnny Walker, aka Baffling Johnny."

There was never any "outside" patchwork children. They really seemed to love each other. Created a firm foundation. When he was dying, the story goes, my great-grandfather asked for a piece of stick, broke it in two. He died with one half in his hand. Celeste had the other half. "As far as I am concerned, I never saw them fuss with each other. Fussed with other people, yes; but not with each other."

*

The will? That is the biggest secret of all. This one says that that one has a copy; and that one says that this one has a copy. No one can see it, the will, though I hear that the small house on the hill, the one that Uncle Johnny lives in, the one that I keep coming back to over and

over again, no matter where in the world I am, should never be sold.
Should always be in the family. It belongs to everyone, though everyone
thinks that Johnny has taken over the place – "almost as if it is his
own! Almost as if he thinks they died and left it to him! One thing I
know, if I plan to build a house, I am building it right up there, and
nobody can say anything to me!"

᳄

No, Uncle Johnny tells me, he is not afraid of seeing Muma or Pupa
now that they are dead; he is a Rastaman and he does not believe in
those things. One day he is going to leave Jamaica and go to Africa
where he rightfully belongs. What he wants is for someone to send
some money to help him fix-up the place. Foreign money. New York
money goes far here. "But yes, Ms Writer Woman Jacqueline, you can
come on a visit; the old house is still there. The one that, without you
even telling me, I know you keep coming back to again and again. The
small house on the hill of your childhood. The small house on the
hill of your imagination. Unfolding again and again, like these Portland
mountains, these Nonsuch mountains. Not only you, but everyone
of us, all of Muma-and-Pupa-generation keep coming back, day after
day, month after month, year after year, one generation after another,
to that small old unfinished house on the hill. So, yes, come on a visit.
Take all the photographs you want. The avocado (is that what you call
pear these days?) tree is still there. Bearing as ever – I got some nice
pears off it the other day. The star-apple trees, so many star-apple trees;
the mango trees, the red gingers, and the bright purple crotons marking
the spot where Lugita is buried are still there. Boy, she was a nice, fat
baby. A nice, fat, fair-skinned baby. Mum used to walk up and down
with her to clinic in the Bay because, from she born, she was sickly.
Doing all she could to save her, Mum did. Still she died. Pneumonia
in both breasts. Just the same way that your cousin Mickey's little girl
died. Little Michala Renee Bishop. Three months and three days old
when she died. Buried right here in Nonsuch graveyard with all her
other generations. Buried close to the small house on the hill; the
mountains, the dark blue mountains. Pneumonia killed her, the doctors
say, but everybody know that her parents were young people, and, anyway,
everybody know that is duppy kill the little girl. Eating with her, the
duppy was. Even when we took her to Children's Hospital where she
died, the duppy was still eating with her. No, I did not let them cut
her. No, I did not want them to cut her. Pretty? Lord Jesus, little Michala
was the prettiest thing. Pretty can't done. Even in her coffin. Goodness
gracious, is in her coffin she pretty! She looked just like a little angel.
Just like a little angel she looked in her coffin. The pretty little angel
who was sleeping."

## STORIES OF A BIRTH

For the first three weeks of her pregnancy she used to spit and vomit all the time and she could keep nothing down, my mother. She got a huge varicose vein on her right leg. "My neck," my mother tells me, "got very dark with you." Still, she was happy to be pregnant. She was hoping for a girl, a sister for the son she already adored; a girl, yes, a little daughter, she would put big red ribbons in her hair. She had a sense, an inkling, that I might be a girl because the front of her hair, her big and beautiful "souls" Afro, kept falling out. *That*, she insisted, had never happened with my brother, and only a girl would do such a thing to her mother.

For his part, my father insists that it did not really matter to him what sex the baby was, he would take whatever came. Though, truth be told, he had a preference for a girl – to this day has a preference for girl-children, who, he insists, "sticks more to you than a boy-child ever do. Boys you have for others; girls you have for yourself."

No, my mother tells me, her mother, with whom she was living, was not upset when she found out that her daughter was pregnant with me, because she, my grandmother, loved my father. Everybody loves my father, tall, handsome, easy-going man that he is, that wonderful laugh in his voice. She laughs at this now, my mother, so many years later, over what her life was like when she was pregnant with me. She must have been about nineteen years old. How simple the world seemed. She used to walk to clinic on Brentford Road, near downtown Kingston. She would talk to lots and lots of people. The nurses and doctors loved her.

"Yes, I was young… unmarried… and the nurses in particular were known to be hard on women like me. But for some reason they treated me good. The doctors and nurses were nice to me."

And then the cravings began.

Green mango with salt. Magnesia block. She ended up having to walk miles and miles to get the magnesia block she could not live without, because, in time, all the shops around where she lived had run out of them. After a while, she had started buying the magnesia blocks two at a time, because she would eat them – "I so loved their crunchy feeling and taste" – right away and would immediately want more. She happened upon a scheme of buying one block and eating it on the way home, then turning around wherever she was to go and buy another magnesia block right away. She didn't eat the blocks only for their taste, my mother admitted, but also for their pale white colour. "People told me," she said, "that if I ate the cool white blocks the baby would come out not-too-black, the baby would have a nice-cool-complexion-smooth-skin" – something she now calls a myth, although, "Look at you, look at your skin, your nice complexion! You have never had a pimple in your life!"

Then there was the doctor fish she had to have, steamed doctor fish with boiled yellow yam. She ate lots of sardines – "brain food" – for the baby, dark-green-leafy-vegetables, and drank lots of milk. She assiduously took all her vitamin and iron pills, rubbed her ever-enlarging belly. She had a very good pregnancy; absolutely no complications. All the time she prayed to have a girl. Night and day she prayed for a beautiful baby daughter.

The day she went into labour she was craving steamed doctor fish with tomatoes, onions, okras and boiled yellow yams – *yet again*. Sorrel, she needed, lots and lots of the blood-red drink. She kept looking down at her stomach. Such a big stomach it was, a stomach that had "dropped" and hung low between her legs (a sure sign she was going to get her wish and have a daughter). But that stomach – my mother kept coming back to it – "all the way down. So big and so round. Like a basketball was that stomach." Almost immediately after she finished eating her meal of steamed doctor fish and yellow yams she started having cramps, slight at first. Those initial cramps "felt like a toothache, but, unlike a toothache, after a while these cramps would wear off and go away." But soon the pain was back, and in no time at all it started getting unbearable. Her mother and her aunt bundled her into a taxi and took her to the Victoria Jubilee "Laying in" Hospital in downtown Kingston.

Her labour was not too long. "All in all it was no more than three hours. The labour and delivery room at Victoria Jubilee Hospital?" My mother laughs at the question. "A lot of crying women; a lot of women in serious pain. I didn't want to cry myself, but I got in with the other women because I felt it was something I had to do. You have to understand, some of those women had been there for days. The things those women would say! 'Mama, I didn't mean to do it! Never, never, never will I do it again!' It was all quite humorous, more of a drama, except you were one of the participants!"

Then I was born. "And once I saw you, I forgot all about the pain. Six and a quarter pounds you weighed. Hair nothing much to talk about. You weren't breathing properly and they had to take you away immediately and give you oxygen. I kept thinking, 'what a good thing she was born when she was born, so they could give her oxygen.' About three hours later they brought you back and you were so pink! The prettiest thing I had ever seen."

I certainly wasn't the prettiest "thing" my father had ever seen.

Rather, "You were a little baby, little and simple."

It was during this time, when my mother was busy in labour with me that Aunt Theresa went to find my father. It was during this time that they found out that my father did not live with his mother, as he had lead my mother to believe, but lived with a woman. A woman named Hyacinth. A woman who had had other children with my father. A woman who would show up some days later to announce herself to my mother.

Still, the day he learnt of my birth, my father made his way to the hospital. My father remembers not seeing me that first day at the hospital, while my mother remembers him seeing me and remarking on my beauty. In any case, who could remember what was going on in the hospital, my mother says, with all the confusion. All the people who came to visit! So much so that the nurses ended up telling my mother that she could have no more visitors.

Two days later, my mother and Aunt Theresa took me home in a taxi. I was wearing a yellow and white sweater set with full white underneath. "Since we did not know what kind of baby you were going to be, we stayed far away from blue and pink clothing. Instead, we kept to 'safe' white and yellow clothing. And when we got home, how your grandmother had set out the room for you! The bed was made up just for you, everything neatly laid out, and she cooked a lot of food, your grandmother, because she was so happy to be getting you! As for your brother, he refused to come from off the bed where his baby 'tita' was; no one could come close to you! Aunt Evelyn, my grandmother's sister's child, would come at 7:00 a.m. every morning and take you away. She would not return you until 3:00 p.m. when she was getting ready to cook dinner. Not much later your grandmother would come home from work and all she wanted to do was play with her first granddaughter. For six months not once did you cry. And for the next six months, just a little. But when you got to be a year old, everything changed! You cried night and day; it seemed you were always crying. Nonstop. Good God you tested my patience!

"I would ask you, 'Jacqueline, what is the matter?'

"'Oh nothing,' you would say, 'I just feel like crying.'"

"No doubt, these days, people would say you were depressed. Not us! At the time we said you were practising to be a singer. Now I *know* that what you were really practising to be was a writer. Though you used to love to sing and draw as well. Your name? I gave you your full name. Your father had absolutely nothing to do with it." ("She is right," my father laughingly tells me, "she gave you your full name. You know how women are with their naming and their ways with their children!") "I named you," my mother said, "for the beautiful sad wife of an American president who had been murdered. The beautiful sad wife of an American president who had so much dignity. I loved the dignity of that woman. Her bravery in the face of trouble. "

Birth: Emergence of an infant or other young from the body of the mother; beginning; origin; descent; ancestry.

# PHOTOGRAPHS ON THE MANTELPIECE

Recently, on a trip to visit her in Jamaica, I walked around my grandmother's house looking at the photographs that decorate her life. As long as I can remember, my grandmother has kept photographs around her, and whether she is aware of it or not, the photographs, and where she places them, give a pretty accurate picture of where she places people in her life. Her dresser, for example, is peopled with photographs of my older brother's second child, who my grandmother adores, and when I opened up one of her Bibles a couple of days later, several pictures of my older brother, her favourite, fell out.

As a child living with my grandmother, I quickly learnt that there were photographs that I was not to touch. These were the ones carefully stored away in the clear plastic bags that would eventually ruin them. These were different from the pictures pushed into the sides of the large, oval-shaped mirrors on the cabinet or dresser that we could take down and handle, though we should be careful not to leave any fingerprints on them. The really precious images were framed, of course, the wedding pictures, for example, and these you would find placed prominently on the mantel-pieces of both my grandmother's and my great grandmother's houses. Sometimes there were images that haunted, of a family member who died young; and there were the ones I was simultaneously repulsed by and drawn to – the images of people in coffins, for example. Then there are the strange images of "Chinese people" that are all over my grandmother's house, that only recently my grandmother told me were people she used to work for years and years ago. I wanted to ask my grandmother about these Chinese people, why she felt the need to keep and display images of people she had not seen in decades, but I suspected she had grown both leery and weary of me and my questions so I did not push the issue.

Her home. My grandmother's home. As I look back at it now I see that my grandmother, as her mother before her, used photographs as a means to keep people who had moved far away close. My grandmother, as did her mother before her, used photographs as a means of holding onto things she feared may slip her grasp, and this, of course, makes sense for people who have watched children, grandchildren and even great grandchildren move away in successive migrations, not knowing if or when they will ever see these loved ones again. My great grandmother would sometimes take up the photographs of her daughter and her daughter's children, then living in far away England, and she would speak to herself in a slow sad whisper, her voice thick with tears, wondering if she would ever see her daughter again, if she would ever see those beloved grandchildren again? Then she would go out to stand on the verandah facing the dark blue Portland mountains, photographs in her hand, and you could hear her calling out every last one of her daughter's children's names.

I think, too, that it was because my great grandmother never knew her own mother, who died when she was but a year and a few months old, that she has been fascinated with photographs. She once said to me, when we were walking somewhere and talking, "Eh, can you imagine it, Jacqueline. Not knowing what your own mother look like? Not having even one teeny weeny picture of what your mother look like? Having to rely on other people pointing out other people to you for you to know what your own mother look like. Can you imagine such a thing?"

For a long time the small photograph towered above me. The small framed photograph of a girl I do not know, but do know, who lived above the cabinet in my grandmother's house. Every time I went to my grandmother's house I would look up to make sure she was still there, the girl I do not know, but do know, the one standing on the chair with the back like a fan, the girl in the pale dress, pale shoes with big pale ribbons in her hair, the girl, staring out as if she was about to cry. Who had taken her to have the photograph taken? It must have been her mother – for the *me* that was in the photograph became transposed as a *her*. I can see it all unfolding in my mind's eye. My mother would have gotten up early that morning, knowing for days if not weeks ahead that this would be the day when she would take me for my baby photograph, for everyone got a baby photograph taken in a studio. Probably she had picked out the white clothes I was to wear the night before, knowing, or having been told, that white clothes would show up lovely in black and white photographs. She would have bathed me, my mother, lovingly combed my hair, and put the two big white ribbons in it.

Then it would be off to the photographer's studio in downtown Kingston. By the time we got to the studio, this or that thing might have come out of place, so my mother would have reached into her bag for the brush or comb she carried with her, and brushed my hair back in place, and straightened out my ribbons. She would have done everything she could do, my mother, to have the photograph come out just right. The photographer would have placed me on his spreading chair and then the two of them would have set to work straightening out my dress, fixing the bangles on my hand, making sure that my socks were neatly turned down. Together they would try to get me to smile, and when talking did not work, they would have started dangling something in front of me, let it be something strange, from the look in my eyes – something I had never quite seen before (maybe the camera?) – because I am sure that if it had been something bright and shiny I would have been reaching for it.

As I look back on this image I am struck by its fragility and vulnerability. Maybe the size of the photograph (at just about 3x5 inches) or maybe the fact that the image is black and white is what adds to its fragility and innocence. The frightened yet vacant look in my eyes.

What draws me most to this image is the small black handbag I am grasping tightly in my left hand. Family lore has it that as a very young child I would watch my mother get dressed, pick up her handbag and leave the house and one day I did exactly the same thing without anyone knowing. I was found at a busy intersection about to step off into the street. After people had gotten over what could have happened to me… If, Lord Jesus, if the child done stepped off into the road… they would then come back to this small black handbag and how tightly I held it, as if I was a little woman going to work. As if, even then, I liked having my own way.

It is a strange thing looking back on yourself as an infant, looking back at another you, a you you do not know, for even as I know the little girl in the photograph has my eyes, my lips, my face, I feel as if I don't quite know her, whereas I feel as if I do know the little girls in my ten-year-old photographs, for example. I am still on speaking terms with some of those ten and twelve-year-old girls, whereas I have absolutely no recollection of the little girl who went off in her pretty white dress to have her picture taken. Yet, I feel instinctively protective of her, want to reach out and touch her. I often use this photograph as a way of measuring the distance between the child who is in the photograph and the woman who is writing about the child in the photograph today.

The picture, as it is reproduced here, is not the picture as it was taken in those long-ago days of my childhood. It was when my grandmother left to spend a few years in Canada, and there was no one to tend to the images on her mantelpiece, that I finally got my hands on this photograph I had always wanted. Over the years, as I delved more and more into the visual arts, and as technology transformed, I was able to use this image in multiple iterations. Most recently I added a flower to the centre of the image and carefully modulated the light and dark shades so it seems as though the child is a flower is a child, and it is hard to separate the images. The image then became part of a larger discussion about childhood memories that I have been working on for several years now.

Most days when I look at this image, I smile at the little girl and reach out to take her hand. Her sister image, the one without the flower, the one that sits on my mantelpiece in New York, is often quick to remind me that not only have I become my grandmother and my great grandmother by keeping photographs on mantelpieces in my home, but that the mantelpiece that she is sitting on in New York is not the mantelpiece where she belongs. Her place, the girl in the photograph in New York insists, is in Jamaica, in a small district called Nonsuch, high in the blue Portland mountains.

That first photograph, the original, the untouched digitised version without the beautiful flower in the centre, speaks of being in exile, in a far away and sometimes brutally cold New York, and that she really belongs with a woman named Emma, with the pictures all over Emma's house, on the mantelpiece where she should be sitting; that is the place where she really belongs.

## SAILING WITH WAYNE BROWN

You got the sense that underneath the gruff exterior, for there was a gruff exterior, was a sensitive man. Someone who cared deeply, but someone who went to pains to hide just how deeply he cared. What did he care so much about? Well, about the writers he was mentoring, about the work that the region as a whole was producing. He was a person who, if he believed in your work, would be out contacting others about you.

"There're two really fine so-far-unpublished writers here, Verna George (poet) and Sharon Leach (short stories). Both are heading for international publication, I've no doubt."

And then later:

"Jacqueline – Sent you Verna George's poems over the weekend, hope you got them. Here now is a sample of five short stories by Sharon Leach. She has, by the way, a huge following here from *Observer* Lit Supp readers. Look forward to hearing from you – Wayne".

When I told this to Sharon Leach recently she was stunned. Really? is all she kept saying to me. Wayne did all of that without telling me?

I don't think I will ever forget the first time we met face to face, for ours was in fact a friendship conducted mainly by email and over the telephone. How that first time we started talking, guardedly in the beginning, before things got easier and then effortless between us. At that time he lived in a medium-sized, airy house that felt to me like a writer's house, a writer's place. I remember the poet of great talent who came while I was visiting, how she disappeared somewhere in Wayne's house to get some writing done. We talked about any and everything; then we stumbled upon our mutual adoration of the ocean, and Wayne started talking about his boat: "Strange, I get the feeling you understand 'the boat' too, in a way no one else seems to have done…"

One of the gifts I will give myself is sailing around the boat of my imagination, swirling out in those many-shades-of-blue waters, having a conversation with Mr Wayne Brown.

Wayne had what was for me then, and still is now, a questionable theory. One which went something like this: you could tell the development of a society by the genre of writing that it produced. A society started out with poetry, advanced to fiction writing, and at the highest level of development expressed itself in non-fiction commentary. Jamaica, he said, was producing excellent poets; Trinidad good fiction writers. He never did tell me where in the Caribbean was producing excellent non-fiction writing.

It goes without saying that he had very strong opinions. That, in fact, he liked having strong opinions. But he was not, as I come to think about it, a man so much of strong opinions as he was a man of fierce loyalties. Over the years this started to bother me a little about this man whom I realised, very early on, that I shared a lot with, because these loyalties seemed to extend themselves to the genres in which authors chose to express themselves. For Wayne, I was a really good poet; he could not understand why I was bothering-bothering with writing fiction. It is true that he would publish my work, in multiple genres, but there was no denying that for him I was primarily a poet.

But his going back and forth between two countries, between Jamaica and Trinidad, was something I could understand, in my back and forth between Jamaica and the United States. For Wayne, Jamaica was beautiful, Trinidad pretty. When he was in Jamaica he felt like a Trinidadian. When he was in Trinidad, he felt like himself. Jamaica. Trinidad. Jamaica/Trinidad. Trinidad-Jamaica. You got the sense that for him it was all a continuum. I told him that in America, I felt like a Jamaican. In Jamaica, I was very conscious of having lived most of my life in America.

But, he said, smiling at me, the more you and I talk, the more you lose that American accent. Is the more you sounding Jamaican. I told him in America I only have a Jamaican accent and I am surprised someone would even "hear" an American accent in my voice. But I can, he told me, I can hear it, but the more you talk and talk to me, is the more you lose that American accent. Is the more you sound Jamaican. We were looking out at a beautiful flamboyant tree flaming orange/red across the street. I sighed. Jamaican accent. American accent. The dilemma of belonging.

"Hi lady, good to hear from you. Xmas was a family affair, but here, not in Tdad – after which I was in Boston for a fortnight, teaching a low-residency MFA in Boston. Broken wrist still a nuisance, tho still improving; otherwise I'm okay.

"So – when next are you in these parts? I'm remembering a contract to take you sailing!

"The "first draft" of our online literary magazine website is up, tho not for public consumption – we're now tweaking the million little details that need tweaking and hope to be able to go public in about a fortnight – at which point I'll of course send you the link. Meantime here's a review of yr book that should be appearing in *The Gleaner* this Sunday."

The magazine: *Caribbean Writing Today*. He called me up in New York to tell me he was starting the magazine. What buoyancy I heard in his voice!

I should send him a couple poems. He was actually in a position to pay authors for their submissions.

"Hi beautiful – here it is, finally – let me know if you hit any glitches. And tell me what you think of it when you've had a chance… Of course I hope you'll subscribe, and send it on to yr list with a big recommendation! Love, W."

"Jackie – forgive minimalist prose: broken wrist, 1-finger typing. Would like to phone you, if you'll send me a number. W."

"Jackie – CWT has US$20 for you for yr poem in the sample issue; what's yr mailing address?"

"Jackie – yr phone call gave me a lift. Seriously – come and see me in Boston in June –"

The violence on the island troubled him enormously, and for him formed one of the tropes of contemporary Jamaican writing: That such horror, such depravity, could happen in such a beautiful place! I don't know if I read it somewhere or he told me, of the gunmen who entered his home one night, how they wanted to kill him, and how, after that day, he realised that he could not continue living on the island as an observer. Because, he either said to me, or I read somewhere, he realised that he *could* die "in this damn country". Jamaica. Trinidad. Jamaica/Trinidad. Trinidad-Jamaica. All a continuum.

"Let me tell you a story about that half-tree you so busy looking at, that same flamboyant tree across the road that you done falling in love with; yes, let me tell you something about that half-tree, that half-flamboyant tree there, the same one with those pretty pretty flowers; let me tell you what those wicked people across the street did to that half-tree. That tree used to be much bigger than it is, and spread out all over the place, and it was like a lady in a nice orange dress. After I finish my workshops, the students, they would go out to discuss things under that tree, and you know what those wicked wicked people do? They chop down the tree! Yes, chop down the tree so the students wouldn't be able to gather under the shade of that tree. Isn't that a terrible thing to do?"

I looked at Wayne closely. Did he know that trees, like butterflies, like the wide blue ocean, were some of the great loves of my life? I groaned, for I knew that image, that story, his telling voice, would never leave me alone now, knew that somehow I would have to recoup what he told me into a story.

Months later, when I wrote asking about the tree, he sent me back an email in which I could hear the triumph in his voice, for if the people across the street think they killed that tree when they chopped it down, they were wrong, for see it there now, that tree was like a phoenix, springing back to life.

I pulled all the elements into a short story, the first draft of which, when I presented it to him like a carefully wrapped gift, Wayne Brown flung back at me.

"I appreciated the tree; didn't love it, in the tender-personal way you describe. I'm not the tree-hugging type, lady!"

Later, when I decided to dedicate an issue of the journal I founded, *Calabash: A Journal of Caribbean Arts & Letters*, to Wayne Brown, for the tremendous work he was doing developing a new generation of Jamaican writers, I wrote to him again.

"I am sure you have heard by now, since news travels so fast, that I am trying to put together a feature in *Calabash* in honor of someone we both know!"

"Yes I heard. Hope yr story about me hugging some tree won't be in it. Everybody here would know at once it was me and look at me quite oddly."

I did not put the story in the issue, not because Wayne Brown hurt my feelings by saying that – as a writer you get used to hurt feelings all the time – I did not put the story in that issue because it was not ready, had been nothing but a barely thought-out draft when I first sent it to him. When it was ready, when it was a story that had its genesis in talking to Wayne Brown, but became a story outside of that experience, I sent it off to a magazine that published the story.

"New issue of *Calabash* including the works in tribute to you published. Know how famously difficult you can be, so I hope you like it. Love, J."

"Hi Jacqueline – I saw the issue, including the tribute. Nice of you; it was good to read some "oldies but goodies" again. Stay good, Wayne."

I guess what I am trying to say is that Wayne Brown was a bit of a curmudgeon and a lot of a perfectionist. But he was the kind of reader of my works that made me into a better writer. I agreed with a lot of what he said, but not all of what he said. He was a man of such strong opinions, of such fierce loyalties. And I guess what I am trying to say is that the gruff exterior hid a terrible vulnerability. Here is our email exchange over the failure of *Caribbean Writing Today*:

"Too bad about CWT! But, that's how these things often goes. That is why, frankly, *Calabash* is an online publication these days. Too much rass problems with funding!"

"Thanks for yr commiseration… We're going to leave the site up for now; on the off chance it becomes viable in the not too distant future."

This is how it got started: a friend of mine sent me his email and told me to send Wayne Brown some poems for *The Observer Literary Supplement*. I did send him some poems, which he accepted; not only did he accept them, but he also asked me to send him some more, which I did. He published those poems too. Listen, I can still hear him saying to me, I think you are a really good writer. That you have a lot to say. That was how it got started.

And this is how it ended:

"Hi Wayne: No word from you, and I long always to hear from you… Jacqueline."

When I got no response from him – very unusual for Wayne – I wrote to Sharon Leach. The shocking news came when she wrote back.

"Hey Girl: Here depressed. Wayne died this morning. Trying to scramble to put an obit together to send in to the paper so they can carry it tomorrow. Distraught."

"Whey yuh mean Wayne dead??????????????"

"Lung cancer. I thought you knew. He was diagnosed beginning of the year. He was doing treatments and though he was terminal he thought he'd buy some time till maybe year end… Alas…"

Even today I am still so tempted to write to him, to say to him, Wayne, my darling, how you going? I have written some new poems, some new stories. Won't you take a look at them? You know you do a great edit! And waiting for him to write back and say, "Send them Jacqueline, you know you can always send them. And tell me: How you doing lady? You coming to visit me this summer in Boston? When are we going to go sailing on the boat? I'm remembering a contract to take you out sailing…"

## LOVE SONGS TO MOROCCO

When I went to Morocco on a Fulbright Fellowship in 2008 I was surprised to learn that almost no one knew that the celebrated African American writer Claude McKay had lived and worked in that country. Even more surprising were the people who knew of Claude McKay's importance as a writer, without knowing that he had written most of his books in Morocco. Back in the United States, almost no one seemed to take seriously the author's time in Morocco. To date there hasn't been any examination of the influence living in Morocco had on his work and the development and clarification of his anti-colonialist and anti-imperialist ideas. This is a lacunae still waiting to be filled. This is but a brief introduction to Claude McKay and some of the work that he did in Morocco.

When he first came to Morocco in 1928, Claude McKay was in an upbeat mood. His first novel, *Home to Harlem,* had just been published and was steadily climbing up the *New York Times* best-seller list, one of the earliest such feats for an African American writer. McKay had money in his pocket and was well on his way to writing his second and perhaps most celebrated novel, *Banjo,* which he would complete in Morocco.

In fact the time McKay spent in Morocco, roughly from 1928-1934, would see the author producing an astonishing body of work. Not only did he complete *Banjo* on his first trip in 1928, but he would go on to complete the short story collection *Gingertown* and the novel *Banana Bottom* while living in Morocco. He would also revise the novel *Savage Loving* (which would later be re-titled *Romance in Marseilles*) while living in Tangier. Sometime in 1933, McKay thought of a new novel and began to write what would eventually become *Harlem Glory: A Fragment of Aframerican Life.* In addition, he wrote several poems and various sketches of Moroccan life while still living there. Later he dedicated a significant portion of his autobiography to his time in Morocco and the country kept showing up in subsequent works as well. Though McKay eventually left Morocco to return to the United States, Morocco would not leave McKay and he remained preoccupied with the country, and all the relationships he forged there, until the end of his life in 1948.

What made Morocco, more than any of the other countries that McKay lived in, so conducive to his producing such a substantial body of creative work? I believe the answers can be found in his biography.

Born in 1889 in Jamaica, McKay came to the United States as a youthful twenty-two-year-old, after having published two collections of dialect poems on the island. More publications would follow in the United States, but McKay was an ever-restless and wandering person; after only a few years in the United States, he set off for Europe, where he would end up living for a decade and a half, primarily in England and France. But always there was the pull to Africa. McKay writes in his autobiography that he was first invited to visit Morocco by a sailor from Martinique he met while working in France. In time, McKay would take the sailor up on his offer to visit Morocco.

From the start McKay fell in love with Morocco, and his published works – particularly his moving poems about Morocco – give us some sense of why the country became so meaningful to him. There was, of course, the colourful landscape, so reminiscent of his native Jamaica. His poem "Two Songs of Morocco" is a love song to the northern landscape of Morocco, where McKay lived for most of his time in the country. Here, in the beautiful cities of Tetouan, Chefchaouen and Tangier were the flaming "yellow daisies" that McKay remembered from his Caribbean childhood. Here too was a landscape of abundance, in which "fishes leap up like tumblers in the air". In his lovely poem "Xauen", McKay is particularly taken with the tiny all-blue mountain municipality, where the waters kept "…flowing like the dawn… [in] the gem the Moors call Xauen."

Morocco emerges as a place of personal rejuvenation for a world-weary author who had encountered mind-numbing racism in Europe and America. In "Two Songs of Morocco" he references the theme directly when he writes of how attuned he was to "…the rejuvenated land". Similarly, in the poem "Xauen", the landscape emerges as a "…lovely fountain bubbling up in my breast… cleansing all the bitter memories… of life… bathe me always your wandering guest." In another poem he locates himself on the Moroccan landscape of "…wild honey come from wandering bees."

The sense of Morocco as a welcoming place to a wanderer like McKay is particularly poignant, for by the time McKay came to the country, he was looking for somewhere to settle permanently – and for a while he thought he had found that place in Morocco.

Morocco was also a sensual experience for McKay, one that he linked to the women of the country, whom he never quite gets to know, but whom he admires nonetheless. The women of the country engender "a ripened passion" in the poet. They also represent the "Womb of time". So smitten was McKay with the women in the poem "Fez" that he conflates the city with the female body and the city becomes one of "labyrinthine lanes and crooked souks / And costumes hooding beauty from men's sight." Marrakesh, on the other hand, is a "Salome-sensual

dance" while Tetouan is a "...fountain bubbling up with new life..."
In other poems Morocco is a "beauty pregnant of life's pristine womb
... on your bosom, asleep... I have felt the breaking wave on wave..."
The poem "Tetuan" conceptualises Morocco as a miraculous place since
here is where "Africa's fingers [are] tipped with miracles." While in
his long poem titled "Morocco", the country, "[t]ouch[es] caressingly
my inmost chords." The women of Morocco, as representatives of his
feeling about the country, are sensual, intoxicating, and life-giving, but
at some level remain mysterious and unknowable.

As an African American, what attracted McKay most to the country was
his connection to the local people and in turn his connection to Morocco
as an African country. Time and again he would write about how free he felt
in Morocco, how liberated, and how he could "...drink the eager wine/
fermented strongly in the native cup". His time in Morocco was one of
many "returns". A "return" to the continent of Africa, a "return" to the
Motherland, and indeed a "return" home. Peppered throughout his poems
about Morocco is the sense that the blood of Morocco flows deeply
through his own veins, and over and over again he identifies himself as an
offspring of the African continent.

As both a Jamaican [at the time British subject] and an African American, McKay identified with the injustice perpetrated on the native population and empathised with the local people as they fought against the twin-
headed monster of colonialism and imperialism. Morocco – then a French
Protectorate, though parts of the country were under Spanish control – was
a "... severed head, is Europe's ball... kicked from goal to goal and all
around... in the African game of the European..." But McKay's story of
Morocco is ultimately not only, or even primarily, a tragic one, because the
city in which he lived the longest, Tangier, retained the "symbol of the
Berber brave!"

Perhaps the most moving of the published poems McKay wrote about
this country is the one that shows his dream of African return. When he
wrote the poem titled quite simply "Morocco", McKay was again living in
the United States. The poem describes in moving terms that being outside
Morocco is for McKay a "stone upon [the author's] spirit". He misses the
country's strong "native colours". But it is so much more than this that
McKay misses. Throughout this "wistful and heart-rending" poem is the
constant refrain of return:

> Oh friends, my friends! When Ramadan returns
> And daily fast and feasting through the night,
> With chants and music honey-dripping sweets...
>
> My thoughts will wing

On airy waves
With you to be.

◆

For some time now I have been documenting the places in Morocco
that Claude McKay wrote about, in an effort not only to develop a
visual archive of Claude McKay's Morocco, but also, in effect, to return
Claude McKay yet again to that country. I tracked Claude McKay all
over Northern Morocco. In particular I wished to locate the lovely
small house near a river leading out to the ocean, just outside Tangier,
where the author lived and worked and wrote many glowing letters
about. With the help of Dr James Miller at the Fulbright Foundation
in Morocco, I came to understand that McKay's little house "outside
of Tangier", where he kept a vegetable garden, was now deeply folded
within Tangier proper, the city having grown so much over the years.
However, with the further help of staff from TALIM, I was able to
pinpoint the place where Claude McKay's house would have been.
But whilst no small beautiful house still stands at the "place of peace
for wandering bees" where Claude McKay made his home in Tangier,
the water from the river, where he so enjoyed swimming, still makes
its way lazily out to the ocean.

## "COVERING" FEMALE SEXUAL DESIRES

I fell in love with it the moment I saw it. For the longest time, a photocopy of the image of three nubile women hung over wherever I was writing. At one time, I walked around with a replica of it in my purse. When I fall in love, I really fall in love, and I love having my love objects close to me. That's just the kind of girl I am. And so, yes, I admit it, Koren der Harootian's painting, "Three Graces", had me hooked from the first time I laid eyes on it.

Now, I realise that the painting took me back to the idyllic landscape of childhood, of summers spent in my grandparents' and great-grandparents' houses in the tiny district of Nonsuch, high in the purple-blue mountains of Jamaica. Here, in this gorgeous little district, all the cousins would meet up on those hot lazy days, eating fat stalks of striped sugar cane, making guava jam with my grandmother, catching crawfish in the now heavily polluted river that runs through the district, and going on walks with my great-grandmother, that wonderful maker of patchwork quilts, as she went about selling milk early in the mornings. It was a time of bliss.

Closing my eyes, I can still see stars so big and bright, and seemingly so near that the first time I took my then baby sister on a trip to the island from our New York home, she asked a friend of mine to reach up and pluck one the stars from the night sky for her. The stars seemed that close. All of this came back to me the first time I saw Koren der Harootian's "Three Graces", and the painting remains for me primarily an image of childhood, of innocence, so much so that when it finally came time to choose the cover for my first novel, *The River's Song*, a story about coming of age in Jamaica, I knew exactly which imagine I wanted – and subsequently got – for the cover. It was Koren der Harootian's beautiful painting.

So in love and happy was I with my book, with its cover, with my life in general then, that I was wholly unprepared for how that particular cover – of all my to-date five published books – would become a smorgasbord of issues about female sexuality and the problems of representation of the female body.

To begin with, there was the day I walked blissfully into my office on campus and, with hands trembling slightly, showed my book to a co-worker. It was a point of arrival, after all. All the years I had worked on the book, first as a grad student, and then on my own, chipping and chipping away at it; after the trips I had taken to the mountains of Mexico, the beaches of Morocco, talking to my characters, trying to get to know them better, trying to get them to know me better, letting them know it was okay to trust me with their story. I especially wanted Annie and Gloria, the main characters of the book, two girls on the cusp of womanhood, to know that they could trust me as they explored their developing bodies and their burgeoning sexuality. I knew that if I allowed the girls space to tell me their story, it would become a story that the right publisher would publish, which is exactly what happened. The right publisher liked the book and decided to publish it and finally, after much listening and learning and rewriting, it was time to decide on the cover and Koren der Harootian's beautiful painting popped right into my mind. The publisher agreed immediately with my suggestion.

But I have digressed long enough and it is time to get back to my co-worker, a linguist from India, who had only one question about my book when I showed it to her: "Why are the characters on the cover of your book naked?"

I should have seen the comment as a harbinger of things to come.

I thought it only curious when the book was described as "atypical of Caribbean literature because of its description of a young girl's sexual awakening". Of course, teenage girls in Jamaica are like teenage girls anywhere else, I remember thinking to myself, and they have sexual feelings that they want to explore and express just like teenagers anywhere else do. But even then I started hearing, deep inside myself, voices from my childhood, all the things that had been said around me about the female body and female sexuality, the constant exhortations from the nuns at the Catholic girls' school I attended, that we girls should be wise, not foolish, virgins, for "what sweet nanny-goat will surely run her belly".

But here again, I digress from talking about the cover of the book.

It so happened that, shortly after *The River's Song* was published, someone was looking for books by Jamaicans to take to a trade show. I happily asked my publisher to send along my book and my publisher happily complied. I waited anxiously to hear how all the books, mine included, did at the show. The woman who attended the trade show was a nice woman, quite generous and diplomatic. She had gotten my book, yes, and it had even made it with her to the trade show, but, well, the cover.

Jamaica, for sure, I thought. Where else could there be problems with what for me was a pretty benign cover?

Then I ended up in Morocco on a Fulbright fellowship, and the cover did not go so well over there either. That's to be expected, I told myself. Although Morocco is a fairly liberal Muslim country, it is still a conservative society. Morocco, okay, I understand that, I told myself.

But when my book cover started causing arguments at a large liberal arts college in one of the boroughs of New York City, it dawned on me that there might in fact be something highly problematic or even challenging about the cover, and maybe now, in hindsight, I thought I ought to take a firm and long look at the cover again. Maybe there was something that I should take note of for next time. After all, could people in such disparate parts of the world all be wrong? There had to be something to this that I was not seeing.

It took me a while to see past the idyllic images of childhood that the painting represented. Surely it wasn't the "nudity", because outside of the barely visible nipples, nothing really was showing. Then slowly it started to dawn on me that what might have caused the problem was the self-contained world that the women inhabit; how the girls reference each other for an understanding of their bodies and their sexuality; how abandoned they seem in exploring not only their bodies but the bodies of the other girls around them. Here are girls, I finally realised, who are wholly liberated in an entirely female place and an entirely female space. Here was power inherent in a positive female sexuality that needs only the company of itself for its own enjoyment. Oh, yes, I could see now why this cover would bring so much trouble.

As I look back on the covers of my books, all of which I chose instinctively, I'm astonished how much they mark the changing moments of my life so far, this journey that I'm on, whether it's me looking back on my island-home from a distance, and being completely stunned by its amazing flora and fauna; or whether it's my embrace of community or even my embrace of the other. Now, in looking closer and closer at the cover of *The River's Song*, I see my years-long interest in female sexuality. This searching, this yearning, this wanting to know more. This self-enclosed and strangely beautiful world; this forging ahead and along; this doing it together as a strong community of women. The danger and the desire and the beauty of it all.

## SURVIVING WHOLE: ROGER MAIS' BLACK LIGHTNING

The woman wanted to know how I had done it.

"Done what?" I asked her, a little alarmed, searching my mind for what I could have possibly done wrong, for there was, it seemed to me, a slight accusation in her trembling voice. She was shorter than I was, older, and she leaned against a cane. I loved her name – Spirit – as much as I admired her warm brown complexion. She reminded me of my grandmother. The woman reached into her bag and pulled out a copy of my novel, *The River's Song*, encased in a transparent plastic covering that she lovingly fingered.

"Rachel..." the woman said after a while, bringing me back to the moment, "I want to know how you knew all those things about Rachel..." she lowered her voice in the hushed sanctuary of the church. Service had only recently ended and several people were milling about. "...You know who I am talking about... the prostitute in your book."

The prostitute in my book.

I can't recall what I said to the woman, though I remember instinctively flinching, wondering if she thought that I was at one time, if not now, a prostitute, and that was why I was able to write the prostitute so well for her.

Tears started streaming down Spirit's face. "You see," Spirit said after a while, "at one point... at one point" she was searching for words, "at one point I was a prostitute." She stopped and searched my face again, no doubt looking for judgment, before she continued. "At one point, I was Rachel." She was having a hard time talking now and I was having a hard time concealing my surprise.

"I have carried that shame with me for a long long time," Spirit continued. "A long time now. But in this book... that Gloria [the narrator] loved Rachel, and it did not matter to Gloria what Rachel did or that she had been a prostitute. That little girl loved Rachel anyway. I wondered how you did that."

All I could tell Spirit was that I too love Rachel, that I was glad she chose me to tell her story, even as I marvelled that something that I created, or maybe I should say something that I helped bring into being, since I strongly believe that writing a novel is a conspiratorial thing between characters who choose authors to tell their stories and authors who take up the challenge, that a character in my book had moved from being among the pages of a book to forcefully entering someone else's life. The same thing had happened to me in the books I most loved, and I was humbled by the experience. I mentally thanked Rachel and all the other characters in *The River's Song* again.

My encounter with Spirit is probably the most memorable but certainly not the only encounter I have had, when I would come to the realisation of just what it is that art can and should do; that the characters that one helped bring into being could be out in the world meeting and talking to other people. It would not be the first time that I would wonder about the role of the artist in society, and what responsibility the artist has to his or her creation. In time, as someone would come up to me after a reading, wondering where Gloria and Annie are these days, if they got reunited; or that time a niece of mine insisted that she knew exactly where the book was set – in Nonsuch, our maternal and ancestral home, high in the blue Portland mountains of Jamaica – in time I would wonder about the role of the reader in the artistic compact. Art is nothing, I eventually came to believe, if it is not a transaction.

Imagine then, my delight, when I started reading Roger Mais's amazing *Black Lightning* and realising that it was precisely the very same questions about the role of the artist that I, as a barely begun artist, was asking myself, that Mais fully explored in this his triumphant third novel. I felt that I was simultaneously talking to and taking the hand of a father, an elder, an older brother, a friend even. The novel could not have arrived at a better time in my life.

❧

The outlines of the novel are well known: the protagonist, Jake, is a sculptor and blacksmith who is fascinated by the Biblical Samson as a symbol of man's independence, and of a man who is amongst strangers. Deciding to carve a mahogany tribute to Samson, however, becomes a more complicated affair when Jake's wife leaves him for another man and the issue of deception by a woman becomes more central to his thoughts. In the biblical story, Samson is of course blinded by the Philistines because of Delilah's treachery, and is left leaning on a young boy for support. In the novel, Jake is struck by lightning and left blind, forcing him to rely on his friends, particularly Amos, to survive. After leading him on a journey to discover just how reliant on humanity he really is, Jake's despair in his blindness ultimately drives him to suicide.

Those are the broad strokes.

But this is a novel that is concerned not only with the broad strokes, but increasingly with the smaller more delicate or intimate strokes. Time and time again in the novel the artist is positioned as the outsider, the one cursed or blessed – it was, I believe, the poet Adrienne Rich who said – "to see for others what they cannot see for themselves." The issue of sight, sightlessness, insight and vision is invoked throughout the novel. The novel makes the point that even those with clear eyesight and even insight sometimes cannot see what is in front of them.

Take for example Mother Coby, a prophetess, who consistently exhorts Jake to repent his sins and cease making a "graven image" – in this instance the statue of Samson that he is carving out of mahogany. For Mother Coby, and too many people like her, the only creator is the almighty and to seek to be a creator is to equate oneself with the almighty.

Yet I find it hard to believe that in a Jamaica of tourist trinkets, indeed a Jamaica of pale-faced Christs in just about every church, that this is the first time that Mother Coby has been confronted with art-rendering. Yet Jake is the only person we know whom she chastises. So the question becomes: What is it that Jake is creating that is so bothersome to Mother Coby? For farsighted Jake, who rejects all the trappings of what his education could give him, to settle among his people and be a blacksmith and carver, the question is: what indeed would his carving look like? No doubt his creation is a reflection of the people around him, and it is perhaps this particular and local reflection that so bothers Mother Coby.

The difficulty that some have with the idea of artistic creation becomes even more evident when Jake is visited by his late father's friends Massa Butty and Tata Joe. These men, as representatives of the larger community, cannot understand why Jake, with all his good learning and education, has settled into his father's old business of blacksmithing, doing some carving on the side.

"I'm not trying to say it isn't a fine thing for a man to be able to do them things," Massa Butty says, "But what's it get you? That's what I would like to know." This discussion exposes a significant ignorance as to who the artist is and what he contributes to his society. Neither men can appreciate Jake's art form or the struggle it takes to create art. This issue is further disclosed when Jake offers a gift to Tata Joe for Jake's goddaughter Esmeralda. While Jake is busy getting this gift both Tata Joe and Massa Butty say the gift is "sure to be something that ain't a sight of good to anyone."

Again the reader is forced to ask, what indeed would "good art" look like to Massa Butty, Tata Joe and Mother Coby and what is it that makes Jake's artwork so worthless? Whatever Massa Butty means by the pun embedded in his "ain't a sight of good" (it won't have any utility and it will offend the sight), the reader is forced to conclude that what Jake makes reflects something back to the society that members of the society have a hard time accepting.

Yet Jake, the artist, continues creating his work, knowing that it is as important for the artist to make the work as it is for the society around the artist to interpret and make sense of the work that is created. Indeed, for me, the novel gives one of the most moving descriptions of how an artist works: the intense concentration needed to create a body of work; how the artist is always alert to his vision slipping away; how the artist perhaps can see what nobody else can see. When Jake's helper Miriam, for example, looks at what the artist has created she has sight but no vision, no matter how hard she tries to look. Miriam, like Mother Coby, is a representative of a society not sure about what they are looking at, or looking for – at what is coming into form. In so many ways these characters are a stand-in for a newly independent Jamaican society only beginning to imagine its future.

But if this novel details the hopes of the artist and does an admirable job of showing what it takes to make a satisfactory work of art, it also details the worst thing that can happen to an artist. Jake, as I have noted, loses his sight in a bizarre accident. Or is it, as Jake's estranged wife Estella insists, that Jake loses not just his eyesight, but his insight? In any case, the loss of but one of these two characteristics is detrimental to an artist. And, for me, this is ultimately why Jake decides to take his own life: he feels, having lost his vision, in the second sense, he has nothing more to contribute to his society. The question then becomes, if we take the physical loss as symbolic of the deeper loss of insight, why does Jake lose his vision?

In this novel the artist emerges as someone who questions his society, and does the supremely blasphemous thing in Jamaican society, of questioning God. The novel shows us Jake's role as creator in a society that might not fully appreciate his creations even as Jake ruthlessly examines the role of the artist. It is fascinating the way in which this novel, published in 1955, anticipates some of the challenges that would take place in Jamaica in subsequent years.

For example, in 1981 the sculptor Christopher Gonzalez heard that the Jamaican government was planning a sculpture in tribute to the late great reggae superstar Bob Marley, who had died in May of that year. Gonzalez submitted a winning bid to do the sculpture and turned in a rendition of Marley, with locks and feet curling into roots that seemed to be spreading out all over the world, which was vigorously rejected by the Jamaican government, the Marley family, even members of Marley's band. The public outrage was particularly vociferous and intense. As a child in Jamaica at the time I remember the furore of a large cross-section of Jamaican society (myself included) who felt that Gonzalez's work was a failure because it looked nothing like Marley. Who was this hallucinatory scary figure, eyes sinking into holes, I remembered thinking, that Gonzalez had offered us as Bob Marley? It was certainly not a Marley I could identify with then.

But in a strange kind of way Gonzalez's Marley stayed with me – much more so than the Bob Marley offered and accepted by another artist, the Marley that looked like Marley. Gonzalez's Marley was not a Marley that anyone could walk by without reacting to in one way or another. His was a Marley that caused people to stop and think. A Marley that was not obvious. A Marley that I carried inside me off the island, a Marley that informs my own work as a writer and visual artist these days. For I too wish to create work that makes people stop and think. And this is what Mais's character Jake hoped to do as well in the art he created. He wished to get the people around him to stop and think.

Yet Gonzalez's story is a cautionary tale, for the artist, it is said, became embittered by this experience, and, for the most part, withdrew from making large-scale sculpture again. The public rejection hurt him deeply. He felt he had offered a gift to his people that had been promptly rejected. The artist Laura Facey faced a similar predicament in 2003 when her sculpture of a naked man and woman, which today graces the entrance of the Emancipation Park in Kingston, sparked intense and international discussion. Many felt that because of the artist's racial and class background (she is a white Jamaican identified with the upper class), she should not have been the one to land this emancipation commission. What could anyone of her background have to say about emancipation anyway? Weren't the vast majority of Jamaicans glad to be emancipated from people who looked exactly like Ms. Facey? These are some of the questions that Mais anticipated in *Black Lightning*. As painful as they might be I still appreciate the furore that public sculptures can engender because it gives us a chance to discuss what a commission should look like and what responsibility, if any, the artist has to the people they are representing. Too often, however, the answers to the profound questions being asked are conservative, even reactionary. The Marley commission was eventually given to an artist who produced a work so like Marley that most people walk by it without actually seeing the work at all. Having us Jamaicans reflect on our troubled past, asking how the nation should be represented and who should do the representing, is an exercise we still need to encourage. This is what Mais's courageous book encourages us to do.

And then there is the question of what becomes of what the artist has created. Does the creation take on a life of its own as Jake seems to suggest? Does the artist become his creation? Or is the creation able to stand alone? I want to believe that it is a little bit of both, that the creator is changed in the process of creation, and that the creation should be able to function on its own.

At the end of this novel, however, there is a tragedy. For Mais seems to suggest that his Jamaica has no use for the art created and the artist is forced to destroy his own creation. My hope is that this tragedy says more of Jamaican society in Mais's time than it does of Jamaica today.

For art to be art there has to be a transaction.

&

In the story of Samson and Delilah, a good man is brought down by a bad woman. It is a theme that runs through all of Mais's published books.

It is a temptation to read the story of Samson as that of Jake, especially because of the parallels of both stories: Jake is seemingly betrayed by his wife in the same way that Samson was betrayed by Delilah. Both Samson and Jake end up blinded.

But the Samson and Delilah story acts as a foil for some of the larger questions that Mais is asking about Jamaican society.

For example, instead of heaping shame or scorn on Delilah, Jake wonders why does Delilah ultimately betray Samson? What is missing from the Biblical account? A woman never betrays a man for money, Jake concludes, refuting the claim that Delilah betrayed Samson for however many pieces of silver. For a woman the betrayal most likely has to do with love. Perhaps, Jake thinks, all along Delilah had been in love with one of her own people. I appreciate so much this rereading of the Samson and Delilah story because it complicates who Delilah might have been. It makes Delilah a more noble character, a Judith who is more concerned with the survival of her own people, as Mais, too, is concerned with the "survival whole" of his people.

The reader becomes aware that Jake, in thinking about Delilah's motives for leaving her husband, is thinking about his own situation, about why his wife, Estella, has left him for another man. It is the story that is not told. It would almost be palatable, even explainable, if she had left him for a man who has more money, but there is no evidence for this. More problematic no doubt for Jake is the realisation that his wife left him not because maybe she loved someone else more, but because of a flaw in his own character. As Estella comments on Jake: "He lived for other people's adulation, without even knowing it. Without it he was… nothing."

In so many ways Jake's estranged wife Estella, as a reformed Delilah, is one of the most arresting characters in the novel. Estella, like her husband, asks questions about the society around her; she takes risks, including risks with love, and at the end of the novel, pariah though she is, she is left standing while her husband decides to take his own life. Estella as an outcast, a woman who leaves a husband who was not abusing her, who still loves him, becomes a means to challenge woman's roles in the emergent Jamaican society, and for the society to know and understand itself some more. What is it, the novel seems to ask, that women will do in a new Jamaica? Estella's becoming a social worker after leaving Jake provides some answer to this question.

And then there is the role of an education in this society. Tata Joe and Mass Butty feels that Jake is "fit for better things" than to be a blacksmith – "things that fit your kind of education." But Jake challenges their notion of what education should be and do, insisting that he "fixed old Mother Bado's bedspring … [and] her pains left her." The reader is left to ponder the question: What indeed is the role of an education if not to help with the suffering of those around you?

But maybe the biggest question that the novel poses is that of homosexuality in Jamaican society as is expressed in the homoerotic tension between Jake and Amos. It seems to me that the Samson story of a man being betrayed by a woman is a creative foil in which to hide a homosexual love story for a society that might not have been prepared then, as too many are not prepared today, to face this love that dares not speak its name. Time and time again a subtle eroticism rises to the surface: Amos does not laugh when Jake suggests that he gets married; indeed with Jake, Amos is "like a patient dog waiting for his cue." Throughout the earlier part of the novel Amos is "meek" and receptive to Jake, assuming the stereotypically female role. Jake chides Amos about always being "so touchy" around him, while acknowledging that after all they are a couple of "queer ones", they are "kin", which is why they get along so well. Jake acknowledges that despite the fact that he treats Amos like dirt, still Amos keeps coming back.

At the beginning of the novel, Amos looks up at Jake "humbly", "imploringly", and gets upset that Jake is "still worrying about that woman" (his estranged wife). There are many moments of awkward silences between the two men. When other friends of Jake's, particularly men, drop by, Amos jealously slinks away. Furthermore, there is always eagerness in the voice of both men when they see each other.

Amos buy's gifts for Jake "[w]ith my own money that I saved up – special for that purpose." The very air around Jake and Amos "seemed to be subtly charged with electricity… there was a kind of restless excitement in both men." And when Jake is in one of his "black moods", "there was no one but Amos could do anything for him." It is interesting to peruse why, despite the hinting at undeniable homoerotic desires, this is never made explicit in the novel – but then again this is a novel that is throughout rife with unrequited and frustrated love: Bess's love for Jake is not reciprocated; Estella leaves Jake for another man whom she eventually leaves as well; Bess cannot stand the feelings of love in her daughter that she recognises in herself; then there is Glen and Miriam, Miriam who is always cutting herself in a symbolic representation of the hymen that refuses to be broken in her relationship with Glen.

The novel begins and ends in the woods and some of the most significant events take place there. Readers of Thomas Hardy will note echoes in the prose of Hardy's pastoral under threat, *Under the Greenwood Tree*, also a novel about art (in this case music – and the novel is subtitled *A Rural Painting of the Dutch School*) and repressed desires. In *Black Lightning*, the woods emerge as a place of possibility, a refuge, a place of hiding and secrets, even as it is a place where love takes place. Estella meets her lover Steve in the woods, she also follows Jake into the woods on his way to killing himself, and she has a significant discussion with Amos in the woods that sheds light on aspects of Jake's character that are not readily available in any other part of the novel. In myth and folktale, strange and fantastic creatures inhabit woods, as strange and fantastic creatures inhabit the enclosed world of *Black Lightning*, an important novel that asks important questions of Jamaican society and anticipates some of the society's challenges in the years to come. What an absolute joy to have this novel back in print again.

## CLAUDE MCKAY'S SONGS OF MOROCCO

McKay made two trips to Morocco: one for several months between 1928-1929; and the second when he lived and worked in the country from 1930-1934. The question of "home" and belonging was always a complex question for Claude McKay. The identity of which he was surest was being a Jamaican, but he had left Jamaica at twenty-two, never to return. In a sense, McKay's second stay in Morocco was a return "home" – a return to Africa. In his letters to good friend Max Eastman, he mentions how much he feels at home in Morocco. In fact, there was a time when McKay thought that he had found a place in Morocco to settle permanently.

McKay had a sense of Africa as the ancestral homeland long before he came to the United States. Growing up in Jamaica, his father spoke of an Ashanti origin, while his mother's people were thought to have come from Madagascar. The time he spent in Marseilles among various Africans had whet his appetite to know more about Africa. In Morocco, he often talked about going further and deeper into Africa. His intention to travel to West Africa and beyond never materialised and we can only wonder how such a journey would have impacted his writings.

Getting to know Morocco, had, no doubt, something to do with getting to know himself better. One of the things that immediately impressed itself on McKay is how much Morocco reminded him of Jamaica. In his autobiography, he writes:

> At last I arrived in Casablanca. On the afternoon when the Martiniquan took me to his house in a native quarter, some Guinea sorcerers (or Gueanoua, as they are called in Morocco) were performing a magic rite. The first shock I registered was the realisation that they looked and acted exactly like certain peasants of Jamaica who give themselves up to the celebrating of a religious sing-dance orgy which is known as Myalism. The only difference was their clothing.

In addition, "For the first time in his life", McKay declares in his autobiography, "I felt singularly free of colour consciousness. I experienced a feeling that must be akin to the physical wellbeing of a dumb animal among kindred animals."

In essays written earlier, particularly "He Who Gets Slapped" (1922), it becomes evident that race had become a burden for Claude McKay while living in Europe and America. He described, for instance, how his race had placed a burden on his friendships with white people. The phrase "among kindred animals" is thus significant as it implies the extent of isolation that McKay had experienced in the United States and Europe. Still, as someone who grew up in a predominantly black country, it is a curious idea that McKay reports feeling "singularly free of colour consciousness" for the first time. Though Jamaica is by no means a racial paradise, one would think that he would have had similar feelings as he grew up on the island. Perhaps being in Morocco marked the distance McKay had travelled from the island to where he was in his life by the time he arrived there. Perhaps the racism that he suffered in Europe and America had marked him so much that Morocco represented a breath of fresh air.

For McKay, Morocco was authentically African. We sense his disregard for those who saw it otherwise in his description of an incident on the ship to Morocco. Some Europeans were arguing that Morocco was not a Negro country and McKay remarks, "Themselves divided into jealous cut-throat groups, the Europeans have used their science to make such fine distinctions among people that it is hard to ascertain what white is a true white and when a Negro is really a Negro." By the time he gets to the city of Marrakesh, McKay is not surprised to find the city overwhelmingly black. During his first few months in Morocco, McKay becomes preoccupied with connecting Morocco to West Africa. When he travels to Rabat he visits the tomb of the Black Sultan, at Chellah, "who, to the native legend, was the greatest ruler of Morocco, having united North Africa under his rule, conquered Spain, built the great monuments of the Giralda at Seville, the Koutabia at Marrakesh, and the Hassan Tower at Rabat." It is as if in Morocco, i.e. Africa, McKay encounters a great ancestor and its contingent peoples of whom he could be rightfully proud.

The presence of the African ancestor who is a learned man and leader becomes a trope throughout McKay's writings about Morocco.

McKay repeatedly describes how much he feels at home in Morocco, but, at times, this "feeling home" is questionable. The writer Paul Bowles, who met McKay in Morocco, speaks of an incident in which a very irate McKay came to see him one evening at the hotel were Bowles was staying. McKay believed that Bowles was responsible for his house being broken into and his passport stolen. However, McKay was not allowed by the Spanish proprietor past the desk in the courtyard to see Bowles because of his skin colour and his Moroccan dress.

Though he was most sure of his Jamaican identity, McKay could not give a coherent answer as to where exactly his home was. When asked by a doorman one day whether he was American, McKay gave this garbled answer: "I said I was born in the West Indies and lived in the United States and that I was an American, even though I was a British subject, but I prefer to think of myself as an internationalist."

What McKay chose to think of himself stood in stark contrast to his actual legal status as a British subject as opposed to what he was not – an American citizen. As a British subject he was required to register with the British Consulate, something he did not do. One day, however, a French police inspector accosted him and insisted that McKay accompany him to the British Consulate. Following a tense and unpleasant confrontation with the French police officer (who was all for expelling McKay) and the British Consul, McKay is finally permitted to leave. "The personal unpleasantness," he wrote, "opened my eyes a little to the undercurrent of social unrest... That incident spoiled my native holiday... And now even in Africa I was confronted by the specter, the white terror always pursuing the black. There was no escape anywhere from the white hound of Civilisation."

In his autobiography *Without Stopping*, Paul Bowles writes of a man named Abdeslam ben Hadj Larbi, whom he felt had been paid by some government to put Claude McKay in an "untenable situation". This Abdeslam ben Hadj Larbi later denounced McKay as a communist, thus causing him great difficulties in Morocco.

Several months later, in 1929, his first trip to Morocco came to an end and McKay was faced again, as he was throughout most of his life, with the question of where he should go. Following the success of *Home to Harlem* (1928), he was being told to come back to America. The writer James Weldon Johnson invited him to come back "home" but McKay was reluctant to return to the United States, especially to Harlem. For one, he did not want to face what he considered the harsh censure of the Negro Press that criticized the down-and-out working-class characters he chose to write about in *Home to Harlem*. He also felt unfamiliar with the new Harlem that had sprung up since he left some seven years before. Instead, he chose to go to a Paris that was "dull" after "the strong dazzling colours of Morocco." He stayed in Paris 1929 - 1930 and despite not being much enchanted by the city, he had a good time there. He looked up old friends, went to cabarets, saw copies of his new book *Banjo* (1929) decorating a shop window and met some of the African-American artists then visiting or living in Paris. But after a while he decided to go back to Morocco where the living was cheap, where he could get work done and continue with his "experiment in wearing bags, bournous and tarboosh."

We gain much insight into McKay's time in Morocco in 1930 - 1934 from letters he wrote to good friend, mentor and compatriot Max Eastman. At first when he returned to Morocco, McKay settled in Tangier and it is easy to see his love and exuberance for the country. Said McKay in a letter to Eastman dated December 1, 1930, "I quit France in September for Morocco... I had really arranged (I must hastily add) to return here however, because I love the country..." He continued, "Tangier is lovely and if they don't... boot me out I shall take a house here, where I shall be... able to visit easily all Morocco... I need to settle down and no place has satisfied me since I left home as much as Morocco. There are many things in the lives of the natives, their customs and superstitions, reminiscent of Jamaica."

By 1931 McKay was settled and working steadily, hoping to have a new book published shortly. On July 19th of that year he wrote to Eastman: "I feel like settling here for good. I am a good Moslem now, wearing the tarboush – and [...] I have a little house [...] in an Arab village [...] Living is cheap". In addition to adoring his little house, he continued to fall in love with the country. Soon he was repairing a "dilapidated old barn" in the "Arab village" near "the mouth of the Suani River" and farming the two acres he had to spare. Trying to entice Eastman to come for a visit, he wrote in a letter dated December 1, 1931:

> The house is right on a river which divides it from the sea and at high tide when the sea rides up the river water the water washes the foundation. It is deep enough for good bathing especially when the sea is high, with a little stretch of sandy beach, and next summer I want to build a runway right into the water... It commands a most lovely view of the sea, the town of Tangier and Spain.

In a little under two years, however, things begin to change and McKay quickly moved from exuberance to despair tied to health problems and money troubles.

By 1932 he put his typewriter into pawn and felt miserable doing so. On May 10, 1933 he wrote to Eastman, "I haven't a cent and... I have been selling my few [sticks] of furniture in the native market [...] I have just heard from Jo Bennett [...] A nice letter but she didn't send me anything although I told her I was disappointed, ill and broke."

One is struck by the petulance if not downright immaturity in McKay's letter. Why should others send him money? Perhaps this was in keeping with what one of his biographers has called "that peculiar combination of dependence on others and aggressive independence" that McKay displayed throughout his life.

By 1933 McKay wanted to leave Morocco. In a sense this was not an indictment of the country so much as an indictment of Claude McKay. Throughout his letters, one is struck by his dependence on others to do for him what he really should be doing for himself, and how frustrated he gets when African-Americans do not deliver on his behalf. Before long he started feeling lonely and cut off in his little house in the country. More than once he asked Eastman to send him American magazines so he can have a sense of what is going on in the world. During this time he abandoned his third novel, *Savage Loving*, and instead sent a collection of stories, *Gingertown* (1932), to his publisher. Another novel, this one of

Jamaican life, *Banana Bottom* (1933), followed. But *Gingertown* and *Banana Bottom* did not sell well and when he finally sent *Savage Loving* to his publisher, it was not accepted for publication. To compound an even more precarious financial situation, McKay now found himself indebted to his publisher.

With his world collapsing around him, McKay became increasingly depressed and began to feel trapped. Trying to lessen his feelings of isolation, McKay moved from his house in the country back to Tangier and at first he felt a little better but his confidence had been badly shaken by the failure of two books, as well as the rejection of his last novel. Moving from the countryside to the city improved his mood for a while, but soon Tangier became "an international wasps' nest" that he wanted to leave.

In his letters to Max Eastman, we see the tangible uncertainty about whether or not he will eventually be allowed to return to the United States. This uncertainty stands in stark contrast to the boastful tone that McKay adopted in his autobiography, in which he acted as though he did not care if he returned to America. His letters to Eastman reveal that just the opposite was true.

McKay was, though, still reluctant to return to what he disparagingly called the African-American intelligentsia. He had genuine admiration for working-class African Americans, dockworkers, railroad workers, waitresses etc., what he called "the rough body of the great serving class of Negroes", but he also realised that what he had become effectively separated him from working-class African Americans. If he returned to the United States, he reasoned, he would have no choice but to live among the educated elite of African-American society, against whom he levelled several cutting attacks. In a letter to Eastman dated June 28, 1933 he wrote:

> I was planning another novel. To cover the field of my experiences of the period centring around the time we met when you returned from Russia. It is fermenting in me the way "Home to Harlem" was five years ago. The leading characters will be the Aframericans abroad and our antics [...] The only trouble about it is that I don't know how much I can let myself go about that class of Negroes. They are all so touchy. And if I go back "home" I'll have to live among them. I don't want to do anything more than assemble the facts and get down to the truth, but that is just what those people cannot stand.

While it is true that some in the African-American elite criticized and at times attacked McKay's "negative" portrayals of "the race" in his books, it is equally true that members of this group also came to his defence and tried to help him. There are numerous examples of James Weldon Johnson, Langston Hughes, Arthur Schomburg, among others, who stretched out a helping hand to Claude McKay.

For all his problems though, McKay did complete an astonishing body of work in Morocco – his second novel *Banjo* on his first trip in 1928; the short story collection *Gingertown* and the novel *Banana Bottom*; and he also revised the novel *Savage Loving* (which would later be retitled *Romance in Marseilles*). Sometime in 1933, McKay began to write what would eventually become *Harlem Glory*. In addition, he wrote several poems, essays and various sketches of Moroccan life while still living in the country. Later he dedicated a significant portion of his autobiography to his time in Morocco and the country keeps showing up in subsequent works as well. Even after he physically left Morocco, Morocco did not leave McKay, and somehow having lived in Africa permanently altered him.

What are some of the themes that arise in McKay's writings about Morocco? For one, there is a wholehearted identification of the country as an African country. McKay was also doggedly and determinedly anti-colonial. He always mounted a fierce defence of the natives against European domination, and celebrated Moroccan freedom fighters such as Muhammad Ibn and Abd al-Karim el-Khattabi. He shows how France and Spain colluded to defeat Abd al-Karim; he shows European repression and domination in Morocco.

In the essay "North Africa and the Spanish Civil War", McKay links North African problems to similar issues in the southern United States, while the essay "North African Triangle" highlights the fact that although Muslims are more numerous than Europeans, they have no power in their own country. He talks admiringly about the commingling of Christians, Muslims and Jews in North Africa and he makes a genuine effort at trying to see the world through native eyes.

The letters he wrote in Morocco stand in sharp contrast to the tone in *A Long Way From Home* (1937). Indeed, the letters, when set against the published autobiography, make for interesting reading, for McKay is not the hero in the letters that he portrays himself to be in his autobiography. As mentioned above, in the autobiography, he writes as if he did not care if he returned to the United States, when, in fact, the letters show that it mattered greatly to him.

In his short fiction pieces about Morocco, we notice a narrative of development, starting with the young American woman in the short story "The Little Sheik," who, out of absolute ignorance of Moroccan ways, ends up getting a young Moroccan into trouble in his own country; to, further afield, the Moroccan prostitute in Marseille making a living by her wits; to, even further afield, the presence of North Africans living and dying in the United States, while integrated into the Negro community in Harlem. Here McKay gives a wide spread of Moroccan life both inside and outside of the country.

The poems McKay wrote about Morocco are notably female and erotic. In "Two Songs of Morocco," there is sensuousness, fertility, fecundity, and "ripened passion". The moving series of poems he wrote about cities in Morocco commingle the erotic and the exotic – Fez is a place that "can be taken whole", yet it is also a place he cannot know in its entirety, with its labyrinthine lanes and costumes that are "hooding beauty from men's sight." The poem "Marrakesh" references power and strength and "is an African drum beat sung to oriental songs." These poems also show us a place where the African, Oriental and Arabic come together as in "Tetuan". Morocco is also a "place of cleansing" as in "Xauen". At some level, Tangier remains a mystery to him, and he asks, "What thoughts are hid behind your lowered brow?" Despite the fact that Tangier is still "in chains" and an overtly touristic place, which "stands at the opposing span of two opposing continents," McKay finds within Tangier's mist a "beauty pregnant of life's pristine womb" and in the city he can still "hear the drum beat of Africa and a symbol of the Berber brave." The poem "Morocco" is wistful and touches "caressingly my innermost chords". In this poem, McKay admits that he was "brought beneath [the] spell" of Morocco and is a "captive, within your sphere." It is the author who is "[t]he hungry spirit within your midst."

As a Fulbright fellow (2008-2009) in Morocco, I participated in a series of lectures arranged by the United States Embassy, in which I talked about who Claude McKay was and of his stays in Morocco. It was at one of these talks that I came to realise that Claude McKay remains essentially a misunderstood writer. Right after I finished giving a talk/reading at the Tangier American Legation Museum, a middle-aged American man approached me. The man identified himself as a scholar and said that, unlike everyone else in the room that I had quizzed, he knew who Claude McKay was and also that McKay had lived in Morocco. The man wanted to caution me. "McKay's work, it is quite exotic. If you really look at it you will see that it exoticises Morocco". This encounter best encapsulates some of the confusions that abound about Claude McKay. McKay believed very strongly in "natural instincts" with no sugar-coating. He valorised the primitive, the instinctive, the savage, as more true to life than the educated. It is within this context that his works, particularly *Romance in Marseilles* should be read.

For McKay, assimilation was the death of blacks; the worst thing that could happen to black people was "civilisation". Therefore he launched a multi-pronged attack against what he called "civilisation" and instead chose to celebrate the streetwalkers and boys lounging about the docks, who, he felt, were more instinctual and alive.

At another of the talks I gave, this time at a university, a young Moroccan woman read, in its entirety, Claude McKay's long and beautiful poem, "Two Songs of Morocco". I can still hear the surprise and delight in her voice, and I remember feeling, as this young woman read, that the notoriously difficult Claude McKay would have been happy to be back in Morocco, a country and a people that he loved so much after all. I remember the satisfaction, somewhere far inside myself, of feeling that Claude McKay would have been pleased to hear this young woman recite, in her strong and lovely voice, his "Two Songs of Morocco."

## A CLEAR BLUE DAY

The train was at the 14th Street station for the longest time and I worried that I would be late for my 9:00 am class. Would the students wait? Why couldn't the train just crawl to the next stop, West Fourth Street, which was my stop, so I could get off the train and hurry to my classes? I remember now that the train conductor kept saying something about some problem at the World Trade Center. After what seemed an agonisingly long time the train eventually moved on to the next stop and by the time I got out of the train, I knew that something was terribly wrong. You could see it on the look on people's faces. The fact that New Yorkers looked worried, worried me. Plus why were so many people milling around? The resident beggar at the West Fourth Street train station who I'd had a run in with a few weeks before came down into the station chanting, "Jah… Halleluiah… Jah… Jah come… people you all have to come outside and see this! Babylon!" I climbed the steps out of the train station with a heavy heart and turned around to the two cavernous holes in the World Trade Center's twin towers. The two cavernous holes that led from nothingness into nothingness. I kept wondering if I was dreaming. It was such a beautiful spring day. Cool and bright and blue. In fact, that would be one of the ironies that would stay with me, that something so atrocious could happen on such a clear blue day. I looked around, shaken, before I started my block and a half walk up to NYU. But how could such an accident have happened and happened not once but twice? I kept asking myself, for I was steadfast in my belief that it was nothing but a terrible accident, though the fact that it was two and not one plane rattled me to the core. Much hushed talking was going on around me. Someone wanted to know how planes could be flying so low over the City as to fly into a building. Even if they were getting ready to land, shouldn't they be further up in the sky? It was then that I started wondering what I would say to my students when I saw them, because, college students that they are, they still expected instructors to have all the answers to all their questions. Every now and again as I walked I stopped and looked up at the buildings with the two cavernous holes. *How could this have happened?* Soon fighter planes were flying low over the city. More and more people kept coming out on the streets, milling around, confused, unsure. Then, out of nowhere, the words "attack" and "World Trade Center" started floating around. A woman stopped and said loud enough for those close to her to hear, "I wonder what good the star wars programme is now... eh? You tell me. All that money on some star wars programme and they couldn't stop something like this?" I did not know what to say to the speaker, an older woman, frail and frightened. She tugged repeatedly on a denim jacket she was wearing before drifting off to accost some other person with her unanswered questions.

What I remember next is standing in front of my class with students as dumbfounded as I was. I tried to teach, but could not. I let the students go even as I did not know where I was letting them go to. I remember too that my class was on the ground floor of the Stern building, the business school, and that over the next couple of weeks Stern would keep compiling and recompiling what seemed an endless list of business students and alumni who had died in the attacks. As I walked aimlessly out of my class, marvelling at the instructor in the room next to mine who, it seemed, was handing out papers for an exam, I made my way back out to West Fourth Street and now people were everywhere, in the streets, lining up at the phone booths to make phone calls, because cell phones were not as ubiquitous then. And then the words... Pennsylvania... plane coming down... Pentagon... and it was then that we all knew, that we were all sure, Jews and gentiles alike, that *we* were under attack. By now people were visibly shaking. Fear and panic was everywhere. All the phones were in use. My then supervisor, when I made my way up to my office, kept saying, "Evil... evil... this is just all evil." I tried calling my mother but I did not get her. I tried calling a friend but I did not get him. Someone needed the phone I was using and I handed it over. A guy was holding a young woman, telling her it would be okay. It would all be okay. But looking at the television that had materialised in the centre of the room, we all knew that it would not be okay. We all watched, a chorus of "Oh no! Oh no! Oh God no!" erupting out of us as the two buildings, like a great big terrestrial animal, buckled under its own weight, a mammoth down on one leg, then another, then down on all fours. I will never forget this. It was alternately happening too fast or it was happening in slow motion. The dust, the rubble, the tremendous smoke. The persistent feeling of being trapped in a nightmare from which I could not wake. I tried calling my mother again. I thought about my family in Jamaica. I finally got a hold of my friend, who told me to come and meet him in midtown Manhattan. By then the trains had stopped running, and so I walked with a large group of people stunned silent up to midtown. It seemed that stunned silent people were on the move all over the City. For the first time since I lived in New York, I had the eerie feeling of walking in the City without the constant sound of the subway below. I learned that day that the sound of the City is the sound of the subway, with its constant rumble below.

Everything went by quickly after that, walking in silence to my friend's apartment, the two of us watching the same footage over and over again that night, the planes entering and entering and forever entering the buildings. I eventually got a hold of my mother. For the most part the eerie silence continued, though later that night, in my friend's Chelsea apartment, there would be another sound, the fast intermittent *swish* of vehicles going up and down the street. "What is that?" I asked finally, after the swishes began to get the better of me. My friend got up to check the window. "Ambulances," he said from the window, "ambulances ferrying the dead to the morgue."

Over the next few days the city would be in lockdown. No one was allowed below 14th Street, so I could not go to work. Not that I wanted to go to work anyway. I was listless. A pall had descended over the entire place, and when I eventually went back to work there was the debris, the debris that had blown up to NYU from the busy multi-tasking lives that had once populated the World Trade Center – key chains, lockets, letterheads, rolodexes. Paper, so much paper, was blowing about the streets of not only Manhattan and Brooklyn, but also Queens and had even found its way, some insisted, to the Bronx. The detritus of the World Trade Center, it seemed to me, was finding its way all over New York, all over the United States and via its waterways from the United States to the rest of the world.

And then there was dust, for weeks and weeks, then months and months, it felt as though the city was covered in a thick layer of dust. American flags were everywhere. My first day back at work, as I walked the block and a half from the subway to my classes, I saw two friends meet on the street and collapse in tears into each others arms. They could not stop crying. I knew instinctively that they had worked at the World Trade Center. An older gentleman rode by on a shaky bicycle with a huge radio in the basket of the bicycle that played the national anthem over and over again. By then my vocabulary had been irrevocably changed… al Qaeda … Bin Laden… Taliban. I thought it incredible that almost no one was pulled from the rubble alive.

Not long after, leaflets and tributes started sprouting up. The missing lined the walls of the City. I would stop, read a few of their stories and tears would fill my eyes. There was a dull, hollow feeling inside. People spontaneously gathered in groups. Flowers and candles were left outside fire stations.

For months after the attacks I wanted to do something, but was unsure what I could do. Eventually I took a part-time job teaching creative writing to students in the public school system, but as I looked at the students I wondered what writing could really do.

Maybe it would help me in some way to go to the site of the destruction. People I knew went down to the World Trade Center site, as if in homage, but I ended up not doing that. What would I be looking at? What would I be looking for? What did I hope to gain or understand in looking?

Since I had no answer I stayed put.

I remember distinctly a little girl, no more than about six years old, whose aunt-mother had died in the attack. She had written a tribute poem for her aunt-mother in one of the creative writing classes I was teaching. "I guess it is alright to tell you," the teacher said when I showed her the poem, "but when it first happened…" the teacher's voice started to break and her eyes glassed over, "when it first happened… I had to have her here, by my side, all the time. She could not stop shaking."

Another student – older, a teenager, and very angry – wanted to know in his poem how did it feel when the buildings came down on you; how did it feel when they took you out in a black body bag, Dad? Where did you go to that day you went to work, Dad? Why did you never come back home? We did not get even a part of you to bury.

What surprised me was how accusatory this student was, not at those who attacked the World Trade Center, but rather at the father who went to work, but never came back home. After he wrote and handed me his poem, this student never came back to any of my writing workshops.

Writing. That has been the way I have sought to process so much of what has happened in my life, and that is how I now seek to process what happened the day the World Trade Center came down. It has been more than a decade since those terrible events. The City, I am told, has largely recovered. But we New Yorkers, for I am a member of the tribe, still live on edge. I still ask myself what is it that writing can do? What is it that writing can achieve? How active indeed is writing? What I do know is that it is through writing about what did happen that I am able to understand how that event changed and shaped me; it is through writing about these events that I understand how that event changed and shaped the City – how put upon some of us in the City still feel, how we almost always feel that someone is out to get us. We cannot get rid of the feeling that something has been taken away from us. We still have a gaping hole inside – a sense of things residing just below the surface. Writing brings understanding. And for as much as I question what I do in trying to make sense of the world through words, and trying to get others to make sense of themselves and their worlds through words, I have always known that the moment would come when one day I would have to tell this story; these words feel as though they were waiting there all along, wanting to come out to shape the images, the memories, the snippets that still lay awake inside. I always knew that one day, if only for myself, and perhaps to exorcise the demons that have come along with that day, that I would need to set this down on paper, tell the story of what that day, so seared in blood, what that day and the days that followed were like for me.

PART THREE

## THE BOOKENDS INTERVIEW

Sharon Leach: You wrote your novel, *The River's Song*, in the United States, right?

Jacqueline Bishop: I wrote *The River's Song* largely in the United States. I worked on it a great deal in graduate school at New York University; it was my thesis.

S.L.  Do Diaspora writers have an altered relationship with their native landscapes when they leave? Is it harder for you, specifically, to write of home in your adopted country?

J.B  For me, no. In fact, I think writing away from Jamaica gives me the chance to really look at Jamaica. I think if I were living in Jamaica and writing about Jamaica, that would be much more difficult for me. I seem to be the kind of writer who needs to put some distance between herself and the country she is writing about. When I was writing about America, for example, I needed to go to Mexico. Morocco. Also, I think it is important to add that my writing career began in earnest outside of Jamaica, since I left Jamaica as a teenager. So I would really be in trouble if I needed to be in Jamaica to write about Jamaica.

S.L.  What is the importance of memory for you writers writing away from home? How is it possible to get it so right? You don't write like someone who has trouble remembering Jamaica! I mean, the Jamaica I remember as a girl is the Jamaica you write about with precision.

J.B.  Well, first I have to say I take this as quite the compliment! Especially coming from you, a writer who has chosen to stay at home. You know Sharon, this is a very interesting question. The best I can say is that I'm writing out of the Jamaica I know – the Jamaica I can visualise, the Jamaica that is most real for me. When I look at my work, for example, I have characters taking the Common Entrance exam, while you, in the story "Midnight Love", have your main character's brother taking the GSAT exam. The GSAT is not real for me. Not now anyway. So my characters would be taking the Common Entrance exam.

I don't know if it is politically correct to say this, but what I am noticing, especially since I am rereading your book *What You Can't Tell Him*, is that you are writing in what I would call the "now" Jamaica – and, indeed, that you seem to be writing "out" of Jamaica to a larger world – while I seem to be writing "back" to Jamaica. I say all of this to say the Jamaica that I try to bring to life in my work is the Jamaica that I know. The Jamaica that I live(d) in. The Jamaica that is most personal to me. Consequently, it is important for me to keep in touch, to visit as often as I can, because I don't want the Jamaica that I know to diverge too radically (in my head) from the Jamaica that exists today.

S.L   Yeats found being "rooted in one dear perpetual place" to be important. Do you, as a writer "from here" but writing "over there" feel that need to be rooted in one dear place?

J.B.   No, I don't. I think you have to make the distinction between place and space. For me, the space I find myself in may or may not be conducive of writing, but not the place, per se. For example, the last time I was in Jamaica I went to visit Wayne Brown. We had been in steady email and telephone contact for a while, but that was our first face-to-face. I liked Wayne immediately. I think he is a brilliant writer. Anyway, as I sat in Wayne's house, I thought this is a space I could write in. A space I could create in. His house just had that feeling for me. It felt like a "dear perpetual space". Later, when I went to Portland to visit my grandmother, I had that feeling again and, in fact, late at night, my grandmother walking around me, I did get out an extended essay that Wayne ended up publishing. I found this odd, because I had never really written in Jamaica before, and did not even know if I could. There is just so much to distract me in Jamaica! The landscape, the people, all those things that fascinate and engage the person who has lived away for a long time. So I don't think it is a dear perpetual place that works for me, but rather, a dear perpetual space, wherever and in which country that space may be.

S.L.   A characteristic of your fiction and poetry is folk legends. How important is folklore to you?

J.B   I LOVE folklore and would love to do more with Jamaican folklore. I remember as a child being told these "tall tales" that would scare me, because it always seemed to come down to you not knowing something, or something not being very apparent to you, even as you had to make a decision between a "real" world and an "alternate" world that co-existed.

I remember my great grandfather telling me a tale of two sisters who were picked up by a kind bus driver late one night by the side of the road, he worrying for the safety of these two girls dressed all in white. No matter how he questioned them, the bus driver, they never said a word. They just kept staring straight ahead of them out into the eggplant-dark night. How, when he tried putting these two strange, non-talking girls off his bus, how they started saying, in a voice he had never heard before, "Take us back to where you took us up from!" Which, of course, was just outside of a graveyard! Now think of the possibilities of such a situation. The possible literary interpretations. The possibilities of translating all of that into characters! I very much like playing with that. For several years now I have been collecting Jamaican proverbs (I am up to several hundred) and I recently completed a children's book that is essentially the retelling of a folktale. The visual arts is also very important to me (I just had a show with Earl McKenzie in New York) and now I find that folklore is working its way into that area of my life as well. Perhaps folklore is important to me as a way of staying close to Jamaica. After all, folklore is the collective wisdom of a people.

S.L.  Do you consider yourself a Jamaican writer? Caribbean? American? Or do you prefer to not be labelled?

J.B.  I consider myself a writer who is from Jamaica. I consider myself a writer who is deeply invested in the Caribbean. I consider myself a writer who votes in America. But first and foremost I consider myself a writer. That is the label I most prefer.

S.L.  You founded the literary magazine *Calabash: A Journal of Caribbean Arts & Letters*. Do you feel the need to be especially supportive of other Caribbean writers, or even writers of colour?

J.B.  I almost want to pass on this question, because in the past this has gotten me into so much trouble! People sending me work that I should, without question, publish. But I think that the founding and doing the very hard work, with wonderful supporters, of *Calabash*, should give you some idea of where I stand on this issue. Plus so many people have been supportive to me that it would almost be unconscionable not to return the favour! But I can only support people who are serious, and people who I believe to be genuinely talented. And in my making those distinctions, decisions, and judgments, that's when I run into trouble with some people.

S.L.  Who are your writing influences?

J.B.  Critics have to tell us who our influences are. I certainly cannot do this for myself. But I can tell you who I like and, in so doing, perhaps I might give you some sense of influences. I start with a little story. Several years ago, as an undergraduate, I spent a year living in Paris, France. That would be a pivotal year for me, since it would be the first time I would be totally and absolutely away from my family. That year I would end up making all sorts of decisions about my life. You see, all my life I had been told I was going to be a doctor (never mind how I struggled in the sciences at Holy Childhood High School!) but that year in France would change everything!

I was an *au pair* and taking classes at the L'Université de Paris. But my French was *encore malade*. To while away the time I made a list of the "classics" and started reading my way through them. One day at the bookstore, I found Alice Walker. Then another day it was Olive Senior. When I found Olive Senior, I sat on the floor of the bookstore astonished. I gobbled up her stories greedily. Alice Walker and Olive Senior would lead me to some of the people I most admire. The list is too long, but I will say, in one form or another, the Caribbean, and Jamaica in particular, have produced some spectacular people.

S.L.  Do you have a specific audience in mind when you write?

J.B.  No, I do not. Actually, that is not totally true. When I hear the word "audience", my grandmother and my great grandmother immediately pop into my mind. Isn't that interesting? I often wonder, for example, what my great grandmother would have made of my books. I plan to sit down one day soon and have this conversation with my grandmother. The fact that I became a writer. But for some strange reason those two, who I am not even sure would have read my books, are the people who come to mind.

But I think I am going to steal and retell Walter Mosley's answer to this question. He says that the way he sees it, he and his favourite cousin are on a bus together. Both of them sitting down and talking, in the way that people who are close talk to each other. His audience is the person sitting behind them and listening to this banter.

S.L.  Does your writing presuppose knowledge of Jamaica on the reader's part?

J.B.  You know, early on in the process I used to worry about this. I no longer do. The first workshop I took was with a really great writing instructor, Tim Tomlinson. He is not Jamaican. One day I wrote a story in total Jamaican dialect, and I was very worried that no one in the workshop would understand it. As we discussed the story that night, I was surprised to see that most if not all the people "got" it. Later, Tim said in class, "I absolutely loved this story." He said it, I can still remember, very quietly. There was such sincerity in his voice! Naturally, he had a few suggestions (and he probably did tell me this), including that I had to trust the reader. And now, when I think about this, I think: Why not trust the reader? I mean, I pick up Shakespeare and Dickens and read them, books written centuries ago, and I can follow along. Not only do I follow along, but I am transported and I fall in love. So I trust my readers to follow along.

S.L.   How would you describe the place Jamaica holds in the North American imagination?

J.B.   There are the usual stereotypes that one has to fight against. The Tourist Board ads etc. Plus, I remember once that Wayne Brown and I joked about the kind of work where "men start giving birth to children!" And by that we were talking about the kind of over-the-top representations that feed into some of the exoticising of Jamaica that I see taking place, especially in regards to some of the more recent developments in the literature. We really do need to guard against this. But still I come back to the strongest and most resilient of writers. The Lorna Goodisons and Erna Brodbers. Surely they have been great ambassadors! Surely they have helped to foster a more complicated understanding of Jamaica in the North American imagination.

## CHARTING A LITERARY JOURNEY

Keisha-Gaye Anderson:  Talk about your literary journey from Jamaica
    to the United States. What characterises your unique expression
    of Caribbean themes in your writing?

Jacqueline Bishop:  In so far as my literary journey is concerned, I first
    boarded the bus to writing in Jamaica. I remember that when I
    was like ten years old I got my first poems published in a small
    church publication, those two poems were called "Flowers" and
    "Children" and so many people liked them! I still remember this
    publication as a bright yellow insert that had the poems and some
    drawings around it within the church programme. Interestingly
    enough, at around the same time, I saw an American magazine article
    calling for poems to be used as song lyrics and I sent my two poems
    off, and had all but forgotten I had done this when a letter came
    back in the mail saying that they wanted to buy the poems for song
    lyrics! I was stunned. I had a great time showing this letter to people,
    but for some reason I never followed up on this.

      As a child, I also used to write poems for friends and the other day I
    found a notebook from when I was fifteen years old and that notebook
    was filled with the most horrendous poems! I can only hope I did not
    hide this notebook in some place where I will never be able to find it
    again, because it did take me back to a person who no longer exists, and
    it did show me that for as long as I could remember I was writing, poems
    in particular.

      But you must have heard the story a million times before, because
    it is an often-told tale by many writers from the Caribbean that
    they never felt they could make a living as a writer, as an artist, so
    I decided I would become a medical doctor, but the science classes
    were always a challenge for me, particularly as an undergraduate.
    By then I was living in the States and one day someone said to me,
    "Why don't you, for one semester, just do the things you love?"
    There was no going back after that semester! Art classes and writing
    classes galore! I would still go on to get my degree in psychology,
    but by the time it came to grad school, I came back home to myself
    as a writer and I went to grad school in creative writing. Probably

I felt I could do this now because in America I saw a way I could both be a writer and make my living as a teacher. So far that has been my journey.

K.G.A. Are there any particular questions that you find yourself continually trying to address or explore through your work?

J.B. The question of place and belonging. I find myself coming back to this over and over again. I find my characters questioning their place in the world and I find my characters trying to find a place for themselves in the world. In the case of Gloria, in *The River's Song*, she ends up feeling confined by the island space. She ends up feeling the need to leave the island. It is as if for her, the only way she can come to terms with herself is if she leaves and goes to find another place for herself in the world. Whereas her friend Annie, who also grew up questioning her place on the island, is looking to be even more deeply rooted in the island space, despite the fact that she too was thinking of leaving the island for college abroad. For Annie, there was always the sense that the move would never be a permanent one away from the island, whereas for Gloria it is unclear when she leaves if she will ever make it back to the island. There is no denying that the questioning of place, of belonging, of finding out the limits to belonging, are found in most of my works so far.

This same theme of journey, of seeking one's place in the world, shows up also, I think, in my two poetry collections *Fauna* and *Snapshots from Istanbul*. In the case of *Fauna*, my first collection of poems, you can see as well the journey away from the island. The collection starts out being heavily rooted in the Caribbean, with poems of tribute to my great grandparents and others on the island and looking very closely at various aspects of life on the island. Many have commented on the section which has flowers speaking in the voice of island women and, through the flowers, detailing what it means to be a Jamaican woman, another great preoccupation in my work.

But steadily the collection moves from being grounded in the "Jamaican in Jamaica" experience out to the lives of immigrants and an exploration of what it means to be Jamaican in other parts of the world, specifically in the United States. There are poems about birds, birds being for me a tangible metaphor for migration. There are so many questions I now realise that I was asking in that first collection, questions about what it meant to come from the Caribbean, from the island of Jamaica in particular; what you take with you when you migrate and what you leave and how you change. I am delighted that reviewers talk about the complicated sense of coming from a place you deeply love, but where you realise terrible, unspeakable things can happen. About coming from a place that will, for the rest of your life and no matter where you go to live, mark you. The last poem in the collection expresses a coming to an acceptance of a dual Jamaican and American identity. Finding a place for herself in America as a Jamaican.

Something similar happens in my most recent collection *Snapshots From Istanbul*. But instead of examining what it means to be Jamaican, I found that I was examining what it means to be American as well, and coming to claim being American as part of my identity. It is significant that this exploration takes place in a far away and distant country, in Turkey, because I have come to the realisation that I am the kind of writer who has to be away from the place she is writing about to begin to see that place clearly. Sometimes I wonder, truthfully, if I could ever have become a writer in Jamaica because when I am in Jamaica everything is so intense for me that I do not know where to focus my attentions. It is almost like sensory overload, the voices, the colours, everything. I need to go to a far away place to begin to make sense of it all. Of course all of that is a long way around to say explorations of a place, and of one's identity, are central questions in my work.

K.G.A.  How do issues surrounding womanhood – particularly Caribbean womanhood – figure in your work?

J.B.  Well, I did a whole book about this when I did *My Mother Who Is Me: Life Stories from Jamaican Women in New York*. In that book I was trying to figure out two things, namely, what it means to be a Jamaican woman, and secondly, how did immigration to New York impact on the trajectory of these women's lives. I was also interested to find out how seemingly different groups of women, let's say Lebanese-Jamaican vis-a-vis African-Jamaican, handled the whole question of womanhood growing up in Jamaican society.

What I found was that the women almost uniformly encountered the same contradictions. As Maxine says in the book, "So the system is set up with inherent conflicts where, on the one hand, girls are told you have got to be a wife and a mother… but at the same time you are pushed to achieve academically… it is all very contradictory and conflicting!" Well, these issues particular to women, and to Jamaican women in particular, these conflicts and contradictions, are what I love to probe, are what I love to test. What are the limits of these contradictions? How far can you push against them? And what happens, God forbid, when you really break the rules! This gives me so much to work with!

K.G.A.  Who are some of the writers that have most influenced you and why?

J.B.  I read this question and I think immediately of Wayne Brown. Like someone said to me the other day, I still cannot believe that Wayne is gone. I was never a member of Wayne's workshop, not directly anyway, but Wayne took an active interest in what I was doing and tried to help me along the way as much as he could. I know that he did the same for many other writers as well, and we miss him terribly. Wayne Brown is definitely an influence, not only because he himself was an amazing writer, but because he would actually sit you down and explain to you which part of a piece was working, which was not, and why. Since I did not live in Jamaica we would do this largely by email, and when what he was saying was not getting through I could expect a phone call from Mr. Wayne Brown.

He was a serious man. Serious about writing; serious about literature. You knew better than to take him anything foolish, because, it is true, he could be quite cutting. He had very strong opinions and took quite seriously the work he did in mentoring a new generation of primarily Jamaican writers. I can only imagine what the workshops must have been like! After his death, I think it was someone at the University of the West Indies in Mona who said, more than anyone else, he single-handedly brought to the forefront a new generation of Jamaican writers. That is the gift that he gave to Jamaica.

So he is a real influence for me, that Wayne Brown, largely because he had such high standards. He held the bar very high and you had to jump up to reach it. My work was always better after it had passed through his hands. He had a knack of pulling out exactly what I was reaching for, exactly what I was going after. It was as if he could see more clearly into what I was trying to do than I could do for myself. I tell you, I still miss Wayne Brown terribly.

K.G.A.  What do you think are the major challenges facing Caribbean literature today?

J.B.  Publication and publication and publication. We need more access to publishing in the region and out; we need more publishers who are willing to publish and promote our works on a regular basis. That is the greatest challenge I see facing Caribbean literature today.

K.G.A.  You are also an accomplished visual artist. Talk about your art and tell us how that creative process impacts or influences your written work.

J.B.  I started out first as a writer, but I have always been interested in the visual arts. The year I spent in France as an undergraduate was spent largely in art classes. But I always seemed to forefront writing. Over time though, the visual arts just did not stop tugging, and eventually I started to give in. By then I had noticed that painters, paintings and other visual arts had a way of asserting themselves in my poems and as characters in my fiction work. Of course, you can always see these things better from a distance, but it took me a while to understand that the preoccupation with the visual arts, with visual artists and with certain colours in my written work meant that I too was a visual artist. In fact, there is a kind of cross-fertilisation between the arts which I tried to examine in the non-fiction book *Writers Who Paint, Painters Who Write: Three Jamaican Artists*.

What I have noticed about my visual arts is that I seem to almost always work in a series and in that way it is very similar to storytelling. It is almost as if I am telling little stories in the three major visual art works that I have completed to date. There is a strong narrative element. I have to strive, however, to meet the artistic challenges of the visual medium that I am creating in, and work so that these works can stand on their own merit visually and do not rely solely on the storytelling element. That is one of the challenges of working in both mediums.

K.G.A.  This is your second Fulbright award. Talk about both awards and describe the work you are currently undertaking in Paris.

J.B.  The first Fulbright I had was for a year in Morocco. In Morocco, I spent a lot of time going around and giving talks and speeches on behalf of the American Embassy. I talked a lot about African American issues, about women's writing and about immigrant issues. I also read from my own works. I had three exhibitions while I was there, and participated in literary festivals and in general was quite active.

Apart from the lasting friendships I formed though, perhaps the most special part of that time in Morocco was bringing back to Moroccan consciousness the fact that the Jamaican poet and writer Claude McKay lived and wrote in Morocco. The Moroccans were very appreciative of this.

Following that Fulbright experience, I was selected to be the UNESCO/Fulbright Fellow to Paris, which is where I am right now. I am working on the Creative Cities Network, which seeks to connect cities within seven thematic foci: Literature, Music, Cinema, Folk Arts, Design, Gastronomy and Media Arts. Specifically I am looking to put together a proposal to encourage the participation of countries from Africa, from Latin America and the Caribbean, and from Arab states into the Network because countries from these regions are currently either unrepresented or underrepresented in the Network. It has been fascinating, in general, learning about how creative industries can be a major force for development. That gives me a whole other way of looking at and managing my own creativity.

K.G.A.  Tell us about your documentary project and what you hope
     to achieve by making this film.

J.B.  Several years ago, as a graduate student at NYU, I started documenting
     a group of untutored artists in Jamaica called the Intuitives. Now
     I have several hours of footage on them. By the time I came along
     and started documenting these artists, several of them were elderly
     and frail and I felt it was urgent that I do this work. Since then
     most of them have died and so the footage has become even more
     precious to me as a tangible manifestation of their voices and
     mannerisms and so on. I would very much like to obtain additional
     funding to get back to Jamaica to document other members of the
     group as well as to edit these oral history interviews into a compelling
     narrative about artists who are integral to modern Jamaica and modern
     Jamaican art. What I hope to achieve with the film is further recognition
     of this amazing group of artists both inside and outside of Jamaica.
     I am thinking now in particular of Leonard Daley and Everald Brown,
     both of whom I had the great good fortune to interview before
     they passed; they have work that is so revolutionary, that asks so
     many questions about Jamaican society, that it would be really
     wonderful to get their voices and visions out there. I would like
     more people around the world to get to know these artists and especially
     to get to know their work!

## A WORLD OF SUPERIMPOSED MAPS

Derek Alger:   So you're back in New York after an extended stay abroad.

Jacqueline Bishop:  Yes, I am back in New York after travelling about
   a bit. I was on a Fulbright to Morocco (2008-2009) and then I was
   selected as the UNESCO/Fulbright Fellow (2009-2010) and placed
   in the Creative Cities Program at UNESCO headquarters in Paris.
   The goal of the Creative Cities Network is to connect cities which
   want to share experiences, ideas and best practices for cultural, social
   and economic development. However, I noticed while working on
   the Creative Cities Network that there was a need to help less
   developed cities become part of the Network; working with the
   U.S. Mission to UNESCO, I submitted a project proposal that was
   awarded funding to support the participation of less developed cities
   in the Network. I was really delighted about this and that became
   a highlight of my time away. Other highlights included travelling
   around Morocco and talking to groups of, mainly, students about
   what it means to be an immigrant to the United States. This really
   gave me the chance to get out and see the country. While I was in
   Paris, I had exhibitions in Belgium and Italy and those were certainly
   highlights as well.

D.A.  I see you were productive while away, completing *Snapshots from
   Istanbul*.

J.B.  *Snapshots from Istanbul* explores the lives of the exiled Roman poet
   Ovid and the journeying painter Gauguin. However, within the
   stories of these men I explore my own notions of what exile means
   to me. At the centre of the collection is a doomed relationship that
   takes place in Istanbul between a Turkish man and a Jamaican/American
   woman. On the one hand, I believe that the collection was inspired
   by trips to Istanbul. But, perhaps more than that, I guess the collection
   started coming together following a programme I watched on television
   about the Roman Empire and particularly about Ovid, once a famed
   poet, but who eventually was exiled from his beloved homeland. I
   could identify with a poet in exile, because I often feel in exile myself,
   though I am not sure where I am in exile from. By this I mean

that the Jamaica I left more than twenty years ago is not the Jamaica that is there today, and I often wonder if I return "home" to Jamaica, how well I would fit into and function in the society, even as Jamaica and Jamaican is the identity I am most sure of, the place I am most engaged with and the space from which I create within myself. So when I came upon this poet, Ovid, writing letter after letter, begging to be allowed back home, that really spoke to me. In some ways, though, I feel that Ovid's fate was much more cruel than mine, because no one is banishing me from Jamaica, and I get there as often as I can.

D.A.  Discovering Ovid helped prompt your freedom of expression?

J.B.  What I learnt in putting together the book is that there is not much information as to why Ovid was banished. At first this was a huge disappointment to me, then I came to appreciate the artistic license this gave to me in trying to make sense of Ovid's story and what might have caused him to be banished. This freedom also allowed me to flesh out the thoughts of the people around him, and this freedom also allowed me to insert my story of exile within Ovid's. I like the description of my book that says "inevitably, [the poet] is forced to think about her Americaness and her Jamaicaness in different ways" and that "there is one constant: Bishop's insistence that the drive to rearrange words is inextricably linked to the act of the rearranging of self", because, believe me, not only was I seeking to understand Ovid's predicament in this book, but the predicament of many different people, including several artists, who feel the need to create and create things that might not be acceptable to their society. And, ultimately, I guess I was trying to understand my own predicament as a creator who is creating far from home.

D.A.  Your grandmother is a huge influence on you. Tell us about your grandmother.

J.B.  Thanks very much for this question. I really appreciate the opportunity to talk about my grandmother. The first female figure I remember in my life is my grandmother. I lived with her from the time I was a baby until she decided to move from Kingston back to Portland and my mother refused to let me go with her because it was getting time for me to take what was then the Common Entrance examination, so I could secure a place in one of the high schools on the island. I remember very clearly that my grandmother did not want to let me go, that she wanted me to come and live with her in the country, but eventually my mother won out. I would go every summer and spend my holidays with my grandmother, and those holidays were some of the best days of my life, and, indeed, some of those summer days found their way into my novel. Not as autobiography, but as feelings. There are many things I remember about being with my grandmother, but one incident more than all others stands out in a shimmering bright light. I remember a day when I was busy drawing something. It was a beautiful Portland day, the sun kept streaming in through the window. Now, years later, colours stand out for me, red, yellow, green. I was sitting around the table at my grandmother's house. My grandmother came up to me, wanting to know what I was drawing. Fruits in a basket. I think that was what I was drawing. Or maybe it could have been flowers, for even then the flower as image and icon was very important to me. My grandmother asked for the slim yellow pencil I had in my hand and she used that same pencil to draw a stunningly beautiful picture that I have always wished I had kept. "Listen," my grandmother said to me that far ago day, "when I was a child at school, not much older than you, drawing was what I did best. I loved to draw." She then laid the slim yellow pencil down next to the picture she had drawn, went off back to what she was doing, and ever since that day what my grandmother did has both thrilled and haunted me. Thrilled me, because she seemed to validate what I was doing. Haunted me, because the drawing was full of so much potential. But more than anything else, what happened that day was that my grandmother gave me permission to be creative and she validated my creativity.

D.A.  Obviously, she gave you a great gift.

J.B.  Another iconic moment I had with my grandmother occurred on my first day of high school. My mother was right in keeping me in Kingston because I was able to secure a place in the high school I hoped to attend. That day, as we were walking to school, we met my grandmother on the way. She had come all the way from Portland, a drive hours and hours away, just to see me in my uniform that first morning. Later, she would sit by the light of a lamp and make me a white cotton apron for cooking classes at my new all-girl's high school. So being with my grandmother was very important.

Other women of my family were similarly creative. My mother could crotchet everything in sight and my great grandmother would stitch together old discarded pieces of cloth to make quilts so beautiful that some have since gone on to be exhibited. I learnt from these women's example that creativity and beauty was somehow important. Necessary.

D.A.  What was it like for you when your mother left Jamaica for the United States?

J.B.  To be truthful, I had no clear idea of what my mother leaving
     Jamaica actually meant. The breakup it would cause in our family,
     the years I would go without seeing my mother, the heartbreak
     and tears. For that day at the airport when my mother was leaving,
     I was actually quite excited. My mother was going off to a far-off
     magical place, America, and she would send for us soon-soon to
     join her in that magical place. I had no clear sense of what life as
     an immigrant in the United States actually meant. I cover a lot of
     this information in my book, *My Mother Who Is Me: Life Stories from
     Jamaican Women in New York*. Consequently, the happiest day of my
     life was the day I was reunited with my mother at Kennedy Airport
     in New York. Goodness, I was never so happy to see anyone in my
     life, because all along I had been secretly afraid that I would never
     see my mother again. I kept touching my mother, my baby sister,
     and myself just to make sure it was all real. That my mother was
     right there in front of me and not just a voice I heard over the telephone.
     My mother and I talked into the wee hours of the night. Years later,
     I came to realise that immigration and separation are intrinsic to
     my family and my mother and I were following in so many footsteps
     before ours. The collection of poems that I am working on right
     now seeks to understand these geographic displacements and I will
     share with you one of the poems from the new collection to better
     explain what I mean.

     HAGIOGRAPHY

        Somebody was always going somewhere;
        that's the story of our family.

        My mother left me a six-week old
        to work as a domestic in Kingston, to work
        for a family where the boys would always touch her,

        You have such pretty legs Emma –

        As for my father, he made the journey beyond
        the shores of the island to England. When he was leaving
        he took with him a woman, who used to be friends
        with my mother, all of them living in the same yard.

        Remember I tell you this as your grandmother:
        Man cubbitch like star-apple leaf.

Your great grandfather, he came all the way from
the other side of the island, from Hanover,
came following two sisters who were pretty enough,
and brown enough, to get work with foreigners.

He spent sometime in the sugarcane fields in Cuba,
your great grandfather.

In Portland, of course, Ferdinand, your great grandfather,
met Celeste, your great grandmother, who was from same-place-there
in Portland, only higher up in the mountains.

I tell you all of this so that you know:

No, it wasn't that hard for me to leave you children
behind and come by myself to America.

D.A.  One could say you've had multiple identities from early on.

J.B.  I guess one could say so. Though my primary identity is Jamaican.
But I would be lying if I did not say that being American is not a
part of my identity as well: Indeed I have lived in the United States
longer than I have lived in Jamaica. I find though that my identities
are more a problem for others than they are for myself. This is not
to say it is easy to go around living in a superimposed world, for
that is how I live, one identity, one country, superimposed over
another, but I find that I, and people like myself, just get on with
it. That is our lives and our reality and we live with it. It is the
people who have various ideas about what an American or a Jamaican
is or is not, that can make life difficult. When I was in Morocco,
no one could believe that I was American, because for them all
Americans are white. And recently, at a reading at the New School,
it was my Jamaican identity that was challenged. Indeed a woman
was pretty upset with me at that reading, and she said to me in the
question and answer session, "You are so educated, you are so polished,
you sound like a broadcaster!" Somewhere in there she said that
she had come for a "Jamaican" reading and clearly that was not
what she was getting. Let me tell you that comment caused all sorts
of ripple effects and discussions about who is a Jamaican and what
they should sound like. Very interesting. It reminded me of a story
a friend of mine, a Haitian writer, told me, about feeling a little ill
and being on a radio show, and the interviewer saying to her, "Haitians
are supposed to be so happy! So full of life! And look at you!" Or
some such thing. What I know is this: when I am in America, I am

very sure of my Jamaican identity, but when I am in Jamaica, I am aware of the fact that I have lived away for a long time. That I have changed and that Jamaica has changed. Neither myself nor the country is static. To keep up with Jamaica, I have to go there, especially if I want to represent the "now" Jamaica in my writings and my visual arts. It is true that with the Internet and Facebook, it is much easier to keep up with what is going on, but for me, it is very important to actually go to Jamaica. I think that the people who live in America and say that they remain fully or only Jamaican are not quite honest. You change and become as the island changes and becomes. As a visual artist I have been able to create an image that best gives a sense of the world as I live in it and that is a world of superimposed maps, the United States over Jamaica.

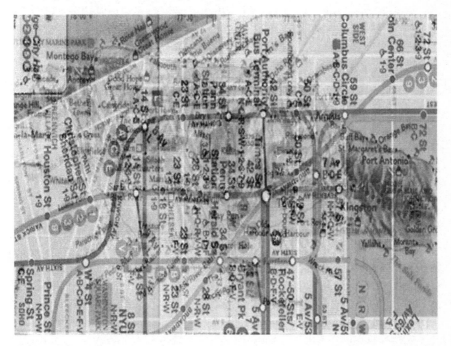

D.A. And when you came to the United States you went right to college?

J.B. By the time I came to the US, I had finished high school in Jamaica and I went right to Lehman College in the Bronx. I LOVED Lehman College. I found it a pretty supportive environment and I think that one of the best ways to integrate into a society is to attend school. At Lehman I started to have an understanding of myself as not only Jamaican but also Caribbean, because there were people from so many of the various islands there. Lehman was also a good place to try and figure out myself and figure out the new society that I was in. I would end up majoring in psychology, but tentatively I started taking creative writing and visual arts classes. By then I had moved far away from writing and painting, and instead, was focused on becoming the medical doctor that I knew my mother wanted me to become. This was a pretty confusing time, because I did not want to let my mother down and I did not want to let down all the people who I had told I was going to become a doctor. Teenage angst, believe me, is very real for the teenager involved. But I was not good in the sciences, and in pursuing the sciences, I was not pursuing the other things that I was most attracted to. I remember talking to someone about what I should do with myself, do with my life, and this person, a nun as it turned out, suggested that I try for one semester only doing classes that I love and that I really wanted to do. That was the end of medical school. I moved right back into painting and writing. And funnily enough, my mother was not as upset by this, as I had feared that she would be.

D.A. You also spent a year studying in France.

J.B. My year in France was a pivotal year. It was my junior year in college when I headed off to a place I had never been before. I knew absolutely no one in Paris. In addition, the few dollars my mother gave me were either stolen or lost the first few days I arrived there. But Paris was the place where I came into myself. In no time whatsoever I found two jobs, one as an *au pair* and another in an office. At the time my French was *encore malade*. Pretty soon after I arrived in Paris, I happened upon an English language bookstore and started reading many of the classics that I had heard of, but never had the chance to read. From the classics I ended up at Toni Morrison and from her and Alice Walker I ended up at the Caribbean women Audre Lorde and Olive Senior. I just read and read and read in Paris, in addition to taking painting classes. Eventually I ended up becoming what is called a *"demi au pair"* to the Flammarion family, which is one of the biggest publishing houses in France. I sometimes fantasise that my books will be translated and published by Flammarion one day, and that story will come full circle. The Flammarion's encouraged my reading, my writing, my painting. That year in France changed my life. I came back and finished up my degree in Psychology at Lehman but I knew then that my life would be in Arts and Letters. That was the great gift that Paris gave me.

D.A. And then it was off to graduate school?

J.B. After Lehman I took a year off working before I enrolled in a master's degree programme at City College. My time at City College was useful in that I took a feminism class with Jane Marcus and in trying to find a subject for the paper I had to write, Professor Marcus turned my attention to the life of Jamaican women in New York and it was in that moment that the book *My Mother Who is Me: Life Stories From Jamaican Women in New York* was born. This is a collection of oral histories from different groups of Jamaican women, explaining how they ended up in New York. That book helped me to understand the immigration process and how that experience is gendered. This work was also facilitated by a scholarship to the Oral History Program at Columbia University where I worked with Mary Marshall Clark. However, I knew I wanted to focus more on my own creative writing and there were people at New York University, such as Paule Marshall, who I wanted to work with, so I left City for NYU, and I have pretty much been at NYU ever since. [...] For several years now NYU has pretty much been home. I first earned an MA in English there, specialising in poetry writing. I later received an MFA in fiction writing from NYU as well. Following my first MA, I started teaching and I have been doing that ever since. Now I am a Master Teacher in the Liberal Studies Program at NYU.

D.A.   How autobiographical is your novel, *The River's Song*, which has been called an "engaging coming of age novel" about a Jamaican girlhood?

J.B.   Whenever I have been asked how autobiographical *The River's Song* is I say that the feelings in the book are more autobiographical than the book itself. Many of the feelings that particularly Gloria has in the novel are feelings that I have had. The sense of feeling confined on the island. Of wanting to go away, stretch one's wings. Those are feelings that I can definitely identify with. One of the great joys in my life as a child, as I indicated before, was to go and spend time with my grandmother, great grandparents, and other relatives in Portland every summer. Who knew that those green days by the river would end up in a novel. One of my aunts has a daughter who is still a teenager who read the novel and she said to me, "All these places that you describe in the place you call Lluidas Vale are really Nonsuch!" – which is really where my family is from, Nonsuch, high in the purple-blue Portland mountains. This lovely girl started naming different places in the novel that are really in the district and that was when I realised how much of the district I had infused in the novel, even if I called it by another name. Certainly the love that Gloria has for her grandmother is the love I still have for my grandmother. But unlike Gloria, I did not have the good fortune of moving into a big house in the hills and I don't remember a friend as rich as Annie at school. So, more than anything else, it is the feelings in the novel that are autobiographical. I know that reviews have talked about the freshness of the voice in the novel, the liveliness of the female characters, and for this I am thankful. For me, *The River's Song* was a novel I had to write, before I could go on to write other novels. I still flip through the book and fall in love with the characters, and these days I still wonder to myself how all those people are doing and if the yard that Gloria and her mother fled from is still standing. That novel gave me the great joy of seeing that I could bring characters to life; that characters would trust me enough to let me into their life and to tell their stories.

D.A.  *The River's Song* was also considered atypical of Caribbean literature because of your description of a young girl's sexual awakening.

J.B.  I know that the sexual awakening of Gloria has been talked about, but what I did not know was that this was atypical. It seemed obvious to me that someone who is eighteen would have sexual feelings, but I guess this is a leftover from our days of being part of the great British Empire and a leftover of Victorian ideals and protocols of behaviour, although that certainly is not the case in too much of our music where sexuality is, in too many cases, overemphasised.

D.A.  A recent book of yours deals with writers who also paint.

J.B.  For several years now I have been intrigued with the fact that so many writers from the Caribbean are also visual artists and vice versa. I started keeping a list of people from the region who were creative in both mediums. When I was invited to have an exhibition by the Brooklyn-based Caribbean Literary and Cultural Center I decided to invite along two writer/painters from Jamaica to be part of the exhibition and my wonderful publisher in the UK, Peepal Tree Press, decided to publish a book of the exhibition, since we were all Peepal Tree Press authors. It is a small darling book that I have come to love a lot. At the time I was putting the book and exhibition together, my dear friend, Wayne Brown, who has since died, recommended Earl McKenzie's and Ralph Thompson's work to me. Earl I had known of before, because he is well known as a writer, but Ralph's work I was being introduced to. Our styles are all different but we are unified in our exploration of the natural world around us and the colours of the Caribbean.

D.A.  How long have you been painting?

J.B.  I would say I started painting seriously about ten years ago. That was when I went back to school to study painting. But in terms of the visual arts I not only paint, I also do some photography (or what I call photo-collage) as is indicated in the image of the two superimposed maps that I mentioned earlier in the interview. In terms of my paintings and photography, however, I find that I engage with pretty much the same themes as I do in my poetry. There is, for example, a lot of engagement with the environment and there is some storytelling and engagement with the folklore of the island. Some of my paintings are abstract, others are not. I tend to work in series when I am creating visual arts pieces, and this I see as a major carry-over from being a writer. It is as if one painting or one photograph cannot contain the entire story.

My most recent series of paintings is entitled "View from Afar". In June 2010, Jamaica erupted in unrest following attempts by the Jamaican authorities to arrest a reputed drug dealer, wanted in the United States. Members of Christopher Coke's west Kingston neighbourhood barricaded themselves and fought back against authorities. At the end of the unrest more than 70 people were dead. At the time this happened, I was travelling around a bit and as I travelled I was desperately trying to make sense of what was going on. I had no choice but to rely on newspaper articles, emails, information on Facebook and the Internet. This resulted in a series of paintings where I am trying to piece together a coherent narrative. Some of the images in the paintings are clearer than others; indeed some of the images are grainy, unfocused and unclear – this being what happens when someone is hearing about something from a distance. Yet the colourfulness and beauty of the Caribbean is suffused throughout. Maps have been used in some of the paintings indicating that the viewer of these events is not on the island, but rather is quite far away. This is the most recent group of paintings that I have worked on.

D.A.  In closing, any major plans for the future?

J.B.  Well I have only just finished a new book, which is a strange hybrid of a book with stories, essays, and interviews. This is a book in which I was trying to find my sea legs in writing essays and short-short stories; I feel as though I was working to establish my voice in genres that I had not really tried before. In addition, I have been painting a lot lately. Next year I am looking forward to an exhibition in New York.

# ART: A SYNAESTHETIC EXPERIENCE

Michela Calderaro: Jacqueline, I would like to begin our conversation talking about your latest work, "The Tempest Poems", which in my eyes is a unique achievement where you succeeded in giving us a synaesthetic experience of your art. We hear and see your work simultaneously, and the effect on us, readers/watchers, is of sheer amazement. Can you tell us about the creative process that led you to such an achievement?

Jacqueline Bishop: This all came about by chance. The Liberal Studies Program at NYU, where I am a full-time Master Teacher, sponsors an annual symposium. This year the theme of the symposium was Shakespeare and I was asked to contribute an essay. I said no to the essay, but yes to a series of poems about Shakespeare's *The Tempest*, a play that has always fascinated me because of its allusions to the Caribbean. I relished the idea of populating the play with Jamaican characters. Once I'd finished the poems I was asked to supply images, any images from anywhere, to illustrate the poems. At this point I chose to create my own images, and when I saw the drawings set next to the poems, I was pleased with the end result. For a long time I strove to be accepted separately as a visual artist and a writer, and now it is interesting to me that somewhere, far inside of myself, I am getting comfortable with bringing the two art forms together.

M.C. What is the source of your inspiration? Do you think writers/ painters are born as such or become ones in later years?

J.B. This is a question I really like, because what writers dream about at night is that somebody in the audience that they are speaking to is going to be a writer. I think that writers know they are writers from very early. That has been my experience, that even before they publish their first thing, they know they are writers. How it was for me is that you even try to get away from it, you are like "Leave me alone", but these characters and these poems won't leave you alone, they keep insisting and insisting and insisting on their way until finally you just go along with the programme. Often times people feel they have a story to tell. You don't know who is ever going to read these stories, but that is not the most important thing for a writer. The most important thing for the writer is the telling of the story. So it is almost as though it is something you have to do. I felt that I had to write *The River's Song*. I felt that I had to write this book to go on to write other books. I had to understand this story of a childhood in Jamaica because then it would allow me to explore other things. It is something you feel you have to do. It is not even asking you, it is demanding. It says, "This is what you have to do" and you can run and become a physicist and do whatever you want to do, but there is still the story to be told at the end of the day.

M.C. Can you define your relationship with words? Do you fight with words or do words come easily to you?

J.B. I don't fight with words as a poet and I still think of myself primarily as a poet. Fiction is tougher. But maybe it is not the words that I am fighting with so much, when I do have a struggle, as it is the thing I am trying to bring to life. I struggle with what it is that I want the words to do. A poem usually just comes to me, oftentimes in a hurry and I have to grab it; it comes in a flash. Then I have to craft the poem. My process of writing fiction is very different from that of writing poems. In fiction I am more straightforward in what I am doing. Oftentimes in fiction, especially in writing a novel (and I have just finished my second novel), I make an outline from beginning to end of the story, so I can have some sense of where I am going with this work. Although I rarely stick to the outline I made, because characters begin to take over and assert themselves, I still find having an outline a good thing to get me going. I write to the end of the novel and then, when I get to the end, I go back to the beginning to craft the story. For me the work is driven by characters, you have characters who begin to talk to you, and they begin to insist on their story and at a certain point the characters begin to take over and drive the story and then there is less of a struggle with words – instead I feel as if I am being written, instead of me doing the writing. This is especially so with short stories. With short stories the only outline I have is a general one in my head, but even here characters take over and they begin to "write" their own story and I become a conduit for their words.

M.C. What about images? How do they form in your mind? How do you transfer them to the canvas? Is it a daunting process or do images just form in your mind asking to be transformed into paintings?

J.B.  As with my poems I might have some general idea where I might be going with a painting, but I end up being surprised with the results as well. I am getting to the stage now with photography where I can frame images in my mind and have a pretty good idea how they will turn out, although there is always the element of surprise, which I like actually. Paintings and drawings, though, are still a little out of my control; they never quite turn out how I have them in mind, and by this I don't mean that they turn out badly at all. I actually often like the end result. I draw free-hand and in ink or chalk, as I did with the Tempest Drawings, because knowing that I can't erase something forces me to give all my concentration to the work at hand. It is a nerve-wracking though thrilling experience as I am going through it. For some visual artists, the process of making their work is the art of it all, while I am exactly the opposite. I can only relax after I have completed the work and see what I have made and that I have not yet again ruined everything. For most of my paintings so far, I have been doing "drip" paintings because I like the sense of not having total control over the medium and this does not lend itself to having an image in mind beforehand. I like the sense of a dialogue between myself and the medium – whether that medium be paintings, drawings, photography, or textiles. Art, after all, for me is an exploration. I use art to understand what I think and feel about something. Art helps me to clarify and understand something. Most recently I have started doing Polaroid photographs and watercolour paintings, which I like because of their immediacy and the fact that things are always a little out of my control. What would be the point of endlessly repeating something you have already mastered or something you already know?

M.C.  In your poems there are extensive references to childhood traumas. Can one describe childhood traumas in such detail without experiencing them personally?

J.B.  Yes you can. I don't think you have to experience death to write about it. And I make use of the experiences of people around me. Oftentimes someone will say something to me and I am so personally moved by it that it works its way into my work. What I have tried to do is to listen very closely, and if I still don't understand, I try to talk to people who have experienced what I am writing about. In this new novel the main character's mother dies of breast cancer. I have never experienced breast cancer, but it doesn't mean I cannot write about it. I talk to people who have experienced it, I do research, and then I try to give life to what I am writing.

M.C.  You often deal with lesbian issues. Can you describe the different approaches to these issues in the countries you have visited or lived in, such as Jamaica, USA and Morocco?

J.B.  The USA is the most liberal on these issues, followed by Morocco, and then Jamaica. In Morocco it is so taboo to actually talk about sex that very few people do. In addition, girls and women are expected to be very close to each other, and I think gay relationships in general benefit from this cover. In Jamaica there was and still is a lot of hostility towards homosexual relationships. If I write about lesbian issues it is because I find this an area that I could shed some light on in Jamaican and Caribbean literature. In fact I just finished a story "The Great American War Story" that has a lesbian couple at the centre of the story. What I learnt in writing that story is that even in the United States ideas "from yard" can still haunt a lesbian couple and there are ways, even in the United States, where lesbian couples are silenced and erased from history. There is just beginning to emerge in Jamaica, and in the Caribbean, a literature on homosexuality and there was an anthology that was published that speaks of homosexual issues. Jamaica is not the best place to live if you are a homosexual. People, especially men, get killed for being homosexuals and lesbians are often thought to be lesbians because they have not met the right man. The head of a Jamaican gay and lesbian organisation got killed some few years back. I think you can disagree with homosexuality, but to go as far as to kill someone is saying a lot. If in my writing I can shed some light on that I will, because that is one of the powers of writers, we get to say things and bring our point across and hopefully one single person may listen to what you have to say and rethink some idea or position they might have had before.

M.C.  How did the women interviewed for *My Mother who is Me* feel about being American? Did they consider themselves immigrants or well-integrated US citizens?

J.B.  As you know Michela, *My Mother who is Me* is divided into two parts. The first part is interviews with African Jamaican women and in the second part there are Chinese Jamaican, Lebanese Jamaican, white Jamaican, Indian Jamaican and other groups of women who call Jamaica home; they were born there; this is their home this is their land. The first half of the book deals with how African Jamaican women really struggled with claiming America as their home; they felt that they had a harder time in America, they were confronted with racism and they never really had to deal with that on the island. So if you look in the first half of the book, home for these women is Jamaica. Most of them might never go back there to live, but they guard it as a place where they felt safe, a place where they felt that they were understood, and a place where they belonged.

The women in the second half of the book have had a different reception in America. The women in the second half were largely more middle class or upper class, a lot of them were very rich women and they were not Black. They had a different reaction to America. Even the reasons why the women in the first half migrated are different from the reasons why the women in the second half of the book did so. The women in the first part are migrating for economic reasons; the women in the second half are going to college, they are going to be reunited with their husbands and so on. So each group of women had a totally different reception in America, with the women in the second half feeling for the most part more at home. But what was fascinating for me with the women in the second half of the book is that even though they had an easier time integrating into American society, they too, like the women in the first part of the book, saw Jamaica as home, as a nurturing place, as a place where they would like to get back to. More than anything else, that is the bridge that connects the two groups of women. Both groups of women gesture towards each other in the book and together both groups share a real love of Jamaica.

M.C.   In literature by writers who emigrated from the Caribbean in the past, one finds at times a use of tropes that are more traditional and conservative in comparison with those developed since in their native lands. How do Caribbean writers who live outside of the Caribbean deal with what was left behind? Are the tropes currently used there newer than those used before they left?

J.B.   I have noticed two types of Caribbean writers – those who are outside of the Caribbean and those who are within the Caribbean. Caribbean writers outside of the Caribbean, like myself, are often writing back to the Caribbean and those in the Caribbean are writing out of the Caribbean to a larger world. If you look at the work of a writer based in Jamaica like Sharon Leach, for example, her characters are very cosmopolitan and her work is largely set in the "now" Jamaica, whereas writers outside of the Caribbean tend to write more historical works.

Claude McKay, who was born in Jamaica and came to the United States in the early 1900s, focused primarily on Black identity in his works, and in the 1920s and 1930s when McKay was writing there was a sense that Black writers should present a collective front to the world, an idea, incidentally, with which McKay struggled greatly, but none-theless he too was caught up in being a bulwark against the quite negative ideas about Black people which were running rampant at the time. But now I would say Caribbean writers are freer to explore issues outside of identity, and the tropes are more nuanced. If indeed Caribbean writers outside of the Caribbean engage in more conservative tropes, this has precisely to do with the fact that we are writing outside of the Caribbean. Maybe we are more anxious about being accepted in the Caribbean, so we "Caribbean up" our works, much more so than writers based in the Caribbean feel the need to do.

Let me confess something: before every reading I do I have a melt down. I think I have been able to locate this fear – it's not the fact that people will show up at the reading, it's not the fear of speaking in front of a crowd, it's the fear is that no one will show up for the reading! This has been a fear I have lived with from the moment I started publishing my works. That no one will show up! That it will just be me and my books in a corner. Anyway, one time I was going to Jamaica and I posted this on Facebook. The poet Tanya Shirley, who lives in Jamaica, contacted me and said you must, must, must do a reading in Jamaica. I tried to talk Tanya out of it because I just did not think that anyone in Jamaica would show up! Still Tanya was not standing for it.

The night of the reading came and sure enough I was panic-stricken. I was sure NO ONE would show up! But by the time the reading got underway the room was packed. What is more, the room was packed even with writers whose work I have loved and admired and even read as a child in Jamaica. I wanted to cry. I really did. To date, that has probably been the most meaningful reading I have ever done in my life, and I can't begin to thank Tanya and all those people who turned out that night for that gift of acceptance in one's own country! All of this is a long way round of saying that if Caribbean writers outside of the Caribbean are more anxious, which expresses itself in more conservative tropes, it is because, deep down, we want to be recognised and accepted in our own country.

M.C. According to narrative psychology, people are driven to write biographical or autobiographical texts by an urge to hear their own personal story told by someone else. Do you think you wrote *My Mother Who Is Me* in order to find your own personal identity, to listen to your own story in the stories told by other emigrated Caribbean women? Do you think it helped you identify an already-existing identity in yourself or helped you discover a newly-constructed identity through the stories of these women?

J.B. I think that in talking to other women I came to a place of understanding regarding my identity. I think the women helped me to understand how I am like them, with one foot in each country.

For the longest time, and even after I finished that book, I didn't know how to place myself. On one hand, I feel that my creativity comes from Jamaica, but there is always this nagging sense of something else. When I get off the plane in Jamaica there is the identification of the landscape and there is your family and you are home and you are so happy to be back on the island, even the voices on the radio and on the television are music to your ears. Everything – every last flower, bird, bee – is enchanting to you. But after three weeks or so "home" reverts to being New York and you begin to miss the comforts of your "home" in New York. By the time you get back to New York, of course you miss Jamaica. So it is a very difficult thing for me, quite a struggle, to try and locate where exactly home is. I just know that the women in *My Mother Who Is Me* gave me a language with which to speak about a "whole" identity that incorporates both places. More than anything else, that is what that book gave to me.

M.C.  You talk about an African American identity. Why is the "American" part of your identity so important to you? Why not just say you are Jamaican?

J.B.  Depending on where you land or were born in America, people are very different. So if you are from Texas it is very different from being from the Bronx, for example. And if you are from a city in Texas it is very different from the countryside. Asking why an American identity is so important to me, is like asking an Italian person why your Italian identity is so important to you. It is who you are. It is what you know. It is how you do and why you do what you do. It would be like saying why is your Jamaican identity important? It is who you are. It is a part of you, so it is important. I hear in this question the subtle question of "Is the African part not enough for you?" The answer is no. I have lived in Africa, in Morocco, and I came to understand that this was not an identity that I could claim for myself. At least not now. I think that what I love about the United States is that there are so many different people in the United States who call it home – Asian Americans, Caribbean Americans, Italian Americans, so many different Americans call it home. What I think is particularly wonderful about American literature is that various groups write out of their various identities. Being an American is a fact, in the same way that being a Jamaican is a fact of my life. To deny that I am an American (or Jamaican) would be denying parts of my identity and I don't want to deny any part of my identity.

M.C.  Does the epigraph you chose for your collection of poems *Fauna* refer to your own soul or can it be seen as a description of African American people's feelings in general?

J.B.  I hate speaking for large groups of people, so let's say the epigraph of the book "turning and turning in the widening gyre. Things fall apart the centre cannot hold" is all about my own soul.

M.C.  The second part of *Fauna* is brimming with flowers' names. Do all these names have a particular meaning? Are they connected to a particular aspect of your homeland? Do they also represent the island inhabitants? Is there any connection with your blue-on-blue series of paintings?

J.B.  These are all flowers of the Caribbean, some of which you have right here in Italy, growing and thriving like the hibiscus. I do not attribute much to the names of the flowers, except when these are names given by the local people. There is a plant in Jamaica that curls into itself when touched called shame-mi-lady and several women poets on and from the island have incorporated this plant into their writings, to make a point about conditions facing some women on the island. Regarding flowers as women and women as flowers, when I was writing the poems I tried to get at something, a fact about the flower that I would incorporate in the poem. Allamanda, for example, is really toxic and the love bush literally grows over everything. I particularly love the love bush, which is a parasite that will grow on just about any living plant that you throw it on. But it does not always "catch" onto the plant you throw it on, and so, local lore goes, if it grows, the person you love will love you back. If it does not "catch", well, you have a problem. All these flower poems then are brimming with some aspect of island life. I did the blue-on-blue series of flower paintings a number of years after I had written the poems. They are not like the *Tempest Drawings* for example, that were thought of in relation to the poems I had written. What I think the blue-on-blue paintings and the flower poems show is my continued interest in telling women's stories.

M.C.  When you went to New York for the first time, did you feel as if you were Eve stepping out of the Garden?

J.B.  Yes I did. I really did. I was entering this whole new world, and stepping outside of a world that I had known for oh, sixteen, seventeen years of my life. If I write about Eve a lot, it is because she too leaves Paradise for another place, another home. Jamaica is not exactly paradise, except it is very beautiful, very, very beautiful, but oftentimes when I write about a Garden of Eden that is damaged, of course I am writing about Jamaica. And since I am really concerned with telling women's side of the story, Eve is very important to me and there is a part of myself that identifies with her.

M.C.  In *Fauna* there is a poem called "Full Bloom". It is dedicated to Lorna Goodison. What does Lorna Goodison mean for you?

J.B.  When I was growing up and when I started to write, Lorna Goodison loomed large to me, she was just who I wanted to be. I wanted to be Lorna Goodison. I never thought a day would come when Lorna and I would be friends, because Lorna was so like a vision. I remember I won a scholarship to go and study with Lorna at the University of Miami, and I will never forget that first day sitting in class waiting for Lorna to come. The classroom had these long low windows and I saw Lorna walking to class in a yellow dress with her hair out. She walked under a blossoming flame tree and I was just speechless. She is a very tall woman you know, very regal. Very majestic. And she was a writer and a painter. She was who I wanted to grow up to be.

M.C.  Jacqueline, you are a multi-talented artist and it is very difficult for me, though we have known each other for many years, to define you... I mean you are a teacher and a researcher, true, but you are mainly a painter and a writer. A few years ago, when you gave those wonderful lectures in Trieste and Venice, we showed some of your paintings, not all unfortunately, and later we held an exhibition of your quilts. We also discussed the connection between your paintings and your creative writing. Can you elaborate further on how you see the connection between your flowers and the paintings, and also the quilts, and your poems and fiction? And, also, how you chose the paintings for the cover of your books?

J.B.  To date I have published five books, and as I look back on the covers of my books, all of which I chose instinctively, I'm astonished how much they mark the changing moments of my life so far, this journey that I'm on, whether it's me looking back on my island-home from a distance, and being completely stunned by its amazing flora and fauna, for example; or whether it's my embrace of community or even my embrace of the other as in *Snapshots from Istanbul, Writers Who Paint, Painters Who Write*, or *My Mother Who Is Me*. The cover of *The River's Song*, which has three nubile women, has caused a lot of controversy, but for me that cover is primarily about childhood, innocence and intimacy. I see my summer holidays in the district of Nonsuch, a tiny district high in the hills of Portland, every time I look at that cover. The covers of my books speak to certain connections among my work in that I am often preoccupied with telling women's stories and I am often in search of community. You see this preoccupation in the quilts I made in response to those made by my grandmother, and great grandmother, as well as in my poems, my fiction works and my other visual art works.

M.C.  Yet you have said that you don't want to be identified as a woman artist, but as far as we can observe in your body of work there is a focus on studies of intimate relationships, on the female body and on sexuality, or on what usually remains untold, unwritten, unsaid. This is arguably typical of female writing; whereas if we think about Jamaican male writers, for instance, their writings usually concentrate more on social and political issues. Can you elaborate on that?

J.B.  I decided that my art should not be all about fighting social justice issues. I am a great believer in fighting social justice issues and I do a lot of work in this area. I worked at UNESCO in Paris around social justice issues, in Morocco as well, and I am beginning to do this kind of work in Jamaica. Quiet as it is kept, I am completing a public policy and politics programme focused around social justice issues. But I started to realise that there were things that I wanted to understand as a woman and as an immigrant that were not necessarily going to end up on a poster per se. I guess, too, that since art started out being for me a way to understand myself and my world, it has continued to occupy that place in my life. Are there differences between the art that women and men create? I would say yes, but that has more to do with what people choose to prioritise in their art. In other words what I am saying is that I am pretty fired-up about telling women's stories, but a male artist could do this as well – should he choose to do so. And that is why I reject the label of woman artist. Art is art and I prefer the title of artist.

M.C.  Back to the connection between your creative and your visual work. When an idea is formed in your mind, does it first come in words or in images, and how do you choose the means to express that idea?

J.B.  I am surprised all the time by my artwork, and sometimes I have to wait to understand how best to express an idea. The most I can say on the subject is that the "feel" of a poem is very different from the "feel" of a short story, which, of course, is very different from the "feel" of a novel. A novel, in fact, is something you have to make a great space for in your life. Because poetry is my primary art form I begin oftentimes with words, although words then conjure images for me. Lately, because I have spent the last few years working extensively in the visual arts, something new is happening and it is that I am now creating images for which I have no words. It is here that the work of people like yourself, Michela, becomes very important. The critic can help the writer and artist see through what she doing. Recently, a curator came to look at my quilts, and because I did not want to cause confusion I did not take out my photographs and paintings, but eventually she saw those as well and she was able to make connections across my bodies of work that I had not seen. I think that art is a way of thinking for me, a way of trying to figure things out; and sometimes it is not clear to me why I am doing what I am doing. And it is hard to separate out what came first, the words or the images.

M.C.  In *Fauna* you write about Gauguin. What kind of influence does he have on your work?

J.B.  Gauguin shows up more in my writing than in my visual arts. I write about him. I don't think he influences my paintings as much as he influences Derek Walcott's paintings; I mean Derek Walcott even has paintings for Gauguin, or in the style of Gauguin. For me it is Gauguin's voyages and how he operated in the world as a male artist who placed his art over and above personal relationships that I was so intrigued by, and the fact that he was rewarded for doing this in ways that I do not think women artists would ever be.

M.C.  Thanks for mentioning Derek Walcott. He is another Caribbean writer who paints as well. There are other writers who paint: Lorna Goodison, Earl McKenzie, Ralph Thompson; then there's Marcia Douglas who creates dolls, and of course Opal Palmer Adisa, who is a photographer, a poet, and a performer. How would you explain the fact that so many Caribbean artists are multi-talented?

J.B.  I am unsure how to fully explain this phenomenon, except to note that almost all of the writers you listed are poets or primarily poets, and so I believe that the concentration that poetry requires – that attention to every last word in crafting images that is a poem – is the same thing that goes on in the visual arts. It is something about the intensity of image-making which is contained in poetry and painting. Those two things seem somehow linked. Another idea that comes to mind, as well, is that literacy levels in some parts of the Caribbean for a long time were not very high because of a legacy of slavery and colonialism and so on. I remember as a girl these big beautiful Bibles in all the homes around me. These big beautiful Bibles had all these grand colourful images that could convey to people who could not read something of what the story was all about. I think, given how prevalent and dominant religion is in the Caribbean, maybe this has something to do with it – using images to tell a story to people who did not have access to the written word.

M.C.  Is there in your opinion a Caribbean aesthetic? And if there is, how would you define it?

J.B.  The most I can say is that a Caribbean aesthetic is informed by its concern with the Caribbean. I remember when I was editor of *Calabash: A Journal of Caribbean Arts and Letters*, a group of us sought to define a Caribbean aesthetic. Was it art created by someone born in the region and writing about the region? What about someone who was born and grew up in the region and was an artist but decided not to engage in any way at all about the region? Would there be room enough for such a person in *Calabash*? And where would you place someone like Edna Manley who was born and raised in England but married her Jamaican cousin and came "home" to Jamaica, which indeed became her home for the rest of her life? She is instrumental in developing modern Jamaican art and her work centres primarily around Jamaica and Jamaicans. If we are to use the criteria of born in Jamaica, born in the Caribbean, to engage the aesthetics of her work that would certainly count her out. So it is all quite complicated and in regards to a Caribbean aesthetic the most I can say is that at some level the work is self-conscious about representing the Caribbean.

M.C.  Do you also feel the restlessness that characterises the women interviewed in your book *My Mother Who Is Me*? Do you also feel straddled between two worlds, namely New York and the Caribbean? Do you still consider Jamaica as your true home, your paradise?

J.B.  To a certain degree I do feel the same restlessness as the women in *My Mother Who Is Me*, which is probably why I did the book in the first place. There is that constant straddling between the United States and Jamaica. It is just a way of life for me now. Yes, I still consider Jamaica my true home, except when I go home there, I always long for the United States.

M.C.  Almost all female characters in your work share "a longing to travel", a desire to leave their homeland even if it means leaving behind friends, loved-ones and children. Where do you think this longing comes from? What opportunities can contemporary Jamaica offer to women? How did you feel when you left the island?

J.B.  I think this longing comes from the fact that Jamaica is an island. There is just a natural curiosity to know what life is like beyond the shores of the island. Jamaica is a pretty forward-looking country in so far as educating girls is concerned. Jamaica's current Prime

Minister is a woman and there are no large distinctions in segregating women and men in the professions. That said, I believe I had to leave Jamaica to become an artist and I still do not understand how I could make a living as an artist on the island. I have met other Jamaican artists who tell me I am wrong, but I am not so sure of this. Truthfully, when I left Jamaica I had no idea I would be gone for so long. I fully believed that I would return to the island after getting my college degree. That day, on the plane heading to the United States, my number one concern was seeing the mother I had not seen in years and meeting my baby sister born in the United States. After the reunion with my mother I did not want to be separated from her again. By the time I finished college, almost all my immediate family members were out of Jamaica and I had built a life for myself in the United States. I still dream, though, of going back to live, even part of the year, in Jamaica. That is still a dream I hold near and dear to my heart.

M.C. Through the "calabash", Caribbean women have always been the most important figures in passing on tradition to younger generations. Today, where communication is mainly based on television, internet and mobile phones, do you think women still hold this peculiar matrilineal function?

J.B. Yes, we still do. I will tell you a story. For the longest time I resisted getting a cell phone. I just did not want to bother with even more intrusions in my every waking moment. I enjoyed the times I was disconnected. Then I went to Jamaica to visit my grandmother who had a cell phone that she was constantly talking into. Instead of technology making her less connected, it did just the opposite and made her more connected. Of course, I was a little embarrassed that my grandmother should have a cell phone and I did not, so I eventually got one and once I did I wondered why I resisted so long. It does make life that much easier. Now my grandmother and I can talk on our mobile phones, and though she remains incredibly suspicious of me and all my questions, none the less, she still uses that cell phone to dispense wisdom and knowledge.

M.C. When writing, how do you fuse nation language with standard English?

J.B. It depends on the point I am trying to make and the characters that I am writing about. In my short story "Brown Girl in the Ring" that entire story is told in nation language because it is all happening in this one little girl's head and this is the language she would use. Whereas in another story of mine, "Letter To My Children" you have a mixture of both Nation Language and standard English because one of the other characters in that story is an educated white American woman, so it would make sense that when she speaks she is not using Jamaican nation language. Speaking of nation language though, what I have noticed is that it is oftentimes not given the due it should get in Caribbean literature. By that I do not mean to suggest that nation language is not used in our literature – it is used quite often – but it is often used with characters who are the butt of many jokes and so on. I find that it is often not thought through in its use. It is kind of like – here is some local colour to colour-up or lighten-up this piece to make the reader laugh.

M.C.  Do you think the Caribbean reading public is increasing? What can be done in that context, in your opinion?

J.B.  I should hope it is, especially with increasing literacy rates and such events as the Calabash Literary Festival in Jamaica. But it is not only the Caribbean reading public that should be increased, but also the reading public in general I would hope would become more interested in Caribbean literature. One idea that I am playing with is to work with a school in Jamaica to get more books by local authors into the hands of schoolchildren and to see how the children respond to that. I am wondering if that might be a way to generate more lifelong interest in the things that come out of the countries in the Caribbean.

M.C.  How would you define the so-called African-American tradition in both writing and visual arts? Is there a difference between African-American, African-Jamaican and European-Jamaican traditions? And if there is one, how would you define it?

J.B.  The most that I can say about the African-American and African-Jamaican traditions are that they were most likely created or maintained by people who are somehow engaged with the continent of Africa. I don't think I can say much more than that. Regarding the European-Jamaican tradition, it is hard to separate this out from a distinctly Jamaican tradition. In other words, all the people who have populated Jamaica have added something to the Jamaican identity and we, as Jamaicans, partake of it even sometimes unknowingly. I read somewhere once that bar-b-que is actually a Native American way of cooking and I thought, who would have thunk it? We participate and engage in Jamaican Taino aspects of ourselves without knowing it. I think the same is true of other groups that have set down roots in Jamaica; they have all contributed to the Jamaican identity but it would probably take an anthropologist to tell us how they did this.

M.C.  Did the life stories told to you by Jamaican women in New York inspire some of the characters and situations in your novel *The River's Song*?

J.B.  To the best of my knowledge it did not. I had long finished *The River's Song* when I went back to work on *My Mother Who Is Me*. *The River's Song* came out of a conglomeration of my experiences, the experiences of people I knew, and my own imagination. It would *not* be a stretch, though, to see similarities between *The River's Song* and *My Mother Who Is Me* because many of the women's experiences in *My Mother Who Is Me* are similar to experiences that I have had and know about and that I have written about in the novel.

M.C.  What are, in your opinion, the main features that characterise Caribbean women artists?

J.B.  Our concern with the lives of women and girls. We are still preoccupied with writing and righting the long historical wrong of the absence of Caribbean women characters that we know and understand into Caribbean literature, as opposed to the caricatures and stereotypes of Caribbean women that for too long populated the arts of the region.

M.C.  Do you think that each Caribbean woman has a unique story that awaits telling?

J.B.  No I don't think so. I think every Caribbean woman has a unique story for sure, but all stories are not stories to be told. Take my grandmother, for example, she has had what I would consider a pretty interesting life but she hates it, simply hates it when anyone, in her words "broadcasts" her business. By *that* she of course means me. For a long time I wanted to know my great grandparents' story; they had such an amazing love story that spanned decades, and there are so many questions I would have liked to have asked them. Then one day I heard something similar to my great grandmother's voice saying to me, "Jacqueline, that is a story that your great grandfather and I want to keep to ourselves, our story, we don't want to share it with anyone else. Let us be with our story and focus instead on your story of us." I can't say I am satisfied with that answer because there are so many things about those two people I still want to know, but I came away understanding that not all stories, not even all unique stories, should be told.

## WRITING ACROSS THE DIASPORA

Loren Kleinman: You're a novelist and a poet. How do you reconcile both genres? Do you ever reconcile them? Do they live independently of one another?

Jacqueline Bishop: For the moment both genres live independently of each other. I started off life as a poet and I consider myself primarily a poet. But always, deep inside of myself, I harboured the idea of writing longer works, fictional pieces. I wanted to write short stories and novels. To do that, though, to write longer fictional pieces, I went back and did an MFA in fiction writing, after I had an MA in poetry writing. That is not the only way to write fiction, but I wanted the rigour of a structured programme.

   I guess implicit in your questions is the question of how you know when you begin a piece whether it is fiction or poetry. I must confess I have not struggled as much with this idea as I know that others have struggled. You see, for me, poetry writing is often intuitive, poems often come to me whole, in a flash so to speak, and then there is the going back and the intense crafting of the poems. By contrast, in fiction writing, I almost never start from a place where I have the story whole. I start from hearing the voice of the narrator and getting to know the narrator, and then allowing the narrator to tell me his or her story. It is detective work, but what that also means is that I am very clear, oftentimes, whether I am writing a poem or a piece of fiction.

L.K. When did you decide to write a novel? What were some of the rewarding moments? Would you write another novel? What were the major challenges after only writing poetry and non-fiction?

J.B. I have actually finished another novel. I finished it some time ago and I have put it away to go back to it with fresh eyes. The process of writing a novel for me is a very involved process, and my characters become real people that walk around with me all day long. They have opinions, different from mine, they have all these mannerisms and opinions! For the moment, I have had to shove them in the closet as I try to get on with other areas – and other people – in my life. But with your questions now, they are telling me they are restless and they would like to see the light of day again!

I guess what I am trying to say is that writing a novel is an undertaking. You have to make a place for all these people in your life. They come bearing the weight of all their joys, sorrows and concerns. The people in my novel are real people to me. I also know that for all of its displacements that I will always be writing novels, because, frankly, it is only in the process of writing novels that I can set these characters free. It is only in writing novels that I, in turn, am free to go on with other areas of my life. There was a time I fought against this, a time I wondered what the people in these novels wanted from me. Now, I just get on with it. This is what I have been chosen to do and this is what I have to do.

In so far as my first published novel – *The River's Song* – is concerned, I started to think about the novel after I had written and published a short story called "Brown Girl in The Ring". Looking back now, I see that this short story was influenced by Jean Rhys' *Wide Sargasso Sea*. In *Wide Sargasso Sea* you have the delicate sensitive Antoinette, who is being hurt, at the beginning of the novel, by the very environment of the Caribbean in which she lives. A playmate is summoned for Antoinette in the form of Tia. But Tia, a black girl, is presented as unfeeling. Indeed she can walk barefoot and barehead in the hot sun without feeling any pain. But I knew that this was wrong. I knew that Tia could and did feel pain, and so in that short story I wanted to talk back to Jean Rhys who herself was talking back to Charlotte Bronte in the novel *Jane Eyre*. Like Jean Rhys, I too felt the need to set the record straight about the "maligned mad woman in the attic". I wanted to say to both Jean Rhys and Jane Eyre, here is another side of the story, the story that neither of you are seeking to tell. So I wrote "Brown Girl In The Ring" to tell the other half of the story, that the great poet Lorna Goodison has written, that some of us must tell.

After "Brown Girl in the Ring" fell out of me, because that was what it felt like, that the short story fell right out of me, I wondered about the two girls in the story, and in wondering and thinking about them, that was how I came to write *The River's Song*.

The most rewarding moment in writing that book was the moment when I realised that both characters trusted me to tell their story. That moment meant everything to me. I guess, too, when I realised that I could use words to recreate a place, that meant a lot to me as well. I studied with Paule Marshall at NYU and she always talked about the power of words in making you see what is not there, and as I wrote that novel I became increasingly confident with myself as a fiction writer, in using words to make people see the world of these girls.

I would say that writing non-fiction was more challenging for me than writing fiction or poetry, because, oftentimes, in both fiction and poetry, it is not "me" so much that is on the line as it is the characters. I see myself, afterall, when I am writing poetry and fiction, as nothing more than a conduit who the characters use to tell their stories. With non-fiction though, I have found that to be more difficult, more challenging, because it is me, Jacqueline, that is on the line here. It is my thoughts, my experiences, and feelings, and so I struggled more to find my non-fiction voice that my poetic and fictional voices. But these days I am getting more comfortable in embracing myself as an artist and a writer who creates in more than one genre and medium. I am not totally there yet, but everyday I get more comfortable with this, and so I am becoming more and more comfortable in writing non-fiction pieces.

L.K.  Your novel, *The River's Song*, explores the sexual awakening of a Jamaican girl, which you mention is "[a]typical of Caribbean literature." Can you discuss this "atypical" nature? Why did you decide to break those boundaries? Is there any connection to your own personal experiences?

J.B.  I was not the one who talked of *The River's Song* as being atypical of Caribbean literature; that was something that was written about the novel. This was said in the context of coming-of-age Caribbean novels not really addressing issues of sexuality and the sexual awakening of their female narrators. I think too, hidden in that observation, is the fact that one of the girls in the novel is clearly in love with the other girl and her breakdown comes when her love object decides to leave her. I think this is what makes the novel atypical, because homosexual love remains taboo in Jamaican and Caribbean literature.

A friend of mine who has taught the novel in the Caribbean says that it generates some wonderful discussions among her graduate students about what is hidden and how it is hidden in Caribbean literature, and I think that is just great. Really, quite a compliment. Her comment also made me think of another book, Roger Mais' *Black Lightning* that I just had the great joy of writing a new introduction to. This book was first published in 1955 and it is being reissued by Peepal Tree Press in the UK. This book, too, is about homosexual love, but here too, the work speaks in parables because it was the love then, as it still remains so, for the most part in Jamaica, that dares not speak its name. In so far as *The River's Song* and *Black Lightning* are both atypical in that they get us to talk about what is hidden and what is difficult and charged and at times painful for us to acknowledge and speak about in society, then I am glad that I decided to, in your words Loren, "break those boundaries" and write about this subject. Because I believe that one of the jobs of the writer is to get us to look at and try to face and think about things that we would rather not. And there is a lot of looking away from certain subjects in Jamaican and Caribbean literature, because, to be frank, there has already been so much collective pain in our story.

The question of whether the girls in the novel reflect me in some way is always a difficult question to answer. In so far as the main characters are young girls who came of age on the island of Jamaica, that too is my experience. I also went to an all-girls Catholic school on the island, and the love, for example, that Gloria has for her grandmother and her grandmother has for her, mirrors my own relationship with my grandmother a great deal. But I think that is where the similarities stop. To a degree our characters are our creations, in so far as they come from us, but they have a life and lived experiences outside of us. As a student of mine astutely observed in class one day, you do not have to die or have ever been pregnant to write about those things! So I would say that there is little in the novel that is overtly autobiographical.

L.K. How has your mother influenced your writing (all genres)? What is your relationship like?

J.B. You know, my mother was the first audience for my work. I used to write these poems as a little girl and I would show them to her, and she would praise these terrible things and she would encourage me to keep writing. I remember once that I had two poems published on a church flier and she was oh so proud of me and the work that I had done, and I think about this often these days, how her encouragement made me actively pursue my goals.

More than anything else my mother gave me freedom. Freedom to pursue what I wanted to pursue. I remember once, when I was in college, I was having an argument with my mother about something or another related to my college career, and I said something to the effect of, "Stop controlling me! Why are you trying to control me? Why are you telling me what to do?" And my mother took a deep breath and she said, "If I were trying to control you, I would tell you to study nursing, like all the other Jamaican mothers are telling, sometimes forcing, their children to do, because then I would know you will be alright for the rest of your life. You will always be taken care of and you would always have a well-paying job!"

Well, that comment stopped me in my tracks.

Here was this woman who had to shell out every single penny to pay my tuition, on a nursing aide's salary. I. Will. Never. Forget. This. And yet she was giving me free reign to study whatever I wanted to study. My mother (and my grandmother too) made all of what I am doing now possible, because more than anything else they believed in the value of an education. They prized an education, even when at times I am sure they were confused about what I was doing. I remember a time, for example, when I wanted to study French in Canada, in preparation for going to live in Paris for a year, and it was my grandmother who paid for that.

So yes, these women, my mother and my grandmother, have both been a huge influence on my life, on my writing, and that is why my non-fiction book, *My Mother Who Is Me: Life Stories From Jamaican Women in New York*, is dedicated to both of them.

These days my mother and I have a pretty good relationship. In the past it has been more difficult. But we are both grown women now, and I think she takes pride in what I have gone on to do with my life and we have a clearer, lovelier relationship these days.

L.K.  I've always been fascinated by the idea of "the other" in literature. Do you feel that is something that is over-represented or underrepresented? Why? Why not? Do you feel that all writers feel that sense of "non belonging", which is why we tap into creating a sense of belonging via the literary arts?

J.B.  I think that literature allows us to live vicariously the lives of others. Think about it: when you are reading a really good book, you become invisible and there is total identification with the character. I remember being a student in Paris, many moons ago, and, without the benefit of language and television, I just kept reading and reading and reading everything I could get my hands on in English. I particularly remember reading Toni Morrison's *Song of Solomon* because I started that book in the morning and just could not put it down, and when I came to the end of the book, I just turned over and cried. I mean really cried. I loved Pilate so. I totally identified with her. I did not want what happened to her in the end to happen. It just broke my heart. So I think in one way or another literature is about the "other", so to speak. And this is even the case for the writer. You come to know your characters as others from yourself. They have ways of speaking, mannerisms that are different from you. And, of course, they insist that you call them by their rightful names. Not some name you made up for them – but their rightful names.

I think that at the very least writers, and artists in general, are obliged to turn a critical eye on the society that they are writing about. In turning a critical eye on their characters and the society in which they live, the writer is forced to be an outsider. And to be clear, by critical I do not mean only negative. Twice in my life as a fiction writer I have written stories that came to me in one go, as a poem usually does. One of the stories, "Brown Girl in the Ring", I have talked about already. The other story is "Love Story in Two Parts", which was published a few years back when I was in graduate school. People who have read that story have compared it to Zora Neale Hurston's *Their Eyes Were Watching God* because here too is a story of love, told in the vernacular of the Jamaican dialect. Here is a woman in "Love Story in Two Parts" who triumphs in love, not once but two times over. Maybe, as I think about it now, a little bit of Zora did find its way into that story, though I distinctly remember writing that story before I read Zora's wonderful book. The point I am trying to make, though, is that by critical eye I mean what you can see and acknowledge and fall in love with, the things that are absolutely beautiful about the people you most identify with. This too is turning a critical eye on something. And what is more challenging and ultimately triumphant than love? What is more mysterious and confounding than the things we do in the name of love? How it stretches us, teaches us, shapes us into who we are to become. I am often surprised at how much I come to care about my characters. So yes, I do believe that writers are often acutely aware of a sense of non-belonging, because we bear the burden of so many other lives, so many other stories, within our selves, and I do believe that we use our art to create a community in our works.

L.K.  You are also the founding editor of *Calabash: A Journal of Caribbean Arts & Letters*. Do you feel the journal represents writing across the diaspora? Talk about the original intent of the journal – who is the audience?

J.B.  When I look back on *Calabash* I must say I take pride in so much that it accomplished in the ten years that I worked on it. I want to believe that *Calabash* gave impetus to paying closer attention to the visual arts in the region, for example. I see more and more journals of Caribbean letters these days and they all are showcasing the visual arts and I think *Calabash* had something to do with this.

I also wanted a journal that made an effort to represent parts of the Caribbean that we did not usually hear from, the Dutch-speaking Caribbean areas for example, and I was also interested in hearing from voices that were often submerged. That was very much the intent of the journal. To bring the Caribbean closer and to bring more voices into the discussion.

Time alone will tell how much we, who worked on *Calabash*, succeeded in doing all the things that we dreamed of doing. We really gave it a good faith effort in representing "writing across the diaspora". I have to say though that every time I talk about *Calabash* I feel a twinge of regret and I get a bit teary-eyed. It was and still is my baby. I hoped it would live on forever, and in a sense it will, because it is archived on the Internet. But as I started travelling and teaching and writing and creating more, I had to make a decision as to what to do about the journal and so we have not published in several years now, but I am loathe to give up on the idea that we will never publish anymore.

The audience for *Calabash* is those who love great art and literature, particularly those who love the arts and literature of the Caribbean region.

L.K.  Do you miss home?

J.B.  There is not a day that goes by that I don't think about Jamaica, even though my home is several places now, including New York and Morocco. But Jamaica is my grandmother and my great grandmother. Jamaica is the district of Nonsuch, high in the purple blue mountains of Portland. Jamaica is the food I most love to eat, the language I speak. Jamaica is the timbre of my voice. Jamaica is intimacy and love and worry and pain and understanding and misunderstanding. Yes, I miss home a lot in fact, and by that I mean that I miss Jamaica.

## THE HAUNTED SELF

Natalie Bennett: Your work, Jacqueline, is very much a part of an ongoing dialogue among Caribbean artists and writers, especially the women. Looking at your photography – and it's so redolent of the roots you and I share – I'm reminded of a phrase we often heard growing up in Jamaica: "being haunted". Our elders used it – still do – to silence children, especially girls. The phrase aimed make us "tan tuddy", sit still, stay in place, to behave, be orderly, and be predictable.

Jacqueline Bishop: I remember it well. And "being haunted" was not a place we were encouraged to go.

N.B. "Being haunted" meant that you were ill at ease, an uncertain child, susceptible even to communing with "duppies".

J.B. Yes, consorting with the spirits.

N.B. A distinctly un-Christian idea in a country that constantly struggles against its own duppies. And yet I see in your photography – your poems too, but let's stay with your photographs here – I think I see you being haunted. Are you haunted? What, if anything, haunts you? As an artist, I mean.

J.B. I think I *am* haunted. I'm haunted by memory, by personal memory *and* historical memory. I think it stems from being an immigrant artist here in America, often looking back to where I'm from. I feel refracted. Always setting one place alongside another. Here in New York, where I've lived much of my life, I'm always superimposing landscapes. I see a landscape up in Connecticut and simultaneously I see a Jamaican landscape superimposed.

N.B. A kind of double vision.

J.B. I visited a friend up in Canaan recently, a friend from Jamaica who shares my landscape back at home – the Nonsuch landscape. Do you know it?

N.B. Not well.

J.B. It's a tiny district high in the purple-blue mountains where both our families lived. As we drove that day through the landscape around Canaan, with all its greenery, the surrounding mountains, the rivers not far away, we both thought how much it felt like Nonsuch. We were both superimposing our Nonsuch landscapes onto this one, the one in front of us. We *must* be haunted. It's not just back then, not just memory. That Nonsuch landscape comes with us, no matter where.

N.B.  So your photographs reflect your interest in engaging your own past and present, the duppies that have gone before, and the ones yet to come.

J.B.  I think so. I know, for example, that in my "Childhood Memories" series, I aimed to reconstruct a childhood that was part real, part mythologised – and at the same time to take a critical look back at my childhood in Jamaica. Childhood, for me, had become a land where other people live. Having moved to New York as a teenager, my own childhood felt like a truncated place.

N.B.  That physical splicing of the images does suggest a sense of displacement. You might have imagined a clean break between Jamaica and here. But it really hasn't been that, has it? Blurred lines, background melding into foreground.

J.B.  Yes, and it wasn't easy. I didn't know Photoshop at the time, so here in New York what I did was to take photographs of my childhood photographs. Then I struggled to collage these Jamaican images with newer ones of my coming-of-age in the Bronx. I don't think those images ever quite worked. Then I experimented putting film on top of film and printing the two films as one. In theory, it was great, overlaying my two lives. But the images themselves, quite honestly, they were blurry, indistinct. But then –

N.B.  Digital?

J.B.  Precisely. And none too soon. I was introduced to Photoshop and I scanned all those childhood images along with images from later trips back to the island. For me the world became a series of superimposed images. That's when I made the "Childhood Memories" series. One of its images is an elderly relative superimposed over a map of the Caribbean. She became a stand-in for so many Caribbean women who've literally propped up the region. Then I made the "Folly" series, which also aimed to tell the story of childhood.

N.B.  Why Folly?

J.B.  Folly was a house in Port Antonio Bay. Portland was where I spent summers with my grandmother and my great-grandparents and other relatives. It was a wonderful time, before electricity, when at night the children would gather around and listen to stories. My great-grandparents told us about this house – a mansion, really – built by a rich and handsome young man, from abroad somewhere. He wanted to entice his fiancée to live with him there.

N.B.  He was using property to assert his worth. I wonder if it worked for him.

J.B.  Well, you've seen the pictures. It's a ruin now. Only the Roman columns are intact. The foundation, so the story goes (or at least did back then), was mixed with salt water from the sea. The locals had warned the young man, they'd told him that building a house with salt water meant that whoever moved in was also made of salt and only problems would ensue.

N.B.  Am I hearing the story of Lot's wife?

J.B.  You mean she yearned for Sodom? She certainly yearned for *something* different. When the fiancée came and saw the house, she cried out, "Oh what folly!" And she ran away and never came back. Or so the story goes.

N.B.  What happened to the house?

J.B.  It's been abandoned ever since. The story was great, especially there in the dark. The house, it turns out, was actually owned by the Tiffany family, the jewellery-makers, all those wonderful lampshades, the *art nouveau*… and a house so elaborately designed. When they built it, locals thought it an "architectural folly". Yet for years the family lived in it, flourished in it, I guess. Then the patriarch died and the other members of the family returned to the United States, and the house fell slowly into ruin. As an adult – and now an artist – I went back to the house, which was indeed in ruin, and I walked around it, snapping photographs. Looking later at the images, well, talk about haunted! I felt compelled to understand the history of the place.

N.B.  In a sense, you'd heard several versions of its history that you needed to reconcile.

J.B.  Precisely. I'd become enamoured with competing histories. And in the "Folly" series, I'm aiming to dramatise this duality, with the Folly house as both an architectural folly and a folly in the local mythology. At the centre of this is *perception* – How do we see? And how do we multiply sight through imagination?

N.B. Your photographs, then, are answers to these questions?

J.B. Not really. The photographs don't answer these questions – but they do pose them. I want them to be open-ended provocations to discussion. That's the artist's role, to provoke discussion. Both series, the "Childhood Memories" and the "Folly" series, want viewers to ask about, and differentiate between, what is transient and what endures. This helps people make sense of themselves, of their pasts, and of the worlds they live in. These are some of the things which haunt me as an artist.

N.B. And how does that haunting manifest itself in particular images?

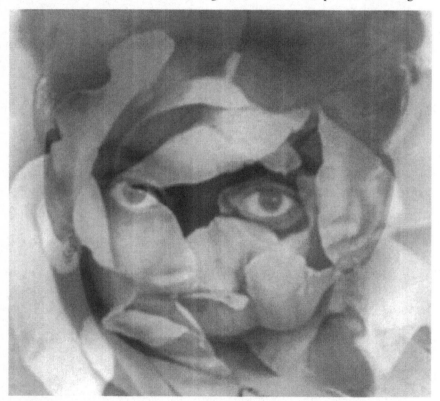

J.B. Well, there's an image in "Folly" that's particularly meaningful to me – called "Folly Flower". It's the image of a woman almost obscured by a flower. Doing my research for the "Folly" series I found all sorts of evidence of the people who worked at the house – as servants and such – people's payment slips, the thank-you letters they wrote to their employers. But, you know, in the hundreds, if not thousands, of photographs the family took, there wasn't a single one of the black people who waited on them, and maintained that way of life for them. My picture aimed to put these servants back into the story, even if obscurely. I couldn't help but think, as I did the work, that some of those absent faces could have been relatives of mine from Nonsuch. And I wanted them back in the story of that house.

N.B.  "Folly Flower" seems to ask us to question the beauty in a rather sordid history.

J.B.  Yes, there is that duality.

N.B.  It also reminds me of how the Caribbean landscape, both the physical and human landscape, was often imagined by earlier British writers as so untamed that it reduced outsiders, mostly white ones, to their basest selves. But your pictures also bring together, quite hauntingly, women and vegetation. It's a gentler, more humane perspective. Say a word, if you will, about reflections of gender in your work.

J.B.  About women you mean?

N.B.  Yes, in particular.

J.B.  In "Childhood Memories" there are images of girlhood and the "wetness" of female friendships that give way to a merging of woman and the landscape. And finally, one of the last pictures in the series: my great-grandmother – within whose image you see that of a younger woman. Regeneration, continuity. And there's a similar exploration of womanhood in the "Folly" series. In "Annie", for example, you have a woman almost hidden, not in a flower, but within and beneath this big house. In "Folly Violin", you see a woman with a violin, and the house is in the background, and there's a big X over it. I didn't put that X there, but I think it helps make my point – which is a counterpoint to still another image from the series – I call it "Folly Dancer" – in which I've collaged a dancehall woman with the house. "Violin", for me, represents the past of this house, and the "Dancer" the present. The images look toward each other, they collide. They offer competing images of what it means to be a woman in Jamaica, a woman of a particular race and class, at different times.

N.B.  So there's race and gender in your pictures. And class, of course. And history, the passage of time and its effects on us. Multiple strands of history, and memory. What I'm seeing, then – and saying – is that your photographs are full of meaning and implication, some of it open, some very personal.

J.B.  You flatter them, but yes. And I'd like to think you've overlooked yet another dimension, one that's very important to me.

N.B.  Which is?

J.B.  Call it the mythic. I want to make permanent the transience of the world, to invoke Arcadia, the lost paradise. Eavan Boland, the poet, wrote that "Arcadia was once a real place... but it quickly became a fiction." Like the Garden of Eden, followed by Man's Fall. Arcadia, a lost world of idyllic bliss, but remembered only in regretful dirges. Modern day Jamaica is my Arcadia. It's a lost world that re-emerges – in my photographs anyway – as this phantasmagoric landscape.

N.B.  And yet, you seem to identify closely with New York as well.

J.B.  I do indeed. I am a New Yorker. I've now lived here longer than I lived in Jamaica. It, too, is home for me.

N.B.  As it is for several generations of Jamaican émigrés. New York does offer another kind of rootedness, a different place in which to navigate our Jamaicanness. How do you account for the effect of New York on your work, if at all?

J.B.  New York is the place where my identity expanded. No, exploded. I am Jamaican, but here I became so much more. In Jamaica –

N.B.  In Arcadia?

J.B.  Yes, in Arcadian Jamaica, I was someone's daughter, and someone's great-grand-daughter, and I was someone else's friend, and so on. My identity was anchored. Here in New York I got to find out who I was beyond those territorial anchors. New York enabled me to understand myself – and hence my art – as that of a Caribbean offspring. It forced me to confront race and gender in ways I'd never had to confront them before. Sure, it's true, there are many Jamaicas down there, and so many ways of being Jamaican. But here I really had to confront my differences and my otherness in ways I'd never had to before. It was challenging, but ultimately very rewarding. When you confront all the differences of this place, different people, different ways of doing things – a cornucopia, really – you discover what is singular, yes, and really beautiful about yourself as a Jamaican, as Caribbean. I teach now at NYU and oftentimes have students try to grapple with this great big city, and make those discoveries about themselves, by themselves. That, I think, is what New York brings to my work.

## INTERVIEW, WITH JOHN HOPPENTHALER

John Hoppenthaler:  For this particular set of poems, you've chosen to
    work in long-lined couplets. I notice as well that, even though there
    is stanza and line, the breaks don't show any particular stylistic agenda
    other than length; that is, the pieces read like prose poems but look
    like pieces that are more structured. This creates a sort of tension
    between a reader's expectations about the poems, as created by their
    visual appearance, and the actual experience of reading the poem,
    where line breaks and each line as an individual unit do not seem to
    have been considered. Can you speak to these stylistic decisions in
    relationship to subject matter and artistic intent? Why couplets? Why
    long lines? Why the disconnect between appearance and experience?

Jacqueline Bishop:  Thanks for your question John. I wanted to try
    something different in my poetry. I wanted to try and see if I could
    sustain the momentum of much longer lines. I wanted to see how
    far I could push the lines, or hold the lines, without losing the
    tension that I require in a poem. I was very much also concerned
    with retaining what I call the musicality in a line. If a poem is not
    taut and if it is not musical, and if I cannot quickly pick up on its
    momentum, I lose interest. Consequently I have to lovingly quarrel
    with your suggestion that line breaks for each line or couplet was
    not considered. In fact, just the opposite is true, and I worked a
    great deal at getting the line-breaks just where I wanted them. Now,
    in fact, I have found myself to be engaged in a whole other problem
    altogether, and that is I do not have enough space on my computer
    screen to break the lines in all the places that I want to break them
    because, in one or two of the cases, the lines are just too long for
    what I want.
        In so far as the couplets are concerned, I set myself a challenge, and
    the challenge was similar to that of the long lines, which was to see if
    I could maintain the momentum, the tautness and the musicality in
    couplets. But, too, the lines in the couplet had to not only work as
    individual lines, but also as couplets, even as the entire poem had to
    work together and retain both its musicality and its momentum. I can't
    begin to tell you how much I have laboured over these poems because
    they felt new and exciting and different for me, and I felt that in these

poems there was a shift in my work and I had moved into a new stage of writing poetry. And this is all due to me lengthening my lines.

In so far as there being a disconnect between appearance and experience, I can't really say that I see that in the works. I am very clear when I am writing a poem from when I am writing a fiction piece. Poems for me often come in a flash – and then there is the intense crafting that begins in getting at the poem that is hidden within that first draft. Truth be told, even though today I am known as a fiction and non-fiction writer in addition to being a poet, I really started life as a poet and I often primarily think of myself as a poet. I am still inescapably caught up in the musicality of words, and now, when I am writing fiction or non-fiction, I am always listening for how the words sound together. That is something I think that poets in particular are sensitive to and preoccupied by. As well as how a poem actually looks on a page. So I really don't see a disconnect between appearance and experience in these works.

J.H.  These are historical poems, based upon research and documentation. How, for you, does the experience of writing this sort of poem differ from that of writing, say, a more personal poem based upon your childhood in Jamaica? Is a different process in play?

J.B.  They really don't differ that much at all, because, all along, my work has been about understanding the human predicament. In so many ways, my poems about my family act as a foil to get me to understand the island of Jamaica. And this as well is true in these poems where I am trying to understand who the people were that would come to let me have the understanding that I have today of my Jamaica. People like Christopher Columbus, for example. I have been fascinated by Christopher Columbus for a long time, and so I decided to research and learn more about him outside of what I had been taught in school. And it was interesting some of the things that I found out about Mr. Columbus, and this in turn forced me to rethink some of the things I thought were gospel about this particular historical figure. In my recent work, he is emerging as a beleaguered and confused man.

In my research I became particularly fascinated by the ways Columbus kept trying to make sense of the new world that he was confronting when he got to the Caribbean, and how, when people around him challenged what he was saying – challenged in fact what he was seeing – how upset he became to the point of forcing people to sign declarations that he was correct! He loved naming things, and this assigning of names to things that he "discovered" was a particular past time for young men of means in Columbus's time, this voyage of discovery that they went on. I decided I would, in a sense, go on my own voyage of discovery to meet some of the people integral to my understanding of Jamaica, the larger Caribbean, indeed the Americas. As my interests kept broadening, it was not too much of a jump for me, for example, to go from Columbus to Charles Darwin.

But always hidden in these grand narratives are other stories and so Darwin's wife, his beloved Emma, became very important to me in the telling of his story. In researching Darwin I became fascinated by Emma and how supportive she tried to be, even as she was afraid of some of the things that were coming into being by her husband's discoveries and findings. In time I came to learn a lot about how the Caribbean has long been seen by Europeans, and I also learnt a lot about my own beloved Jamaica. But I also learnt much about the human condition. So at the end of the day, the writing process was not different at all, because as problematic as some of these people were and are, they are ultimately human, and my work is very much concerned with telling human stories.

J.H.  In addition to being a poet, you also are a novelist, a writer of non-fiction, and a visual artist working in a variety of mediums. How do you juggle these differing forms? In what ways do they inform one another? How do you make the time to work in so many genres of art, as well as teach and edit?

J.B.  You know, I feel like I have finally come to the place I want to be, living the life I wanted to live. To get there, though, there was a lot of juggling. Because I wanted to treat each art form with the respect that it demanded of me, I often ended going back to school to study. Just today I was joking with my students that you will never know a person with as many degrees as I have! They cracked up laughing. First I went and studied poetry, then fiction, and then I went off and got degrees in the visual arts. I do not believe that this is the only or even the best way to attack the problem of having multiple callings in one's life, but I have always appreciated the structure of being in a programme.

What this all means is that I have a firm grounding in all the art forms that I am presently engaged in. Consequently, I am never one of those people who struggle to understand which art form I am working in. In the same way that what I am doing now is answering questions in an interview, I know quite clearly when I am writing poetry, fiction or non-fiction. A similar process goes on in the visual arts, though there is more cross-fertilisation.

I have great respect for the work that critics do and feel that a critic would be better placed than I am in talking about how my work informs one another. I am not being cheeky about this. A curator came to look at some of my quilts recently. Because I know that the many things that I do might be overwhelming, I was careful to only show her the quilts. But in these quilts I have used photomontages of my family members. The curator looked around my tiny apartment that doubles as my studio and she asked about some drawings that I had up. Then she started to show me how my painting, photography and drawings had worked their way into my quilts. I was fascinated! Absolutely fascinated! Because without her help I would not have seen this.

The question for me then is not how I juggle these multiple art forms, but rather, could I live with myself if I did not? Because after studying to be a poet and finding my poetic voice, the fiction goddess raised her head and decided to speak, and then the photographic and painting goddesses. In short I am doing what I feel compelled to do, and it does not exhaust me at all; rather, it energises me. At the very least, there is always something for me to do.

J.H.  You have done a good deal of travelling in the past decade or so. What do you bring back from these travels, both to your art and to your teaching?

J.B.  It is so hard to be self-reflective about one's self and one's art, but I want to think that one thing I bring back is a greater understanding of the things that join us as human beings and some of the things that pull us apart. We all look up at the moon, for example, and wonder about her luminescence and beauty, though in some of the places I have ventured I might find myself in a great deal of trouble for calling the moon "her". These are some of the things that I try to get my students to understand. This semester I am teaching an oral history course, and students have arranged themselves into groups to do various oral history projects. Each group has to turn in a proposal for their project, and this is where the fun really begins because you can see the students' biases a mile away, that they are writing as if they have all the answers already to the questions they are posing. This is one thing my travels have sensitised me to, and it is that I do not have all the answers to all the questions. And this is one thing that I try to impart to my students.

The other thing that immediately comes to mind is that travelling gives me more, as an artist, to pull from. It just allows you more experiences and people to write about, and I want to believe that travelling allows me to have a more complex and nuanced rendering of the, let's say, "other", than I might have had if I sat in my home and tried to do this without the benefit of travel. I know for a fact that I could not have written my second collection of poems, Snapshots from Istanbul, had I not gone to the country several times.

J.H.  Off the top of my head, I can think of only a few other Jamaican poets with whose work I'm familiar; a few have published here in *A Poetry Congeries*: Kwame Dawes, Shara McCallum and Ishion Hutchinson. And I think of Claude McKay, of course, and Lorna Goodison. You've been the editor of *Calabash: A Journal of Caribbean Arts and Letters*, so you are in as good a position as anyone to let our readers know about the Jamaican writers we should be reading. Who are the fine young (or not so young) writers of Jamaica? Ishion has brought Edward Baugh to my attention, and I've received a note from Baugh suggesting that he will send work at some point, but I'm eager to learn of others.

J.B.  Jamaica is just blessed when it comes to having artistic talent in my view, and it is especially blessed when it comes to having poets. The poet whose work gives me goose bumps at the moment, whose work is sooooo good, is Tanya Shirley. She is a young poet based at the University of the West Indies, and I mean the woman's work is like thunder-clap! So strong, so powerful, so good. She came out with a very good first collection from Peepal Tree Press, but in that first collection there was a sense that she was not in full command of her voice. Now, there is no question that she is in full command of her voice, and her most recent poems are mesmerising and amazing. I can't wait... absolutely cannot wait... for Tanya Shirley to come out with a second collection of poems.

 Velma Pollard's work has also been consistently strong, as is the work of Geoffrey Philp and Aza Weir-Soley, both based in Florida. I also like a great deal the work of Ann-Margaret Lim, another poet based in Jamaica, who just came out with her first collection of poems. Opal Palmer Adisa and Marcia Douglas have both been writing and publishing solid poems for many years now. And then there is Mervyn Morris who remains an amazing poet. There are of course many other poets doing really good work, but off the top of my head, those are the ones I can think of.

## "INSIDE I ALWAYS KNEW I WAS A WRITER"

Opal Palmer Adisa: When did you know you were a writer or wanted to be a writer?

Jacqueline Bishop: As contradictory as it might sound, I think I knew that I was a writer before I knew that I wanted to be a writer. Being a writer – being an artist – for me is instinctive. I am fully convinced that I was just born this way. Being an artist for me was never a condition that I struggled with or against. It was this thing that was thrust onto me, like my gender, like where I was born, like my skin colour and I just had to get on with it. Wanting to be a writer though is a whole different matter, to take on that title, to professionalise my art and to be somehow compensated for the work that I do; getting my work out there into the world – that is where I struggled. But deep down inside I always knew that I was a writer – from a very young age actually.

O.P.A.  How do you think being Jamaican or Caribbean has and continues to shape your writing and what you write about?

J.B.  Being a Jamaican is definitive to what I write about. It is true that I have written characters and poems about people and places that are not Jamaica(n) or Caribbean, but what shapes my writing, that primary Jamaican identity, is the tiny district of Nonsuch, high in the purple blue mountains of Jamaica where my family is from. Being Jamaican is always the place I come back to in one way or another in everything that I create. So even stories and poems and writings in which the island does not feature, my particular experience as a Jamaican immigrant woman still informs that work. So when I look at my second collection of poems for example, *Snapshots from Istanbul*, even though many of the poems are about Ovid, it is also about the condition of being in exile and being sent away to an unfamiliar landscape while all the while missing one's home. In other words, the book is all about my engagement with Jamaica, even though most of the book is set in New York, Turkey and ancient Rome.

O.P.A. Is Caribbean writing relevant today and if so why?

J.B. I think Caribbean writing remains incredibly relevant and important today. Every generation is handed a set of issues that it is forced to confront and to try and solve. Artists are often at the forefront of those discussions. When I look at the Caribbean, and see for example the recent ruling by the High Court of the Dominican Republic making stateless Dominicans of Haitian descent, many of whom were born and have lived in the Dominican Republic for decades and know no other home, I am reminded anew of the relevance of Caribbean writing. News reports, sociologists, anthropologists and historians can only tell us so much about the lives that are being touched by issues such as the people now made stateless in the Dominican Republic; it is up to the artists, to the writers of the region, to make those lives real and genuine and palpable for readers. The gift and burden of being a writer is the ability to breathe life into characters and make a reader empathise and understand the issue before this character and its relevance to one's self. Lately, for example, I have become incredibly politicised about the issue of climate change. Because I am convinced that the way the world is going with climate change, we in the Caribbean may very well loose much of our biodiversity within our own lifetimes, I have taken to photographing the flowers of the island of Jamaica. My flower portraits are an attempt to hold onto these images of beauty for myself, yes, but also maybe for others into the future. This is what I as an artist can do. Literature can help us to understand and hold onto and make sense of a Caribbean world that in many ways is rapidly receding; as such, Caribbean writing is not decreasing but rather it is increasing in relevance.

O.P.A. Your novel, *The River's Song*, is a rites-of-passage work that seems appropriate for adolescents. How did this book come about?

J.B. This book was my thesis when I was graduating from the MFA programme in Creative Writing at New York University.

O.P.A. Do you remember when you had the initial idea to write it and where you were?

J.B. I wrote this book primarily in the United States, Mexico and Morocco. I believe that as a writer I am simply a conduit to the stories of others and so I am unsure if there was an initial idea to tell this story so much as the characters latched onto me and insisted that I tell their story.

O.P.A.  Select a character from this work and discuss what you wanted to say, or are saying through this character.

J.B.  Understanding friendships among young girls and women was very important to me in this book. The friendship that stands out the most for me in the book is that of the main characters, Annie and Gloria. Through both these characters I wanted to explore two of the many Jamaicans that exist on the island. Annie comes from money and has had a more privileged life than Gloria, yet, their high school becomes the place for them to meet on somewhat of an equal ground. I was intrigued by how their friendship developed, how close indeed they became. And I was saddened when the relationship fell apart. In a sense, I guess that I was looking at what would bring two girls, from such different socioeconomic backgrounds, together and what would ultimately tear them apart.

O.P.A.  What were some of the feelings/emotions you experienced in writing this book?

J.B.  I went through many, many emotions, especially since I felt that I had to let the characters lead and tell me their story. For me characters are real people somewhere out there in the world and they tap the shoulders of those who they want to tell their stories. At first there was the getting to know these characters, the initial curiosity – what did they look like and what were their names? After I got a sense of them there was the families that they came from and how they ended up at the place they were at in their lives.

Sometimes I absolutely fell in love with the characters as I did when Annie visited her grandmother in the country and she and a group of girls went bathing in the river. And then there was the shock when one of the girls almost dies at the river. Also, I wondered whether Annie and Gloria would be able to be friends when they first met at school, and was gratified when they managed to sustain their friendship through so many difficulties. Still, in the end, when they separated I was crying as I wrote that section.

Oftentimes, teenage girls will ask me, "Why did you do that? Why did you let them part? Why couldn't they be friends forever? They have been through so much together!" You can hear the hurt and accusations in the young adults' voices, as if I have done something that they would never do. That they would never abandon or betray a friend. I smile at this, because I see so much of myself in them. Indeed I can identify with their sense of outrage. But it is here that I have to say no to my outraged and hurt readers, and explain that I did not do that, that was the characters' story, I was just chosen to tell Annie's and Gloria's story. I try to get my readers to understand that I am as saddened about the separation of two characters I love as they are. Sometimes I can still see the accusation in their faces, but it is the truth: characters take over the telling of their story at a certain point and you simply cannot force this. Lastly I will just say one thing that I struggled particularly with – the title of the novel. The title went through several incarnations before it became *The River's Song,* at which time the characters stopped rebelling, settled down and said, yes, that is the title of our story.

O.P.A.  How does it feel to have work out into the world that will live on long after you?

J.B.  I am thrilled about this. What could be better? To have a work that lives on long, long after you do? It is like having a child that will live forever. That is just beautiful.

O.P.A.  Finally, what projects are you currently pursuing?

J.B.  Presently I am working on a collection of short stories and a collection of poems. My most recent work as a visual artist is a series of "Babylon" and "Zion" paintings. These are about the Rastafarian ideas of Babylon being a place of captivity and oppression while Zion symbolises a utopian place of unity and peace. In the Babylon series I write the lyrics from songs and poems to create text-based drip paintings leading up to the "Hanging Gardens of Babylon", in which I use popular dancehall posters to evoke the inner-city Babylonian "walls" of Kingston. The Zion series is comprised largely of monochrome paintings to delineate this symbolic paradise. Glitter is present in these works not only as a representation of the paradise that Rastafarians seek in the Biblical homeland of Zion, but also as a commentary on the "bling and glitter" culture that has enveloped much of Jamaican society.

## RELIVING, REWRITING, REIMAGINING

Leanne Haynes: I wanted to pick up on a response you gave in an interview with Derek Alger (2011). In this interview, you speak about the poet Ovid in relation to your 2009 collection *Snapshots from Istanbul* (Peepal Tree Press) stating:

> "I could identify with a poet in exile, because I often feel in exile myself, though I am not sure where I am in exile from. By this I mean that the Jamaica I left more than twenty years ago is not the Jamaica that is there today, and I often wonder if I return "home" to Jamaica, how well I would fit into and function in the society, even as Jamaica and Jamaican is the identity I am most sure of, the place I am most engaged with and the space from which I create within myself."

I wonder if we might address some of the issues in this response and talk through this feeling of exile. Is this something you still experience? Is Jamaica home? How often do you return? When was the last time you visited? What was it like? Do you still have family/ friends out there?

Jacqueline Bishop: Yes, this feeling of being in exile is something that I still very much experience. Here is what happens to me every time I go to Jamaica: First I cannot believe that I am home, and Jamaica is very much home, home for me being a place of acceptance, connection and belonging. I start having this feeling once I begin to see the island coming into view from the air; there is this feeling that it is all real after all, Jamaica is real and it is not a dream, because oftentimes I wonder if it all isn't just a dream, this longing that I always walk around with inside of myself for Jamaica.

By the time I land and start to hear the voices around me, those Jamaican voices, I start to silently give thanks that not only is it all real, but it is all still here. The drive in from the airport is not as lovely as it used to be since they dug up all those lovely sand dunes for a roadway that looks pretty much like any other roadway anywhere else in the world, nothing at all distinctive about it, but I start looking out at the ocean, at the trees and flowers and it is all a powerfully emotional feeling for me. Usually some friend or family member has come to meet me at the airport and all I want to do is hold them so close, as close as I want to hold the island of Jamaica, and all I keep thinking is it is all real, it is all real and it is still here.

I would say I get to Jamaica every two years or so. I would like to get there more often, and hopefully I will. Almost all of my family is still in Jamaica – my grandmother, my father, so many aunts, uncles, and cousins. Almost all of my high school friends are in the US now, but a few of them are still on the island and I go to see these friends and family member every chance I get. A mandatory part of the trip is going to the district of Nonsuch, in Portland, to see my grandmother and all the relatives I have there. I do this every time I am in Jamaica. It just does not feel right if I don't go to Nonsuch. I totally adore Portland, which is the parish where my family is from in Jamaica. Portland is my favourite parish on the island, and I always say if I go back to live in Jamaica, I will live in Portland. Going to Jamaica for me is a very emotional experience. Everything is heightened. Everything is fascinating. All the colours are bright.

L.H. I think being away from your birthplace always adds an extra dimension to one's writing about the place in question. In your 2006 collection of poems, *Fauna*, also published by Peepal Tree Press, we see how you creatively engage with Jamaica. Here, I am thinking of poems like "The Picture". I am particularly fond of the lines: "All my mysteries reside in this place, / small dot of an island, / the restlessness and the need to always return / to my great grandmother's river" (15). Tell me more about this poem. Did you write this in Jamaica? Can you talk more about the restlessness you mention? And what of the mysteries? (We'll talk about your grandmother a little later on, if we may).

J.B. Very little of my work gets written in Jamaica, because I find being in Jamaica so overwhelming. I oftentimes wonder if I could write and create there, to be honest about it, because it is all such a sensory experience, almost like a sensory overload for me when I am on the island. More and more I find that I need absolute quiet to think, to create, and it is very hard to have that in Jamaica, because there is so much of life going on around you. At my grandmother's for example, there is always a chicken scratching about, a rooster crowing, that kind of thing. Plus my grandmother's house is one of the most open places you will find, someone is always sitting on her verandah talking to her, and neither her front nor her back door is ever closed until very late into the night. That is just the kind of person my grandmother is and the kind of household that she has.

So in fact, most of my writing is done in my tiny apartment in New York. And, to be truthful about it, I find it hard to write and create outside of New York, because in my apartment I have everything that I want. When I try to work elsewhere, it is not impossible, but just more challenging, because there is always something that I want that is not around me, and that extends to my two cats who like to lay on my lap as I work, or walk across the keyboard.

In terms of the restlessness that I feel, I guess it springs from being forged and formed in one place – the island of Jamaica – but coming to creativity and having a life in another place. Recently I had to give a talk about my "Childhood Memories" series of photographs and I started off by saying something that totally surprised me about that body of work – which is that, in this series I am trying to get back to a place and a time that no longer exists, meaning my childhood, and I use these photographs to return there. That is where the intense restlessness comes from I think, my seeking to return to a place – a Jamaica – that no longer exists. Within myself I am always searching for this.

In regards to the mysteries that I am talking about in the poem, I am really referencing who I am and the circumstances that came to make me "me". I was quite fortunate to be on the cusp of womanhood when both my great-grandparents died. I knew them quite well. And from them I got a pretty firm grounding in myself. These were people who had their very own cosmology and understanding of the world and they would not hesitate to impart this to me. One time, for example, my great grandfather and I happened to be in the bushes when it was Emancipation day and he told me to look out for slaves and how to behave should we see any. He was not joking. He believed that the spirits of runaway slaves roamed the bushes long after they had died. Then he went on to tell me all about the terribleness of slavery, but ended by saying that the spirits of the enslaved when set free, and particularly on Emancipation day, were roaming around in the bushes.

I grew up at a time in Jamaica where every summer you were sent to the country to stay with your family there, and in the country you were exposed to a whole other world, a mysterious world, that coexisted right alongside the visible world. Another example of what I mean by this: when my Aunt Ann had her daughter I remember being at my grandmother's house in the country, which was like a mile, mile-and-a-half from where my great-grandparents lived. We children would walk that distance all the time back and forth between the two houses. But this time I picked all sorts of beautiful flowers on my walk up to see the new baby, only to have my great grandmother throw them right away, because, apparently, the flowers I picked harboured spirits, which meant, of course, that I now had to turn-my-wheel before going in to see the new baby, so spirits could not follow me in and hurt the baby. Things like that went on all the time in my grandmother's and grandparents' houses and I could tell you countless stories of all these mysterious things that are located specifically for me in the district of Nonsuch.

L.H.  As the title suggests, the Jamaican flora and fauna is a dominant feature in this collection and indeed an important part of your creative consciousness (cocoa pods, bamboos, mountains, mangos etc). You firmly locate this volume in the Caribbean. How important is it for you to poetically connect with the island in this way, especially given your current location (New York City)?

J.B.  It is extremely important. I think a lot of my connection to the land has to do with those summer holidays in that tiny district hidden away in the folds of those purple blue Portland mountains. One of the things that surprised me when I wrote that first collection was how important that time was with my grandmother and my great grandparents in forming both my poetic and other artistic consciousnesses. Almost always that is the place that I am writing out of. My great-grandparents and my grandmother had such an understanding of the land! Almost as if the land was a person! They talked to fruit trees and flowers. Told them it was time to bear, that sort of thing, and lo and behold the trees and the flowers would bear fruit. Now this is not at all strange or laughable, as it used to seem then, and now I watch documentaries all the time about how plants respond to talking and laughter and so on. The world has finally caught up with my great-grandparents!

But I think I can locate for you the exact two moments when the flora and fauna of Jamaica became of immense importance to me as an artist. I have spent some time retracing this in my mind. These moments both happened when I was a very young child and they both happened in Nonsuch.

It so happens that my grandmother is a gardener to the core, a farmer, someone who likes to grow things. This is just something deep inside of her. For a few years, for example, she lived in Toronto and one summer when I went to visit her there, she took me out to show me the tomatoes, onions, cucumbers and pumpkins that she was growing in Toronto. But that is another story. For a long time my grandmother, when she first moved back to Nonsuch from Kingston as a young woman, she lived for a time in her sister Gladys's house. Next to Aunty Gladys's house is a place, a big field really,

called the "centre" which must have been a place at one time, because
there was some kind of concrete structure, but it has long fallen
into ruins. Behind that ruin of a centre is a thick area of forest with
gigantic trees hovering overhead and it was in this thickly wooded
area, that, years ago, my grandmother decided to grow some vegetables,
in addition to what she was growing in her yard.

When my grandmother would go to check on her vegetables,
sometimes I would go with her and I still remember walking into
that forest with my grandmother, walking, in fact, behind my
grandmother. It felt like I was walking into a magical place, the
dappled green light that would come down through the leaves. And
so we walked, me behind my grandmother, following a path, until
we came to the place where she had cleared out and planted her
garden. The soil was moist, rich and dark and the vegetables were
neatly laid out in sections. Then my grandmother did what for me
seemed the most miraculous thing she could have done, which is
that she pulled a fully formed carrot from the soil and checked it
for a while, before she replanted the carrot. All the time I stood
there watching her. God alone knows why that incident became
emblazoned on my consciousness, but it linked my grandmother
so strongly to the land and to the vegetation of the land for me.

The second incident is quite sinister. As a child, in Nonsuch,
there would be bird season and you would have all these foreigners
with long guns shooting day and night in the bushes, and they would
come walking out of the guava piece next to my grandmother's
house with all these beautiful but bloodied and very dead birds
strung together by their feet and there would be much laughing
and drinking as they drove away. It so happened that I was then,
and still am today, something of a worrier and I found myself really
worried about all the birds that they killed, the gorgeous parrots,
and unconsciously I still link that to the disappearance of some of
the endemic birds of the island. What troubled me the most about
the killings, even then as a child, was that they were done for sport,
not that anybody wanted to eat the birds. In fact, I do believe those
men – foreigners all, by the way they spoke – threw away all or
most of the birds they killed. The birds were killed for the sport
of it. And that just troubled me, troubled me enormously as a young
child in Nonsuch for the summer holidays. And I think somewhere
in that moment the fauna of the island started becoming very important
to me.

In so far as me being in New York while writing about these
things, that makes perfect sense to me, because all along I feel as if
in my writing and through my other art forms, I am writing my

way back to Jamaica. You see, when I am writing about Jamaica, I am there, in Jamaica, no matter where in the world I might be as I am doing this writing. I get to relive all those childhood moments again, and I am not so sure if I would have the enduring need to do this if I was still living in Jamaica.

L.H.  There's almost a spiritual undertone to some of the ways in which you engage with the region's flora and fauna. Can you talk more about this? How does poetry allow you to connect with the psyche?

J.B.  In so far as spirituality is a search for the sacred, I think you are very much correct about this. I see spirituality as holding up for veneration that which is outside of the ordinary, which is exactly how I feel about the vegetation, the flora and fauna, the very landscape of Jamaica. Its beauty is extraordinary. I think oftentimes with sadness about the ways in which the landscape is seen by developers and the like as just resources there to benefit them. Whereas people like my grandmother and so many others see the natural landscape as something they have to cooperate with to get through their day. There is the feeling that if they take care of the land, the land will take care of them and there is something very ancient and sacred about that idea for me. But maybe, too, my feelings about the land being sacred comes from having a great grandmother who would leave food outside on plates for unseen spirits to come and eat; a great-grandfather who believed that long dead slaves were roaming about in the bushes; relatives, friends and family members who talk to fruit trees and flowers telling them to behave themselves and to grow. My father's wife, for example, is notorious for talking to her plants, and telling them where they can grow and where they should not grow, and believe it or not, those flowers listen to her. There was, when I was a child growing up in Jamaica, and still very much there today, a belief in the spirit and the soul and there was a belief that this was located in the natural landscape as well.

L.H.  As much as there is a sense of positivity, spiritual connection and comfort in the familiarity of the Jamaican flora and fauna, there is also, on the flip side, undertones of danger and guilt. Here I am thinking of "Litter" and "The Smell of Mango". I wonder if you might say a little about these poems and how place and memory are, in my opinion, intrinsically linked.

J.B.  Jamaica is not a utopia. Even *I* have to remind myself of that all the time. Especially so because I live away from the island and have a tendency to see it in bursts of colours. I came of age in a Jamaica rife with political and other violence. There was and is still a lot of violence being perpetrated on children in Jamaica for example. What I was told time and time again growing up was that children should be seen and not heard! There is a lot of violence being perpetrated on the bodies of young girl children as well. I was not quite ten when a classmate staggered into the classroom, mute; she had been raped on her way to school.

A few years back my grandmother told me that in the very district I love so much, Nonsuch, three men were arrested for the rape and pregnancy of a prepubescent girl, who was somewhere between twelve and fourteen years old. One of the men was 65 years old! I remember being annoyed at some of the discussion about how "bad" the girl was, because she had gotten pregnant so young! All the men arrested I believe were at least twenty years older than this child.

I wish that these things did not happen, but they do, and I feel my job as a writer and an artist is not to overlook these things, but to hold them up for discussion, even as we work to forge the beloved community. To do otherwise just would not be me and the work that I am doing.

In so far as the poem "Litter" is concerned that poem was based on actual events. My family did have a cat who became pregnant and we children were warned not to touch the kittens when they were born. I can see it all quite clearly still in my mind's eye. I am not sure if I was the one playing with the kittens, but someone did and that cat refused her kittens, as we had been told she would, letting them die. I guess I conflated that event with my mother's absence in the home because, by then, she had left Jamaica to make a new life for herself, and ultimately us, in the United States. In fact this was quite a common occurrence in Jamaica then, and probably still is today. We were called barrel children because our parents, which usually meant our mothers, had left for the United States. I missed my mother terribly. I was frightened I would never see her again, and so, yes, I guess there is some residual guilt in that particular poem. And there is definitely an undertone of danger in some of my works, because, in fact, with its sky-rocketing murder rate Jamaica can be a very dangerous place.

L.H. And actually "The Smell of Mango" also makes us realise how important the senses are in evoking memory in creative writing...

J.B. What bothers me about the reception of "The Smell of Mango" is that it conflates the narrating "I" in that poem with the poet Jacqueline Bishop. Reviewers have even said that they feel sorry for me and want to know how I dealt with the issue of incest because of that poem. This is all quite bothersome. I read in the question before this, and this question, the underlying question of how autobiographical is that particular poem, Jacqueline? Whereas all along that poem was meant to make two points really: that despite how much I love Jamaica and feel a certain reverence for its incredible beauty, that terrible and violent things do happen in this beautiful place. What is more, I wanted to make the point that wounding can and oftentimes does come from those closest to you, those related to you. I have a friend who was a nurse for several years in Jamaica, and she would tell me these truly hair-raising stories. She would tell me stories of seven-year-old girls who came to the clinic and their hymens were no longer intact and had not been intact for a long time. And those little girls refused to say who touched them. She told me a bone-chilling story of a little girl who had neither parents HIV positive but this five or six year old turned up HIV positive, because, a man who *was* positive had been told that he should have sex with a virgin and that would clear himself of the disease, and so he ended up raping and infecting this baby. I mean I could tell you stories that my friend told me years and years ago that still give me sleepless nights.

The question for me then, as a writer and a creator, is what do you do with these stories? Do I pretend not to hear them? Knowing myself, I cannot do that. As much as I love and am devoted to Jamaica, there are still several snakes in our beloved garden. So the next question becomes how best to tell these stories? How can I be rigorous with myself as an artist, as a poet, in telling these stories, and that is what I tried to achieve in "The Smell of Mango". I wanted people to understand that terrible things do happen in beautiful places. I wanted to find a way to marry the tragedy of stories like the one in "The Smell of Mango" with poetic rigour, and to do that I knew that I had to invoke the senses of touch, taste, smell. I really wanted the reader to identify with the tragedy of that little girl.

L.H.  Your grandmother's presence percolates throughout *Fauna*. I know you have talked about your grandmother's influence in previous interviews but perhaps you might tell ARC readers a little more about her significance, especially with regards to your creative careers.

J.B.  It is significant to me that I am answering this question on international women's day, because it really gives me a chance to reflect on the women in my life. I feel blessed, really blessed to have known my great-grandmother until I was well into my 20s and I am blessed enough to still have my grandmother and mother in my life. I think once you know yourself back through so many generations, it gives you a firm grounding into who you are, and it is out of that place, knowing myself back through my great-grandmother, my grandmother, and my mother, that I create out of. That is the significance of these women in my life, they gave me something to create out of. But what exactly do I mean by this?

Increasingly I see my art forms engaging their art forms. And so if you look at a poem like "Girl" in the collection *Fauna*, you see immediately of course the influence of a writer like Jamaica Kincaid on my own writing, but more so I believe I was able to catch the language and cadence and words of my great-grandmother. Those are her words. Those are her warnings and instructions into womanhood, and so my great-grandmother and I have co-created that poem together, is how I feel about it.

But there is more.

My great-grandmother had great big red ginger lilies growing in front of her small house in Nonsuch and these ginger lilies have been implanted on my consciousness as both a writer and a visual artist. I write about them in various forms all the time and I have long incorporated floral imagery in my visual art. But outside of her garden and her words, my great-grandmother gave me another art form that I can never thank her enough for: she gave me patchwork quilts. Here was a woman who would piece together these small pieces of cloth to make these things that have since gone on to be widely exhibited. What a gift to get from one's great-grandmother! What an art form! My grandmother tells me that the people in the district knew of my great-grandmother making these things and they would send her pieces of cloth. Dressmakers in the district especially would send her pieces of cloth. Whether they recognised it or not they were assisting her creation, and I tell you, Leanne, that just brings tears to my eyes. I think how fortunate I am to own some of these quilts, and I can almost hear my great-grandmother whispering to me, through these quilts, go on and do your art my great granddaughter, do your work, it is a worthy thing to do if only you do it for yourself, because surely my great-grandmother was making these quilts only for herself. I think she would be surprised to know that they are being exhibited in other countries.

My grandmother, too, was a very artistic person. She told me once that as a girl in school drawing was her favourite thing to do, and she drew a picture for me that long-ago day when she told me her story, which I still keep buried far away in my mind, the long slender elegant lines that made up the apples, oranges and bananas. My grandmother could weave baskets, made me an apron that I needed for school by hand, makes the absolute best guava jelly, and recently, when she found out that I still had her mother's quilts, made some quilts for me to add to my collection. Now I have more than thirty-five such quilts that my great-grandmother, my grandmother, and I made in response to each other. If I can say so myself, the collection is breathtaking!

My mother was no less artistic, but her art form was crocheting and knitting. My mother could crotchet and knit you under a table! That was what I grew up seeing my mother do all the time, and there were crotched doilies, some of them quite spectacular, all over the house. Looking back at the work of these women I see how I became a writer and an artist and I see now why I am so preoccupied, as a visual artist, in using textiles in my work.

L.H.  I particularly like your poem "Calabash" in *Fauna*, both tone and form are just spot on. The visual look of the poem nicely represents the shape of the Calabash fruit and the tone is somewhat like you would find in a botany book (a tone that is similar to your poem "Fauna"). How important is the relationship between the visual look of the poem and the material itself?

J.B.  Very important actually. Though poems come to me in a whole, I spend a lot of time crafting the poem. And it is interesting to me that you reference a botanical book, because I get immense pleasure from reading botanical books, so who knows, probably some of those readings found their way into that poem as well. But in regards to the poem "Calabash", it has a very particular history. I had just started a magazine of the same name at NYU, and was looking for a way to incorporate what I was trying to do in that journal of Caribbean arts and letters into a poem. This was at a time when I was reading quite closely some of Olive Senior's poems and she had poems that mimicked the art form of the object that she is writing about, and so I tried to do that with this poem, and I was happy when it succeeded. I haven't really done this with much of my other poems, because I hate too rigid a structure, but who knows if I will go back to doing some more poems like that in the future.

L.H.  Just as a side note, "Calabash" really reminds me of Olive Senior's "Hatch", "Sweet Bwoy" and "Walking on Eggs", whereby a relationship is created between the physical look of the poem and the words themselves. Has Senior influenced your writing career at all?

J.B.  Yes, she has, in many more ways than with just the poems mentioned. The thing about Olive Senior's work is that she has such a distinctive

Jamaican voice! I read particularly her stories and am left wondering, how does she do that? Anyone anywhere can pick up and read and understand what she is saying, yet her voice remains remarkably Jamaican, and when I first started reading her work that was something I desperately wanted for myself. For a long time I studied Olive Senior's fiction. I would say that her work helped me to find my fictional voice.

L.H. You've written poetry, a novel, short stories and non-fiction. Is there a particular form that you feel most at ease with?

J.B. Poetry I have to wait on. She is quite the task-mistress, poetry. Fiction comes more easily to me than poetry, even though I still consider myself primarily a poet. The form that I am struggling with the most right now is non-fiction writing, which is so hysterically funny because in my working life that is what I do, I get students to write mainly non-fiction essays! To be honest about it, I feel that I can hide behind fiction and poetry in ways that I cannot do in non-fiction writing, because it is me, my opinions and thoughts that are wholly on the line. And because I am the type of person who likes to dive headlong into a creative challenge, I am now working on writing more non-fiction pieces. But doing so is challenging for me in ways that writing fiction and poetry are not. Not so much in finding the right words, or the right imagery, or crafting an essay per se, but more so in negotiating my ideas. The good news, though, is that it is getting easier and easier for me to write non-fiction works, in large part because I have taken on the challenge to do so.

L.H. I wonder if we might now concentrate on your visual art. You experiment with all sorts of forms including photography, textiles, drawing and painting. Tell me more about your gravitation towards the visual arts for the exploration of issues that are important to you.

J.B. I was always interested in exploring the visual arts and even as an undergraduate took several studio art classes. But like with writing, I wondered how in the world would I be able to make a living doing this? In a strange kind of way, the visual arts was and was not a possibility for me. By that I mean my mother would take me to what is today the Edna Manley College of Art for Saturday morning ballet lessons. I don't remember much about the ballet lessons, but I do remember being drawn to the visual arts on that campus. As I was waiting for my mother to come back for me, I would wander around the school and I would always spend the longest times in the visual arts section. As a child, I loved that place, and I would go home and draw and colour to my heart's content. And as I talked about before, the visual arts, particularly textiles was a useful outlet for the women in my family.

But somewhere in high school I had to choose a "serious" profession and that meant that I would become a medical doctor, never mind how much I struggled in the sciences. This goal of becoming a medical doctor followed me until well into my undergraduate career, and, in fact, I graduated with a Bachelor's degree in Psychology. But shortly before I graduated... I think it was in fact my junior year abroad in Paris... I came back to the arts and that was in large part because the arts are venerated in Paris. It was all around me, and suddenly that little girl who always wanted to write *and* paint returned.

I guess that for me the arts can help me to tell the truth in a way that I cannot if I just list facts. With the visual arts, for example, my great grandmother's quilts can best tell you who this woman was, and how she lived and loved life, much more so than her words probably every could, because, in fact, my great grandparents were not particularly talkative people. This is what the visual arts give to us. They can make us pay attention. They force us to look. Ideally too, they should get us to think. I use the visual arts to think through issues and to get to understand how I feel about something. Perhaps this is why I gravitate so much to the visual arts.

L.H.  Perhaps one of your most striking series, in my opinion, is your Childhood Memory photographs. Could you tell *ARC* readers a little more about the motivation for this series? How did this visual and creative journey affect you emotionally, if at all?

J.B.  In this series of photographs I am trying to return to, again and again, a place and a time that no longer exists, and that is my childhood. Specifically, those summer holidays with my grandmother, great grandparents, and other relatives and friends in the district of Nonsuch. Almost all the photographs are set in Nonsuch. At the time I was a little girl there was this lovely river that ran through the district and us children would go to the river from time to time. I have many stories about that river, and it shows up in many of my works, including in this series of photographs. Sad to say the river is heavily polluted these days, but at the time I was a child I remember just being mesmerised by this river. Of course it was dangerous too, you could drown in the river; and then there was always rivermumma, the half-woman, half-fish creature, who loved pulling little girls down into the water. But we would also go to the river to catch crawfish and that kind of thing. A very idyllic childhood, which I try to capture in these photographs.

I too love this body of work because I get to spend time with so many people I love and who are important to me in these photographs, although it took me near forever to get the photographs I wanted. There was a lot of experimentation, and, in fact, it was not until Photoshop came along that I was able to get the images that I wanted. So sometimes we have to wait a little for the technology to develop to do what we want to do. It means a lot to me, Leanne, that you singled out this body of work to talk about, because after many years of work and experimentation I felt I finally started to find my photographic voice in these images. Plus so many of my relatives are in these photographs – my great-grandparents, my grandmother, my parents, various uncles and aunts and so one. Maybe this is a way of staying close to my family, to the district of Nonsuch, and ultimately Jamaica, because when I look at these photographs I am back in this time, this place, and among my family members. It is all a very emotional experience for me.

L.H.  I wonder if you might talk more about your Babylon series?

J.B.  I was finishing up at graduate school, getting a master's degree in studio art, when I started this ongoing body of work. These are about the Rastafarian ideas of Babylon being a place of captivity and oppression while Zion symbolises a utopian place of unity and peace. I think it is significant that these paintings emerged in graduate school because I found the atmosphere in graduate school for studio arts overwhelmingly white in the readings assigned and overwhelmingly oppressive. When I complained about this, some of my fellow students thought I was a troublemaker. One day, as I was sitting in my studio it finally occurred to me that I was in Babylon, a place of oppression, in graduate school, and that was how this body of work came about.

In the Babylon series I write the lyrics from songs and poems to create text-based drip paintings. The Babylon series of paintings are largely all white paintings, while the Zion series is comprised largely of monochrome black paintings to delineate a symbolic paradise and a place of acceptance and understanding. In the past I used glitter in some of the Zion pieces seeking to represent the paradise that Rastafarians seek in the Biblical homeland of Zion. But an interesting thing happened on the way to me creating these paintings, which was that I started to really pay attention to how these utopias and dystopias are created and the work is beginning to morph in interesting ways and I am using colours outside of black and white in the latest paintings. I don't feel that I am done with the series yet though, and I will be interested to see the different transmutations that this body of work goes through!

L.H.  What are you working on at the moment?

J.B.  A million different things! But one body of work that I am working on quite intensely now is a project I am calling, "Claude McKay's Songs of Morocco". The Jamaican writer Claude McKay lived in Morocco roughly five years from 1928 - 1934. In fact, he wrote most of his books in that country. But what I am finding was that virtually no one in Morocco knew who Claude McKay was or his considerable achievements. A similar lacunae exists in the United States and in scholarship about Claude McKay, his time in Morocco is treated as a long vacation.

I set out to develop a visual archive of Claude McKay's Morocco, and I have been working on this project for some time now. In effect what I am trying to do is return Claude McKay yet again to Morocco. Consequently I have tracked Claude McKay all over Northern Morocco. In particular I wished to locate the small lovely house near a river leading out to the ocean, just outside Tangier where the author lived and worked and wrote many glowing letters about. With the help of some folks in Morocco I came to understand that McKay's little house "outside of Tangier" where he kept a vegetable garden was now deeply folded within Tangier proper, the city having grown so much over the years. I was able to pinpoint however, the place where Claude McKay's house would have been and I have been photographing there.

## "FROM NONSUCH TO BORDEAUX: AN INTER-ISLAND CONVERSATION ON THE WORK OF JOHN DUNKLEY"

David Knight:  The Social Media Age, depending on who you ask, either makes us lonelier or connects us with others. It either shatters monoculture by giving everyone with Internet access a media megaphone, or, with its one-size-fits-all templates, filters any attempt at human individuality through a sinister corporate funnel. Either it will bring about the end of thoughtful political and artistic discourse, or it will lead to our enlightenment. In any event the debate is hardly interesting anymore. Very soon we will live in a world run by social media natives.

With so much always made about the ultimate fragmentation of the Caribbean region (its language barriers, its confusing knots of identity formation, its clashing political systems), I wonder if this part of the world is the one with the most to gain from social media. Perhaps platforms like Facebook call attention to the fact that we really are a network of small places, our citizens united in disunity. I often note a chaotic synergy amongst my Caribbean Facebook friends.

When I recently posted an image of a painting by Jamaican Modernist artist John Dunkley on my Facebook profile, I almost immediately heard from Jacqueline Bishop, a native of Jamaica who now teaches at New York University. Bishop is a poet, visual artist, and the founding editor of the journal *Calabash*. We have never met in person, but had connected after another small Caribbean journal *Moko,* at which I am an editor, published an interview she did with Opal Palmer Adisa. Bishop was excited to see that I was a fan of Dunkley. "Best painter Jamaica has ever produced!" she commented on my Facebook post.

Our agreement struck us as an opportunity to learn more about each other's thoughts on this idiosyncratic painter who we both felt drawn to. The following conversation is the result of a week-long exchange, via e-mail, in which Bishop and I talked about Dunkley's life and work. Prompted by a simple Facebook post, we discussed topics as far-ranging as the troubled terminology surrounding untutored artists, intersections of art and nationalism, and the duppies (jumbies, in the Virgin Islands) that inhabit the work of Mr. John Dunkley.

Jacqueline, when and where did you first encounter John Dunkley's work?

Jacqueline Bishop: I think it was in graduate school. There was a graduate course in Caribbean art that was being taught by Edward J. Sullivan, the scholar of Caribbean and Latin American art at NYU. I remember that I dropped E.L. Doctorow's fiction class and enrolled in Sullivan's class. In Sullivan's class I felt I had come home to myself as someone passionately and intensely interested in the visual arts. That course changed my life. When Sullivan presented the work of John Dunkley I could barely breathe. I had never seen anything quite like these moody secretive paintings in my life! These were works that every artist hopes s/he can create, for what is the work of the artist but to create and present a new world? And that is exactly what John Dunkley has done. He has created a whole new world with his mysterious paintings.

And you David, when and where did you first encounter John Dunkley's work?

D.N. I'm fairly certain that I first encountered a John Dunkley painting in Veerle Poupeye's book *Caribbean Art*, which I read when I was an undergrad. I was living in Portland, Maine at the time, and educating myself a little bit about Caribbean visual arts out of nostalgia for home more than anything else. I was experiencing a lot of the usual self-exile problems at the time, and I found that learning and writing about the visual arts granted me a measure of free expression that was lacking in other areas of my life. Dunkley's painting "Banana Plantation" was one of the images from Poupeye's book that spoke to me right away and has stuck with me over the years.

The island I am from, St. John in the U.S. Virgin Islands, is one that isn't often seen represented beyond the sunny and sanitised images that proliferate for the consumption of tourists. I found Dunkley's "land-scape of the mind" (to use Poupeye's terminology) in "Banana Planta-tion" to be far closer to my own mental and emotional landscape than most of the images I was being presented of the Caribbean while living in the States. That got me thinking about why that was, and encouraged me to learn more about Dunkley's work.

I'm curious, Jacqueline, because I have never spoken to a Jamaican about Dunkley's work before, is he fairly well known there? Is his work considered part of a national Jamaican school of painting or is he seen as more of an "outsider" artist? My understanding is that he is thought of as an "intuitive" artist rather than part of the trained art establishment of his period. Is this correct?

J.B.  David, before answering your questions, I want to say why they
      excite me so much. You posted on Facebook that you love John
      Dunkley's work. You posted his image "Banana Plantation". I too
      love this work. This began the dialogue we are having today. I think
      it is significant that Dunkley has arrived in the social media age.

      Dunkley is celebrated and very much appreciated in Jamaica. His
      works sells for millions of dollars, and even then it is hard to come by
      a Dunkley, because so few of his works survive. Dunkley was a barber
      with a shop in downtown Kingston. He painted his works with house
      paint and they have not aged well over the years. His works are a

precious-precious gift to Jamaica. Several years ago, when I was doing some work on Dunkley I found out that each of his paintings had an unveiling in his little barbershop and people would gather around just to see what he had made. I find that so moving, because the visual arts are so often seen as the elite arts, and I love how Dunkley disrupts this idea.

If memory serves me correctly, I read somewhere that Edna Manley, the woman who was the fountainhead of the visual arts movement in Jamaica, went to see Dunkley to invite him to attend visual arts classes and he declined. He was so wedded to what he was doing and we are all the better for it. So yes, Dunkley is very much part of the artistic foundation of Jamaican art and just about anyone on the island or anyone writing about Jamaican art will tell you this.

The terms "outsider" and "intuitive" art, as you know, are very charged terms. On the one hand I am sympathetic to what Dr. David Boxer, then head of the National Gallery of Jamaica, was doing in coining the term "Intuitive" art and rejecting the then used term "primitive" art that was used to describe work like Dunkley's. We really have to give Dr. Boxer credit for this.

The problem with the term, though, is that it separates Jamaican artists into categories, and years ago when I went around the island interviewing "intuitive" artists, they outright rejected the term. Not only did a lot of them not know what it meant, but they also did not like it being applied to them. So the term is really a contested area in Jamaican art. In trying to solve one issue, it seems to me, we have recreated the same issue.

But this is not to say that these artists have not at all benefited from being called "Intuitive" artists. It gave people like myself a way to tackle and talk about the works of what for me are essentially untutored artists. But I think it is time we remove the label from them. A label, after all, that most of them did not take unto themselves. Maybe it is time to let them be just artists.

My question for you, David, veers a little bit off from the discussion about Dunkley. I want to know what is the art scene like in St. John? Do you have museums? Art galleries? Please forgive my ignorance, but I am really curious to know. If yes, which works are shown in the galleries? Is it the work of St. John artists? Are there self-taught artists like Dunkley in St. John?

D.K.  Wow thank you Jacqueline, this is turning out to be a very exciting dialogue for me as well!

So first, I should address your thoughtful words on the fraught terminology surrounding untutored artists, particularly here in the

Caribbean. I agree that the separation between the elite art establishment and untutored artists is one that is socially-created and often self-serving to a certain class of people. But when I use the terms "intuitive" or "outsider" I tend to have positive associations with them. I am not a visual artist, but I am a critic, writer, and editor, and much of what I do I would describe in those terms – I have very little formal training in the things I write about and am certainly an outsider to the art world and academia, even if I take some cues from those places. I think this may be one reason why I instinctively felt a connection to Dunkley's work, which is deeply personal and independent; not a part of any "school" and seemingly resistant to any "nationalist" readings. Dunkley's work seems too idiosyncratic for that. I suppose that's why I asked you what his current status is in Jamaica.

Now I should answer your question about art in the context of the society I am coming from, which is a hugely complicated question. I'll try to be as brief as possible. Historically St. John was the most insular of the U.S. Virgin Islands (former Danish West Indies). Unlike cosmopolitan St. Thomas, and the larger agricultural/industrial island of St. Croix, St. John for much of its recent history had a very small, rural, self-sufficient society. This has all changed as of late due to a very peculiar dynamic created by American philanthropist Laurence Rockefeller's purchase of much of the island in the 1950s, and his subsequent donation of the land to the United States National Park Service. As you can imagine, this has changed the island dramatically. Today St. John is the most "gentrified" of the U.S. Virgin Islands, with the largest percentage of wealthy transplants, the highest land prices, and arguably the most troubling social dynamics.

Within this context decorative art flourishes. We have many talented artists on St. John. The vast majority are working in the pictorial. Nearly all are white Americans. With a few exceptions, most do not place themselves in a regional context, so it is difficult to know where to situate them in conversations on Caribbean Art. I would classify much of the work produced here as American neo-colonial art, to be honest. There is one transplant artist, Janet Cook-Rutnik, who often does explore social themes and participates in the broader Caribbean art world. There are a few native St. Johnian artists who are well-known here – among them is Avelino Samuel whose woodworking is certainly fine art. But there is no "national school" to speak of really, as neither St. John nor the U.S. Virgin Islands are nation-states at the current time. And certainly St. John has never been a centre of government, media, or academia in the U.S.V.I., although perhaps now the island functions as the "centre" of our tourist economy.

In the broader U.S. Virgin Islands, there is slightly more discourse on the arts. I am currently collaborating on an overview of U.S. Virgin Islands art history with a contemporary artist from St. Croix, La Vaughn Belle (she works in various media and uses art as a critical tool) and Priscilla Hintz Rivera from St. Thomas, who is an advocate for all sorts of creative endeavours in the territory. Hopefully we will be able to connect the many artists working here with some of their antecedents.

But back to Dunkley. I want to discuss something we touched on in our original conversation on Facebook, and that's our connections to the sort of landscapes found in Dunkley's work. Words like "brooding", "nocturnal", and "impenetrable" seem to be words that are often used to describe his paintings.

For me there is something about this aesthetic that speaks to my experience of "home" which, as I mentioned earlier, is rarely represented in this way in images here or abroad. I grew up on a mountain called Bordeaux, which affected my sensibility very deeply. For me Bordeaux was a world of giant "elephant-ear" philodendrons, enveloping clouds, pitchapples that would unfold into soldier crabs in my young imagination, Birds of Paradise flowers reaching out like long claws, dark gungalos (millipedes) curling into spirals on the polished Guyanese hardwood of my mother's house, enormous moths, the ever-present smell of bay trees, abandoned charcoal pits, sensitive plants that curled up their leaves when touched, and treefrogs wailing as if they were air raid sirens in response to the sound of U.S. Naval bombs falling on nearby Vieques. In short, the environment was fundamentally strange, equal parts comforting and menacing. This is what I feel when I look at a John Dunkley painting.

What about you, Jacqueline? You've described yourself as a city girl. What is your relationship to the aesthetic of Dunkley's work, which I read as solitary and rural?

J.B.  I may very much be a city girl, but I think my heart and my roots are in the country – for I was sent every summer to spend my holidays in a tiny district called Nonsuch, which is very reminiscent of your beloved Bordeaux, which you describe so movingly above.

But I don't want you to think that I am shirking from being classified as a city girl. I was born in Kingston, Jamaica, and my earliest memories are of the houses in Kingston that my family moved around in. It seems we only spent a few years in one house. My father tells me now that the moment I was born my recently deceased grandmother took one look at me and claimed me as her own. I lived with my grandmother until I was around ten years old, in various houses in Kingston, before she decided to move back to Nonsuch, at which time I went to live with my mother.

But my grandmother's move to Nonsuch meant that I would go to the tiny district high in the purple-blue mountains of the parish of Portland every summer holiday. In Nonsuch I was introduced to another world that coexisted with the world I knew in Kingston. This other world of Nonsuch was a world of duppies, and rolling calf, a place where "bush have ears" and a place where flowers, blood red flowers especially, had a spiritual life of their own. I guess, like you, it is this magical mysterious world that I am pulled into every time I look at Dunkley's world and Dunkley's work. It is, in fact, the world of my great-grandparents and my grandmother. His works connect me to that world and to that life. Dunkley's work is not so much brooding for me, as it is magical and mysterious. It is a world that is rich and alive – but yes, mysterious – and a world you have to suspend belief in order to enter.

There is something else about Dunkley's work that I love outside of its remarkable execution, and it is the perspective from which he paints. By this I mean it is as if he has x-ray vision when he is painting and he is taking you inside of a world that you would not ordinarily see with your naked eyes. For should we really be able to see the rabbit burrowing into the earth as we do? No, with our ordinary eyes we should not. But, if we have the gift of not only sight but also insight and imagination, then we will be able to see the rabbit burrowing into the earth. We will be able to see the marvellous that gets overlooked in the everyday world about us, and that is one thing I love so very much about Dunkley's work. That you have to use more than your eyes to see what he is showing you.

So what is another John Dunkley piece that you love, David, and why?

D.K.  I love your point about the "x-ray vision" quality of some of Dunkley's odd perspective choices, Jacqueline! I, too, find this to be a compelling aspect of his style. I could go on all day about "Banana Plantation" – I find his composition there to be very near perfect – and maybe we will return to that painting, which I think is his most well-known. But for now let's move on to another of his works.

During the same period that he painted "Banana Plantation", Dunkley also painted "Jerboa". I would love to know more about his biography, as the details I have been able to find are somewhat murky. I know that he died in 1947, so both "Banana Plantation" and "Jerboa" are works that he created near the end of his life (both are dated c. 1945). Do you know how Dunkley died? It seems to me these late works are somewhat preoccupied with death, and Dunkley was not an old man when he passed. I am thinking about the bone-like colour palette he uses to represent the moonlit scene in "Banana Plantation" as well as the deathly symbolism of "Jerboa".

For me, the landscape of "Jerboa" is certainly Dunkley's vision of the underworld. The long skinny legs and curved tail of the jerboa remind me of nothing if not medieval European representations of the Devil. Perhaps the dark winding river that makes up the backdrop is Dunkley's

Acheron. Unlike the balance found in "Banana Plantation", the composition in "Jerboa" seems to me to be a bit busy and off-kilter, which contributes to the atmosphere of unease. There is, of course, also the very prominent phallic symbol in "Jerboa" which, although not an uncommon element in Dunkley's compositions, is a good deal more conspicuous here than in many of his other paintings. So, even in Dunkley's darkest work we find an unstoppable natural fecundity.

What do you make of this, Jacqueline? How do you read Dunkley's take on natural cycles, on life and death? It seems an important part of his work to me.

J.B.   Well first let me tell you what I know of Dunkley's biography.

He was born on December 10th, 1891 in Sav-la-Mar, Jamaica. His wife has written that because of an accident to his eye, he had to withdraw from school early. As a young man he went to Panama to be with his father who worked there, but found that his father had died and was buried one day before he arrived. He spent the next couple of years wandering about in Central America and the Caribbean as a sailor, and once even headed off to California to study dentistry, but was not successful with that. He started working as a barber in Panama and it is believed that it is in Panama where he started painting.

Dunkley came back to Jamaica in 1926 and set up a barbershop in downtown Kingston, which from all reports, it was a sight to behold. Edna Manley has written that the moment you entered Dunkley's shop you were met with "a blaze of colour". He had decorated and hand-painted everything in sight in his barbershop. "[T]he great centre-piece" of his barbershop, Edna Manley wrote, "was his barber's chair covered with lovely patterns." Apparently, the place where he lived with his wife and children was similarly decorated.

It is believed that he came to the attention of the art establishment in Jamaica through the efforts of Mr. Delves Molesworth who, at the time, was Secretary of the Institute of Jamaica. Molesworth had been attracted by the hand-painted signs on Dunkley's barbershop, which was a gathering spot for the local people, who would turn up for the unveiling of a new painting or sculpture. From Molesworth, Dunkley was brought to the attention of Edna Manley and his works started being exhibited both in Jamaica and overseas.

He died on February 17, 1947.

In regards to the natural cycles of life and death, and also of fertility, I think your reading is very much correct. In fact, Dr. David Boxer has written as such, noting, of Dunkley's work that he could "… speak at length of his obvious phallic consciousness and his obsessive preoccupations of the linkages of eroticism and death…"

So there is much to what you are saying.

What strikes me the most now as I look at several images of Dunkley's work is the sense of claustrophobia in it – how close together everything seems to be. How, for as much as he seeks to impose order in his work, there is a sense that the vegetation and life going on in his work could so easily take over, and overrun the painting. I can't help but wonder if this is not somehow a commentary on island life, this wanting to impose order on something that is inescapably chaotic and unpredictable. The endless roads in his paintings that seem to go nowhere: there is a lot of frustration, anxiety and angst in these dark beautiful works!

And to me, it makes sense that in such a chaotic and unpredictable world, that one would try to control the one thing that is most under one's control, hence the highly cultivated gardens. But those of us who have lived on Caribbean islands know nothing if we do not know that this vegetation stays "cultivated" and "controlled" for only so long, and, before you know it, we are back to where we started in trying to tame and civilise the vegetation on the island.

Indeed this is what I see when I look at a painting like "Back to Nature", one of my favourite works from Dunkley. An effort at taming and containing, but an effort that is eventually futile.

David, I want to gauge how you feel about Dunkley's piece "Back to Nature". I would also at some point like to talk a little bit about some of the carvings that he did, because, in addition to being a painter, he was also a sculptor.

D.K.  Thanks for the bit of biographical info on Dunkley. His time as a sort of wanderer and nomad in his youth interests me a lot, and I think it is here, where my previous comment about Dunkley's work fitting poorly into a "nationalist" school is relevant. There is an aura of rootlessness in his paintings, and I think it is one aspect of them that retains its power. Dunkley's "roots" are all *natural* rather than *national*, which seems to mock, or else have no interest in, the categories of human social organisation. He seems to be too aware of human frailty to care much about the very temporary issue of identity here on Earth.

I love your point about Dunkley's artistic efforts to impose order on the chaotic, and the resulting anxiety in his paintings. There is the line from Horace about "driving out nature with a pitchfork" (or a machete, as it were) and it always coming back. As you note, this is the condition that we live under in the tropics, where there are frequent battles to impose order on a very unruly natural environment.

"Back to Nature" is then the prototypical Dunkley work in that both the qualities mentioned above are in evidence: not only anxiety over society's insignificance in the face of nature, but also a stark awareness of the place of humanity within natural cycles. Obviously there is symmetry in "Back to Nature", but it is not a calming symmetry. It is extraordinary that Dunkley was able to pull off such a symmetrical composition but still give the painting such a disquieting air. The leaves of the background trees appear as flames. The human footprints on the path appear cyclical. And yet where does the path lead or come from?

J.B.  David, do I read an attack on nationalism – Jamaican nationalism in particular – in what you are saying?

D.K.  No, I guess I should clarify. My sympathies, like most U.S. Virgin Islanders I think, are with Caribbean nationalist movements. Here, many of us have a natural yearning for more national awareness and autonomy. But I have a sort of conflicted relationship with nationalism, one that I read, perhaps wrongly, in Dunkley's work. I do not have a lot of faith in "the nation state" as a form of political organisation, nor do I find overtly "nationalist" art very interesting.

J.B.  Okay, then, let's turn our attention a little to one of John Dunkley's sculptures. Dunkley has a small body of wood sculptures, many of which are about animals – birds, kangaroos, squirrels, iguana, and such. Some are of women. But the one that I find the most arresting is "Sandy Gully". "Sandy Gully" was made from the first lignum vitae tree cut down in preparation for the building of an American air base in Jamaica. Speaking of nationalist sympathies, this is the figure of a proud Jamaican man. What I find so interesting about all of this is the fact that Sandy Gully is now a pretty notorious gully in Jamaica, with bodies being found there all the time. So, what I want to know, David, is what do you "see" when you look at "Sandy Gully"?

D.K.  I find three-dimensional artworks incredibly difficult to critique without seeing the object itself. Much is lost in the photographic reproduction of 2-D works, but the problem becomes more pronounced with sculpture.

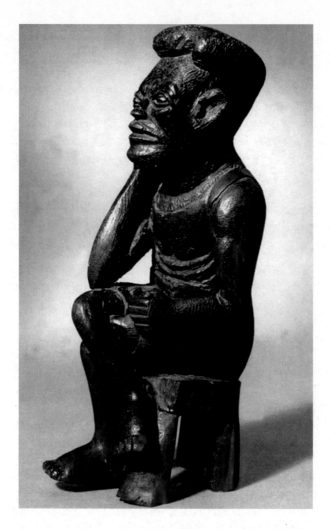

What I can say is that I am very intrigued by the narrative you have given, or the suggestion of one, surrounding this particular artwork "Sandy Gully". It is poignant that Dunkley used a material (the first lignum vitae cut down in preparation for building a U.S. air base) with such weight to it, literally and metaphorically. I wonder if Dunkley himself was making a commentary by selecting the material or if it was a coincidence that was later given meaning. It doesn't seem to matter, as either way the material lends increased meaning to the work, a facet of "Sandy Gully" that has affinities with much contemporary art. The subsequent reputation of Sandy Gully the place, on the other hand, could not have been known to Dunkley. But I do enjoy the dialogue that seems to exist between the work and the history of the place from which it takes its name.

Aside from that, what is notable about "Sandy Gully" to me is how

Dunkley represents the man, "a proud Jamaican" as you point out. Perhaps it is not as striking to us today, but Caribbean artists representing Caribbeanness in the early 20th-century are naturally polemicists against the era's racist and imperialist discourse. Okay, maybe that is not so different from the present context after all. In any event, the words that come to mind when I see how Dunkley has represented his subject in "Sandy Gully" are "sophisticated", "proud", and "poised", which are not necessarily words that metropolitan viewers often thought of in relation to the Caribbean.

And you Jacqueline, I am curious what you see in "Sandy Gully". I also want to close by asking you what lessons Dunkley has to teach contemporary Caribbean creators. What will his legacy be as we enter "the social media age"? What does he have to say to us today?

J.B.  I see very much a sense of personhood in "Sandy Gully". I see also self-determination. I find it fascinating that this was a work produced before Jamaican Independence, because it seems to call for independence.

But I can't help wondering if some of the hopes that Dunkley had for Jamaica, as exemplified in "Sandy Gully", have indeed come true? I say this deliberately referencing what Sandy Gully has become today. The death, decay and despoliation. It certainly gives us something to think about.

I often wonder about artists like Dunkley, who started their art careers without the institutional support that is now more widely available to artists in the Caribbean in general, and in Jamaica in particular. Not enough institutional support by a long way, but at least some structures are in place. How did they do it, these earlier artists? What gave them the impetus to go on? Who did Dunkley initially think he was making work for? Who was his audience in this before-Independence Jamaica? All of this makes me appreciate his work that much more. All of this is his legacy. All of this is what he gives to Caribbean artists, which is to say: stay true to your vision and create no matter the difficulties and misunderstandings of what we create and why indeed we do create.

It is our job as artists and thinkers and people deeply concerned about the place/s we call "home" to tell the stories of our age and time, to engage in the dialogues going on around us, to not only expose problems, but to critique, question, and yes, at times to even propose solutions. That is what Dunkley is doing with this proud, self-determined, self-willed and very independent upright figure. A figure that was long independent before Jamaica got its actual Independence in 1962. Dunkley's job was to call for Independence for his native Jamaica.

Part of the job of the artists of today is to ask the question, what have we done with this "independence?"

And I cannot help, too, to believe that part of our job as artists and thinkers is to see beyond, to use your words David, "the sunny sanitised" images that proliferate about the Caribbean. The man in "Sandy Gully" is a deeply thoughtful, fully realised individual, not a caricature. That is part of the legacy that Dunkley leaves for Caribbean artists today. We should create images – for better or worse – of who we are and who we want to become. And, indeed, who we *have* become!

I don't know if John Dunkley was farseeing enough to see the social media revolution that has occurred in recent times. I rather think not. What I do know is that the fact that you and I, David, could have responded the way that we did to an image of his that we saw on the Internet, speaks volumes to what his legacy will be in the social media age. You and I, for example, have just had an intense discussion about Dunkley's work and its reverberations in the larger Caribbean. That points to what I think the social media age will add to Dunkley's small but magnificent body of work. It will bring more people to know Dunkley's work. It will force questions. And, hopefully, as it did for you and I David, it will start a conversation.

# ABOUT THE AUTHOR

Jacqueline Bishop was born and grew up in Kingston, Jamaica. Her parents separated early in her life, and she lived for many years with her mother and (then three) siblings, but lived with her father for several years when her mother migrated to the United States. As a child she spent her summer holidays in the small district of Nonsuch, in Portland. There she moved among the homes of her (maternal) great-grandparents, her grandparents and numerous aunts, uncles and cousins. She passed many evenings at her great-grandparents home, listening to the stories and folk legends of Jamaica, a prominent feature of her creative work. Shortly after completing high school, she joined her mother in the USA to attend Lehman College, City University of New York, where she obtained a bachelor's degree in Psychology. She spent a summer studying French in Montréal; and a year living in Paris attending the L'Université de Paris. It was in France's 'reading culture' that she started to harbour the thought of becoming a writer.

In 1996 she obtained a James Michener Creative Writing Fellowship at the University of Miami, where she studied poetry with Lorna Goodison. That fall, she started a Master's in poetry writing at New York University. In 1997 she received five creative writing awards from the Cultural Development Commission in Kingston, Jamaica, for fiction and poetry writing. She subsequently won three additional creative writing awards in 1998. She obtained her (first) Master's Degree in 1998.

In 1997 she received a scholarship to the Oral History Summer Program at Columbia University and, in 1998, an Oral History Association Conference Fellowship to New Orleans, Louisiana, for her oral histories on Jamaican women living in New York City. These oral histories were published by Africa World Press in June 2006 as, *My Mother Who Is Me: Lifestories from Jamaican Women in New York*. She was accepted back into the Creative Writing program at NYU to pursue a (second) Master's of Fine Arts degree in fiction writing, which she received in September, 2000. Her thesis, a novel, *The River's Song*, was published in 2007.

Jacqueline Bishop is a visual artist with exhibitions in Europe, North Africa, the United States and Jamaica. She writes a monthly article for the *Huffington Post* and conducts interviews with artists and art professionals for the *Observer Arts Magazine*. She has twice been awarded Fulbright Fellowships, including a year-long grant to Morocco and again as a UNESCO/Fulbright fellow to France. She teaches in the Liberal Studies Program at New York University, and is the founding editor of *Calabash: A Journal of Caribbean Art & Letters*. She is the author of a novel, *The River's Song*, two collections of poems, *Fauna*, and *Snapshots from Istanbul*, an art book, *Writers Who Paint... Three Jamaican Artists*.

## ALSO BY JACQUELINE BISHOP

*The River's Song*
ISBN: 9781845230388; pp. 181; pub. 2007; price: £8.99

Gloria, living with her mother in a Kingston tenement yard, wins a
scholarship to one of Jamaica's best girls' schools. She is the engaging
narrator of the at first alienating and then transforming experiences
of an education that in time takes her away from her mother, friends
and the island; of her consciousness of bodily change and sexual awakening;
of her growth of adult awareness of a Jamaica of class division and
endemic violence.

 The novel's strengths lie above all in the quality of its characterisation
and the dramatisation of Gloria's relationships with her mother,
grandmother and the girls she has always known in her grandmother's
rural village, with Rachel, their neighbour in the yard who is Gloria's
rock of understanding, and, at the heart of the novel, with Annie, the
purest and indivisible love of her adolescent years.

"I LOVE The River's Song! It was so hard to put it down! Gloria's
coming-of-age story is warm and true and bittersweet. Hers is no wide
bridge over the river but a rocky path to womanhood, to friendships
made and lost and to the knowledge that love also requires navigation.
*The River's Song* is a song we've all heard before, but never with such
force and clarity as this."

— Olive Senior

"In this moving and assured debut novel, Jacqueline Bishop sings of
the everyday struggles of Gloria and her mother in their Jamaican home.
The River's Song is a story of ambition and achievement, of the steady
but troubled rise of a bright child who discovers that finding her own
song could mean opposing those she most loves. The River's Song is
tender but avoids sentimentality, and at the end of the novel we find a
young woman living on her own terms and following her own dreams.
An engaging read. You keep leaning closer to the novel to hear every
word as it is being sung."

— Merle Collins

*Fauna*
ISBN: 9781845230326; pp. 84; pub. 2006; price: £7.99

"To render the familiar strange and new again is the task of gifted poets. Jacqueline Bishop's poems do this in wonderful ways. She calls upon powerful sources, including world mythology, her own Jamaican ancestry and her full-woman experiences to create these fabulous, shining songs of innocence, loss, birth, rebirth, wit and wisdom. Good job Miss Jacqueline!"

— Lorna Goodison, author of *Controlling the Silver.*

*Fauna* is not just a collection of individually rewarding poems but a carefully structured whole. Using metaphors drawn from the fauna and flora of Jamaica and images drawn from painting as the over-arching devices, Bishop explores the tensions between plenitude and emptiness, presence and absence, the nourishing and the poisonous in her memories of the rural Jamaican childhood that has shaped her. There is the lushness of scene, but also the way that 'the smell of mango' will always be associated with childhood trauma, or the richness of avocado contrasted with the allamanda who admits, "Everything alive develops a defence… Mine is poison; all parts of me are toxic".
   And from the perspective of New York, Bishop sees herself as another kind of fauna, the Jamaican birds who can be found everywhere. "In North America three or four species/ have been identified from the peculiar way they sing." This is a moving and heart-felt collection, but the siren voice of longing for return is never allowed to become sentimental. Always there is the drive towards the artist's desire to remake the world and to work meticulously at what can be left in, what must be taken out.

"Jacqueline Bishop's debut collection offers us passage into other worlds, both geographical and mythical. These poems define family, home, longing, and exile in profoundly moving and refreshingly new ways. They capture a myriad of voices, from those of the elders to those of the "Fauna" that populate the gorgeous second section of the book. The voices and images Bishop constructs in these poems are haunting in the best possible way: they are the melody we hear that reminds us of who we are, where we are from, and where we are going."

— Shara McCallum, author of *Song of Thieves.*

*Snapshots from Istanbul*
ISBN: 9781845231149; pp. 70; pub. 2009; price: £7.99

Snapshots from Istanbul is another leap forward in Jacqueline Bishop's development of an assured, recognisable voice and extending the range of her subject matter. At one level, the collection has the intimacy of the confessional – recorded with self-reflexive frankness and good humour – but this is grounded within the structure of other narratives and voices that create a counterpoint of dialogue in which the lyric 'I' is only one point of reference. Framing the collection are poems that explore the lives of the exiled Roman poet Ovid, and the journeying painter Gauguin. Between their differing reasons for departure and between the invented Ovid's changing perceptions of what exile means, Bishop locates her own explorations of where home might be. Like Gauguin, Bishop is driven by the need to discover one's necessity and do it; but as a woman she also has room to wonder about those abandoned by such quests.

At the heart of the collection is a sequence of powerfully sensuous poems about a doomed relationship in Istanbul, touching in its honesty and, as in the best poems about other places, vivid in its portrayal of the otherness, highly conscious of the layers of difference, and aware that the poems' true subject is the uprooted self. Here, inevitably, Bishop is forced to think about her Americanness and her Jamaicanness in different ways. There is one constant: Bishop's insistence that the drive to rearrange words is inextricably linked to the act of the rearranging of self.

"Snapshots from Istanbul is a lovely leisurely album, full of love, life and the fire of information."
— Kamau Brathwaite

*Writers who Paint, Painters who Write*
ISBN: 9781845230647; pp. 48; pub. 2007; price: £8.99

"Great writers from all parts of the Caribbean have always created vivid pictures in the minds of the readers of their poetry, novels and essays. What we have here, in this beautiful selection of three contemporary Jamaican multi-talented artists, is a continuation and strengthening of a long tradition of the concretization of literary allusions in visual form. Jacqueline Bishop, so well known for her poems and her 'artistic activism' offers us, in her paintings, a series of delicately evanescent webs. We are reminded here of the random patterns of surf on the sand or the midnight spinnings of a spider. Earl McKenzie's sober still life paintings have the suggestive power of Giorgio Morandi, one of the greatest masters of the simple object. His up-close images speak in a direct, unadorned fashion of the unexpected complexities of everyday life. Ralph Thompson's landscapes and figure studies, reminiscent of such powerful masters as Cézanne or the African-American painter Beauford Delaney, demonstrate a remarkable sensitivity to the expressive power of form and colour."

— Edward J. Sullivan,
Professor of Art History & Dean for the Humanities
New York University

All these and over 300 other Caribbean and Black British titles published by Peepal Tree Press available through on-line ordering on: www.peepaltreepress.com. Or contact us at orders@peepaltreepress.com